ROOSEVELT UNIVERSITY LIBRARY
DA435.H61969   C001
HOLMES, GEOFFREY S., 1928-
BRITAIN AFTER THE GLORIOUS REVOLUTION

W9-DAP-644

WITHDRAWN

/DA435.H61969/

1969

DATE DUE

SEP 4 '75	P Johnson	
OCT 0 5 '92	JUL 07 REC'D	
MAR 3 0 1983		
APR 2 0 REC'D	APR 2 0 REC'D	

DEMCO 38-297

Britain after the Glorious Revolution 1689–1714

Each volume in this series is designed to make available to students important new work on key historical problems and periods that they encounter in their courses. Every volume is devoted to a central topic or theme, and the most important aspects of this are dealt with by specially commissioned essays from specialists in the period. The editorial Introductions review the problem or period as a whole, and each essay provides a balanced assessment of the particular aspect, exploring the areas of recent development or controversy, indicating what firm conclusions can be drawn, and suggesting any further work which may be necessary. An annotated bibliography serves as an up-to-date guide to further reading.

PROBLEMS IN FOCUS SERIES

Britain after the Glorious Revolution 1689–1714 edited by Geoffrey Holmes

Britain Pre-eminent: Studies in British World Influence in the Nineteenth Century edited by C. J. Bartlett

FORTHCOMING TITLES:

Great Politicians and Their Electoral Appeal 1860–1920 edited by Donald Southgate

Aspects of Victorian Liberalism edited by Leyland Lyons

Popular Movements 1830–50 edited by John Ward

The Interregnum edited by Gerald Aylmer

The Republic and the Civil War in Spain edited by Raymond Carr

Urban Studies edited by A. M. Everett

The Hundred Years War edited by Kenneth Fowler

Development Finance in Latin America edited by K. B. Griffin

Industrial Revolutions edited by R. M. Hartwell

Sweden 1632–1718 edited by Michael Roberts

Britain after the Glorious Revolution 1689–1714

EDITED BY

GEOFFREY HOLMES

Macmillan
St Martin's Press

© Geoffrey Holmes, Jennifer Carter, G. C. Gibbs, Angus McInnes,
Henry Horwitz, E. L. Ellis, W. A. Speck, G. V. Bennett,
T. C. Smout, A. D. MacLachlan 1969

First published 1969 by
MACMILLAN AND CO LTD
Little Essex Street London WC2
and also at Bombay Calcutta and Madras
Macmillan South Africa (Publishers) Pty Ltd Johannesburg
The Macmillan Company of Australia Pty Ltd Melbourne
The Macmillan Company of Canada Ltd Toronto
St Martin's Press Inc New York
Gill and Macmillan Ltd Dublin

Library of Congress catalog card no. 76–83201

Printed in Great Britain by
RICHARD CLAY (THE CHAUCER PRESS), LTD
Bungay, Suffolk

JUN 23 1975

2607

DA
435
.H 6
1969Contents

Preface

No selection of ten essays spanning a quarter of a century of British history can hope to satisfy everybody. The choice of subjects offered here was governed in part by the general aims of the series, with their stress on the needs and interests of the non-specialist, in part by the preoccupation of so many late Stuart scholars in recent years with the politics of their period. An attempt has been made to compensate for some of the more regrettable omissions (for example, the absence of a purely economic or a purely military problem from the final selection) by adjusting the emphases of the introductory survey.

All contemporary quotations in this book appear with modern spelling and punctuation, and those originally in foreign languages have been translated into English. All dates are given in the 'Old Style' of post-Revolution Britain – ten days (between 1700 and 1714 eleven days) in arrear of the calendar then in use in most continental countries – although the year is reckoned from 1 January instead of from 25 March.

Owners of private archives who have agreed to their manuscripts being cited, or quoted from, are thanked most warmly for their generosity. The editor has also some personal obligations to record: to the University Court of Glasgow University for granting him a term's leave of absence to complete his work on the book; to his wife for coping so admirably with a voluminous correspondence and with many other chores; to Miss Pat Ferguson for retyping two chapters at the eleventh hour; and not least to his contributors, whose ready co-operation at every stage has made his own task not merely far easier than he anticipated but exceptionally agreeable.

G. S. H.

Glasgow
June 1968

List of Abbreviations

Add. MSS	Additional Manuscripts, British Museum
BIHR	*Bulletin of the Institute of Historical Research*
BM	British Museum
Bodl.	Bodleian Library, Oxford
CJ	*[House of] Commons' Journals*
EcHR	*Economic History Review*
EHR	*English Historical Review*
HJ	*Historical Journal*
HMC	Historical Manuscripts Commission
JBS	*Journal of British Studies*
LJ	*[House of] Lords' Journals*
Parl. Hist.	*The Parliamentary History of England* (ed. W. Cobbett, 1806–20)
PRO	Public Record Office, London
RO	Record Office
SHR	*Scottish Historical Review*
SP	State Papers, Public Record Office
TRHS	*Transactions of the Royal Historical Society*

Introduction: Post-Revolution Britain and the Historian

GEOFFREY HOLMES

I

MUCH of the excitement of history lies not in the narrative of events, but in the process of discussion: in the debate which precedes the elucidation of problems. This book is wholly concerned with problems. It is designed, like its companion volumes, to deal with those challenging questions of interpretation and explanation which stimulate the professional historian to activity, and which interest, and occasionally perplex, the student of history. Individual contributors, each actively researching in a particular field of late-seventeenth- or early-eighteenth-century studies, will pose their own problems and will essay a reasonable interpretation based largely on current scholarly work. This introduction is an attempt to provide an appropriate backcloth to the discussions which follow. It surveys some of the critical fields of Britain's development in the years between 1689 and 1714; and it picks out in relief a number of questions which either have occupied historians of this period in the past, or are currently engaging their attention, or seem worthy of further investigation in the future. Not all these problems, unfortunately, can subsequently be singled out for special consideration. Yet each is an integral part of the attraction and importance of an unusually crowded quarter-century of British history. What follows in this essay, then, seeks in part to inform, but in the main to provoke thought and argument. It invites the reader to join in the debate.

II

It could be argued that by confining our attention to the years 1689–1714 we are defining 'post-Revolution Britain' too narrowly. Of course the limits of any period that suits the historian's convenience are to some extent artificial. In internal politics, it may be said, 1716 is a clearer landmark than 1714; in the history of the Church of England the same may be true of 1717; in the field of foreign policy, of 1718; and our subsequent discussion of specific problems will not be so rigid as to exclude consideration of certain events simply because they happened after the death of Queen Anne. Yet there is, all the same, a coherence and a logical significance about the period 1689–1714. It is a period bounded on the one hand by a revolution which deposed a native but Catholic king who had ruled by hereditary right, and on the other by the peaceful accession of a foreign but Protestant king whose right was entirely parliamentary and whose hereditary claims to the throne were laughably remote. Moreover, this first Hanoverian monarch succeeded to an inheritance different in one highly important respect from that of his predecessors in 1702 and in 1689: he became King of Great Britain. In 1689 the term 'Britain' was applicable to a geographical entity, but strictly speaking to nothing more. Within one island there existed two kingdoms, 'North Britain' and 'South Britain', with only one constitutional link – the crown – and with little else in common save some social and linguistic similarities. 'Great Britain' as we know it today, a political, economic and fiscal unit, though embodying two different legal, religious and cultural traditions, came into being in 1707 and was essentially a post-Revolution creation. Yet it is doubtful whether even the 1688 Revolution did as much to stamp the following twenty-five years with their distinctive character as the overriding fact of war. This was a period of almost continuous war or threat of war. The long struggle carried on by the last two Stuart monarchs against the aggrandisement of Louis XIV's France began in 1689, was punctuated after 1697 by five years of precarious peace, and finally ended in 1713. And when the war tide at last receded it left Britain indisputably a Great Power (a distinction she could not have claimed a generation earlier), equal in status to France herself and with the foundations of her future imperial greatness securely laid.

The Population

Such an advance was a remarkable achievement for a country whose total population cannot have exceeded 7 million in 1714 and may indeed have been nearer to $6\frac{1}{2}$ million.[1] There were of course no official censuses at this time; and although we are exceptionally lucky in possessing a contemporary estimate for 1695, compiled with great care on the basis of hearth-tax returns by the pioneer statistician, Gregory King, it would be unrealistic to endow any of King's findings with the authority of Holy Writ. There were those even in his own day (Robert

Harley, that assiduous gatherer of 'intelligence', was one) who rejected them. Consequently, very few of the basic demographic problems which beset the historian of the post-Revolution period have yet been satisfactorily solved. King, for instance, put the population of England and Wales at 5½ million. Mid-nineteenth- and early- twentieth-century authorities were generally agreed that his figures were too conservative, perhaps by as much as 10 per cent; but at least one modern demographer has pronounced them appreciably too high.[2] It seems widely accepted that the forces responsible for population growth during the sixteenth century and for much of the seventeenth had lost their impetus by 1689. But whether the growth stopped altogether in the next quarter of a century or continued at a more modest pace remains an open question. The birth-rate too has been the cause of expert wrangling; it seems impossible to be certain whether it was rising or falling, or even whether its level was abnormally low or relatively high.[3]

On the other hand we do know something about the distribution of the population at this time. We know, as an axiom, that most of it was still concentrated in rural areas or very small country towns. Apart from the great London conurbation, by now the biggest in Europe, which housed perhaps 600,000 souls by 1700 and which, thanks to a perpetual stream of immigrants, was still growing apace,[4] there were only three towns in Britain with over 20,000 inhabitants. These were Edinburgh, Bristol and Norwich, and together they contained under 100,000 people. Nor was this a period of urban growth: the rapid expansion of Birmingham and Liverpool between 1689 and 1714 seems to have been due to wholly exceptional circumstances. If we assume that only 15 per cent of British people by the time of Queen Anne's death were living in towns of 5000 inhabitants or more we should probably be fairly close to the truth. About the geographical distribution of the population, too, some generalisations are possible. In England, at least, four major concentrations can be discerned, three of them being textile areas. The four south-eastern counties of Middlesex, Surrey, Kent and Sussex and the six south-western shires (Cornwall, Devon, Somerset, Gloucester, Dorset and Wiltshire) were easily the two biggest, with roughly one million people in each in 1700;[5] then came East Anglia,[6] with over half a million, and Lancashire together with the West Riding of Yorkshire, with just below that number. About a quarter of the entire population of England at the beginning of the eighteenth century was to be found in three counties, Middlesex, Yorkshire and Devon. By contrast, the whole of Wales at this period contained under 400,000 people.[7]

Social Structure and Social Conflict

Few and imprecise though they are, such facts and figures are enough in themselves to tell us something about the social structure of England and Wales under the last two Stuarts. (As regards Scotland, unfortunately, they are a good deal less helpful.) Thus if the figures mean anything at all, they must mean that agriculture was still far and away the main national occupation; and indeed it has been plausibly suggested that six or seven Englishmen out of every ten outside London worked on the land. Yet there clearly did exist already what may be called an 'industrial working class', especially in or around London, the cloth-manufacturing towns and the ports; while the urban population, small though it was by post-Industrial Revolution standards, was large enough to embrace a fairly substantial 'lower middle class', compounded of the families of tradesmen, master craftsmen, the more prosperous shopkeepers, and so forth. Correspondingly at the upper end of the social scale, within what is usually called 'the governing class', landowners inevitably predominated; but commerce, finance, industry and the more lucrative professions must nonetheless have sustained an 'upper bourgeoisie' considerably larger in relation to the total population than its counterpart in most continental states of any size.

One of the great advantages of Gregory King's analysis, in which he breaks down English society into its various 'ranks, degrees, titles and qualifications', is that it enables us to put a certain amount of flesh on the skeleton of these very general impressions. For instance, King calculated that well over a quarter of the population was made up of freeholders or tenant farmers in the £44–£84 a year average-income bracket, along with their families. Or again, out of the vast army of 'the Poor' – over 2,800,000 persons who lived at the bare subsistence level of around £10 a year – a high proportion of the breadwinners either worked the land as labourers or cottagers or were employed as out-servants on farms or in country houses. On the other hand, enjoying a standard of living roughly comparable with that of the middling to small freeholders and farmers, there were perhaps 100,000 shopkeepers, small tradesmen, craftsmen and artisans, most of them town-dwellers. With their families they may well have accounted for over 400,000 of the urban population. Higher up the social pyramid the balance between land, trade and the professions revealed by King's 'political arithmetic' is most instructive. Of the 16,500 families 'of rank', with their 150,000 members, distinguished in 1695,[8] we may safely presume that nearly all outside the households of a few City and provincial knights and of several hundred plain 'gents' were landed families. They overtopped by 6500 those whose livelihoods depended on domestic or foreign commerce, but were in turn heavily outnumbered by what could be called, in the broadest sense, professional families, of whom there were possibly as many as 55,000.[9] The latter included thousands who were no more than petty bourgeois: schoolmasters, apothecaries, small-town attorneys, minor office-holders of all varieties. Yet the leading members of some professions – judges and successful barristers, senior army and naval officers, higher clergy, eminent physicians, specialised civil servants or university dons – could justifiably feel that, like hundreds of well-to-do businessmen, they had as good a claim to be considered members of the ruling élite as many a country squire struggling along on £150 or £200 a year.

But did such claims always meet with ready acceptance? How stable, and at the same time how tensile, was this social structure which we have been briefly reviewing? It is widely held that British society between the political revolution of 1688 and the coming of the Industrial Revolution almost a century later possessed exceptional stability without rigidity; that it enjoyed the advantages of rock-like solidity without the disadvantages of petrifaction. For those interested in the social history of the late seventeenth and early eighteenth centuries, however, such comfortable generalisations as these pose unexpected problems. For most of the 120 years following the end of the Great Rebellion in 1660 the social fabric of Britain was not subjected to any special stresses, nor forced to adapt itself at short notice to new phenomena. But between 1689 and 1714 it was. The almost freakish character of these years, in which the slow, measured tread of society's evolution becomes suddenly disturbed and hurried, owed little to the Glorious Revolution. Essentially it was the product of war.

In most societies and in most ages social status has been principally determined by the possession of property. This was unquestionably so of Britain in 1688, where in addition it was generally accepted that there was a direct and rational relationship between a man's place in the social hierarchy and his eligibility for political rights and privileges. One effect on post-Revolution Britain of twenty years' warfare of unprecedented dimensions was to give an extremely powerful, if in some ways artificial, stimulus to the growth of certain types of 'property' – notably that enjoyed by place-holders, serving officers, and above all by those 'plum men' of the City of London whom contemporaries designated 'the monied interest'. At the same time war had – or seemed to many at the time to have had – a correspondingly depressive effect on the social and political value of land, traditionally the supreme hallmark of status and citizenship. Such developments were bound to impose *some* strain on the social structure, at least as long as the wars lasted. But was the strain severe and damaging, or was it merely superficial? Did the men of property continue (as scholars such as Sir George Clark and Lawrence Stone have argued) to comprise a homogeneous governing class in which, despite occasional stresses, all types of wealth and interest were basically fused, and within which there remained considerable freedom of movement between groups and occupations? This is not so much a single problem as two interconnected ones, the problem of 'social mobility' and that of 'social conflict'; and they are explored in depth in a subsequent essay.[10] Here we must be content with two observations on which, one imagines, most social historians would agree.

One is that late Stuart society in Britain was not a caste society: for all its class distinctions, it was not rigidly stratified; its 'privileged' classes did not occupy exclusive compartments in quite the same way as did most of their continental counterparts. On the other hand it is no less apparent that there were 'two nations' in post-Revolution Britain, and that the dividing line between them did not *invariably* correspond with the line between the propertied rich and the non-propertied poor. Above the poverty line, too, social prejudice and discrimination were in evidence. Thus not every door was open to the urban tradesman nor even to the affluent businessman; and if he did not conform to the Anglican Church – and often enough he did not – more still were closed against him as a consequence of the Corporation and Test Acts of 1661 and 1673. To a greater extent than is sometimes appreciated, indeed, social divisions in the Britain of William III and Queen Anne were confirmed and hardened by religious differences and by the cultural divergencies associated with these differences.

III

On the surface it may seem rather remarkable that, by contrast with the wars of this period, the 1688 Revolution played little or no direct part as a social solvent, as the Great Rebellion over forty years before had threatened to do and as the Industrial Revolution a century later unquestionably did. The mystery is quickly dispelled by the briefest consideration of the nature and aims of the 'Glorious Revolution' itself. For this was surely the most conservative revolution that Europe has witnessed in the last four centuries. Indeed it has been argued that the events of November and December 1688 were revolutionary only in the sense that they toppled a king from his throne. So swiftly and so ignominiously was the occupant unseated that those men of rank and substance who led the rebellion against James II were never in the slightest danger of losing, or even of compromising, their control over proceedings by having to appeal for popular or middle-class support. This was a revolution by the propertied classes in the interests of those classes – one which, as a shrewd and often-quoted aphorism has it, 'replaced the divine right of kings with the divine right of property'. In many respects, indeed, the so-called 'revolutionaries' were more concerned with reaction or restoration. To them it was King James and his henchmen who, by trying to undermine the establishment in Church and State, had been the real revolutionaries.

This is not to say, however, that all the effects of the Revolution were as conservative or as retrogressive as many of its architects intended. For both the English and Scottish nations it was a disturbing if not a traumatic experience; and like most revolutions it was followed by changes which few at first envisaged. One of the main purposes of this volume will be to assess some of the most important of its effects in various fields. And it is surely appropriate that we should begin in the field of the constitution,[11] since it was the breakdown of the restored Stuart constitution which made the Revolution necessary.

The Constitution

Discussion of its constitutional effects conventionally takes place under the umbrella of that well-worn phrase, 'the Revolution settlement'. This is one of the most misapplied and misleading terms which historians have ever had the misfortune to coin for the supposed edification of their readers. Too often a convenient blanket thrown over a whole series of changes affecting government, finance, the judiciary and the Church between 1689 and 1701 (even the Regency Act of 1706 is sometimes thought to qualify for inclusion), its effect has been to enshroud the real significance of many of the constitutional developments of the reigns of William III and Anne; and consequently to convey an entirely false idea of the grievances and aspirations of those who chased James II off his throne. The Act of Settlement (1701) provides a perfect illustration of this confusion. Its celebrated restrictive clauses, which cramped the freedom of action of the Hanoverians after 1714, reflected dissatisfaction not with James but with William; they expressed the determination of the governing class that no future alien king would be able to disregard the opinions of his English subjects. So although the law and custom of the constitution both underwent decisive change in the quarter-century following 1688, and it is reasonable to assume that but for the Revolution little of this change would have taken place, the line of thought which it commonly provokes – *post hoc ergo propter hoc* – can be full of snares. The next essay, in which the direct effects of the Revolution are reassessed in relation to the other factors, notably war, which did so much to shape the post-1688 system of government,[12] explores this problem at length.

The system itself has been described and analysed in a rich variety of books and learned articles,[13] and there would be little point in retracing this ground here. But at least two corners of a well-trodden field, somewhat neglected in conventional accounts of the 'Revolution settlement', still invite further investigation and debate: these are the development of the executive and the electoral system.

(i) *The Development of the Executive*. Political developments between 1689 and 1714, above all the evolution of parties, have so monopolised the historiography of this period in recent years that the parallel development of the administrative machine has received less than its fair share of attention.[14] We know that there was a striking growth in the sheer size of the executive under the last two Stuarts, mainly in response to the demands of war. But there are a whole series of questions prompted by this well-attested physical fact which can still not be resolved with complete conviction. Where, for instance, did the growth occur? Does it imply any new concept of the functions of government after the Revolution? Did the new elements in the system bring any corresponding increase in administrative efficiency? How did the cost of governing post-Revolution Britain compare with that of other administrative systems of the day?

At present, because of inadequate data, we still have to be content with tentative or incomplete answers to questions such as these. Take, for example, the pattern of growth. Evidently it was extremely uneven. The Court and Royal Household actually contracted during the reigns of William III and Anne.[15] Nor does the process of expansion seem to have affected in any spectacular way the staffs of the old-established central departments of State, or even of some newer departments, such as the Navy Office, which had already experienced major developments between 1660 and 1688.[16] What Edward Hughes wrote about the mid-eighteenth century is equally applicable to post-Revolution Britain. 'What impresses one about the central departments of government is not the size of their staffs, but that they managed with so few.'[17] The Principal Secretaries' office, with four Under-Secretaries and eight clerks for the Northern and Southern departments combined in 1713,[18] was still ludicrously undermanned; its establishment bore no relation to the transformation in the position of the two ministerial heads, especially in the field of foreign policy, since 1702. The Treasury was not strikingly better off, despite a reform of its establishment in 1695.[19] In such fields as these there are few signs of a 'proliferation of places'. Apart from the diplomatic service, which greatly extended the range of its activities between 1697 and 1714,[20] the real growth areas seem to have been mostly of two kinds: young departments such as the Post Office, the Customs and the Excise (all creations of the period 1657–83), which were still vigorously developing, and completely new departments, boards or offices thrown up in the course of the wars or after the Union with Scotland. Some of the latter, for instance the Board of Trade (1696) and the Scottish Commission of Chamberlainry and Trade (1711), involved little more than an increase in the number of lucrative jobs available to politicians. But others employed very large staffs indeed. The Board of Ordnance (reconstituted in 1702), Salt Office (1702) and Leather Office (1711) were possibly employing about 1300 men between them by the end of the Spanish Succession war; the needs of Scotland alone for local salt officers were put at 103 in 1714.[21] Unfortunately, until the revenue departments, especially, are more searchingly studied, any worthwhile quantitative estimate of the growth of the executive and the civil service in our period will remain virtually impossible.

When one thinks of the great bureaucratic structures which burdened early-eighteenth-century France or Spain or Austria it is probably fair to say that Britain still enjoyed government on the cheap. In the counties there was no army of *intendants* or *steuerräthe* for the taxpayer to support. Much of the revenue was collected professionally; but the law was administered and order maintained by the local aristocracy and gentry, for whom the status and patronage which their offices carried were ample remuneration for whatever duties the State required of them. Even so, post-Revolution Britain was very conscious of the growing expense of its government; and the seemingly perpetual threnody from the back benches of King William's House of Commons about administrative mismanagement or corruption, followed by the more spasmodic wails of protest under Anne, can only suggest that those who footed the bill were far from being convinced that they were getting value for money. How justified were their doubts? Was there no increase in efficiency proportionate to the physical growth of the executive between 1689 and 1714?

This is a particularly thorny problem, partly because of the diversity of the evidence, but mainly because there is no valid yardstick we can use for purposes of comparison. Fighting the two long wars against Louis XIV and paying for them made demands on the machinery of administration after 1688 far in excess of any that had taxed earlier governments. In the circumstances, evidence of inadequacy or bungling in some departments or of peculation in others must weigh less in the historian's scales than similar manifestations during, say, Charles II's Dutch Wars. Another complicating factor is that British government in this period was not merely facing unimagined problems, but was being conducted, in some measure at least, on new principles. An obvious example is the trend towards collegiate or committee government. This was already discernible in the years between the Restoration and 1688, but it became much more marked thereafter. Politically the advantages of boards and commissions were obvious; administratively they were not always so clear.[22]

Perhaps the greatest paradox about the development of the executive after the Glorious Revolution is that the unquestioned advance of more scientific methods in some areas is matched by the persistence of archaic and rationally indefensible methods in others. While Culliford and King in the 1690s were busy applying the new science of statistics to government, producing the first regular trade figures and the first reliable estimate of national wealth, while Newton presided over the Mint and complex actuarial calculations made possible the floating of public loans through the offer of annuities, the Exchequer, cluttered with sinecurists, was still going its age-old, tortuous, ultra-cautious ways, seemingly oblivious of war and change. By and large, however, it is hard to believe that the executive was not a good deal more efficient in 1714 than it had been in 1689. The tradition of bureaucratic immunity from the wind of party change or royal whim, carefully fostered in turn by Sunderland, Godolphin and Harley, was one of this period's most important legacies to future generations. By the time of Anne's death the tacitly-acknowledged permanence of many key appointments had built up a store of experience among senior officials which was of priceless value, and was reflected in the growing 'professionalism' of many departments.

(ii) *The Development of the Electorate*. The rapid growth of the executive, together with the expansion of the armed forces, caused many members of the House of Commons after the Revolution to fear for the independence of their assembly. Their anxiety showed itself in two ways: in their clamour for Place bills, which would either exclude royal officials and officers of the armed services completely from the House or severely restrict the number of those entitled to sit there,[23] and in their determination to put a legal time-limit on the life of every Parliament, which would force 'corrupted' Members to seek re-election fairly frequently. This second objective was secured with the passing of the Triennial Act in 1694 – an Act which during its twenty-two years on the statute-book was to have the most extensive repercussions. Its effect on the political temperature and on the growing virulence of the battle between Whig and Tory is now generally recognised.[24] Less easy to gauge are the effects of the rash of General Elections between 1695 and 1715 (when they recurred on average once every second year) on the system whereby England chose her Parliaments.

Between the accession of Elizabeth I and that of William III the electoral system had been growing steadily more representative. The stampede to create new parliamentary boroughs in the sixteenth and early seventeenth centuries; the widening of scores of borough franchises since the 1620s; a rapid increase in the numbers entitled to vote in the shires – all had played their part in this development.[25] Under the Hanoverians this process was to be reversed: decade by decade the system became more *un*representative, so that between 1780 and 1832 its reform became a political issue of the first importance. But in the reigns of the last two Stuarts, for reasons still not fully understood but clearly connected in some measure with the consistently high level of political excitement in the constituencies and the intense competition for votes among local party managers, the process had reached its climax. Significant pressures to the contrary notwithstanding,[26] the total electorate of England and Wales was indubitably larger, and possibly much larger, by the end of Anne's reign than it had been early in William's. Professor Plumb believes that 'a conservative figure for William III's reign would be about 200,000'; by 1714 it was almost certainly in the region of 250,000.[27] The 'political nation' in fact was far larger in this period than is commonly imagined. A higher proportion of the population of England and Wales voted, or had the right to vote, in the General Election of 1715 than at any Election between 1689 and 1832. After all, an electorate of 250,000 included roughly one in every five adult males in the country, and at least half the remainder consisted of wage labourers, servants or paupers to whom even the Levellers would have denied a vote. If one also remembers the unparalleled frequency of contests, and the activity of election mobs, made up largely of the unenfranchised, not only in the metropolis but in sleepy cathedral cities and small west-country boroughs, it must appear that the Revolution made possible for a time an exceptional degree of political participation by men of 'the middling and meaner sort': the very men who, as we have seen, had virtually no place in the minds of the revolutionaries in 1688.

The Common Man after the Revolution

In what other ways, if at all, did the Revolution affect the lives of ordinary people? Did constitutional and political change bring about any comparable change in the material condition or the human rights of the humble subject of King William III and Queen Anne? It will be argued in a later essay that in the short term the events of 1688 made no appreciable difference to the lot of the common man in Britain; indeed that in some ways – for instance, the greater severity with which the criminal law dealt with offences against property – they worsened it. It will also be suggested that any long-term benefits they brought him were, to say the least, problematical.[28] All the same, it is perhaps worth stressing that the years 1689–1714 were quite important years for the poor and the unprivileged, however little the Revolution itself may have been responsible for the fact. For instance, the period was one of nascent trade unionism in some trades and in some areas, as in the west-country textile towns; and although, like the relatively high wage rates paid in certain industries during the wars,[29] this was made possible by scarcity of labour rather than by any new concern for its dignity, it was nonetheless a development of obvious significance for the future. Then there was the steady stream of pamphlet literature which poured forth in the 1690s and in the early years of the eighteenth century, in which economic principle and philanthropic argument were closely intertwined. Its motivation is not easily established, since the pens at work included those of businessmen and manufacturers, theoretical economists, civil servants and even politicians;[30] but it is certain that it contributed, along with the new attitude adopted by Church leaders towards their social responsibilities,[31] to a notable enlargement of the concept of social welfare, not only in theory but in practice. As the experiments in establishing workhouses and the advance of charity-school education both showed, this concept embraced by 1714 something more than the mundane necessity of keeping the poor from starvation.

Of course, the latter was still the overriding concern. By 1702 the income from the poor rate was around £900,000, an increase of nearly 40 per cent over the previous fifteen years – a fact which probably reflects the prevalence of distress in William III's reign more than any stimulation of the social conscience by the Revolution. Did the government and Parliament themselves accept any responsibility in this sphere? Certainly there is little to suggest that the post-Restoration trend away from regarding social policy as one of the primary functions of government was significantly arrested by the Revolution. But it is possible to be misled by such sweeping phrases as 'the end of Stuart paternalism' into thinking that executive and legislature had abrogated *all* responsibility for social welfare by the late seventeenth century. In emergencies, such as the chronic grain shortage in the winter of 1709–10, or to meet what seemed particularly serious abuses, they were ready and able to act.

IV

The Content and Structure of Politics

Since social policy was not regarded as one of the normal functions of government in the years 1689–1714, it is hardly surprising to find that social issues – at least in so far as these involved the material well-being of the man in the street – played no part in the disputes between contending political forces in Parliament or in the country at large. The grievances of the 'mere gentry' against the *nouveaux riches*, to which we earlier referred, and the landowners' efforts to reassert themselves supplied the only ingredient in post-Revolution conflicts which could be described even broadly as social. Otherwise the issues which divided politicians were mostly either constitutional, or religious, or external (arising out of the wars and the conduct of foreign policy), or simply personal.[32] There was no genuine 'radical' element in these disputes. The Whigs of the age of William III and Anne had parted company with such groups as the London radicals, with their sectarian-Leveller traditions, which had been associated with their cause in the later years of Charles II. Whig leadership was now firmly aristocratic; their chief support in the City came from great business magnates with a heavy stake in the establishment. Even the mob, in its periodic incursions into politics, was content to mouth the slogans of the established parties – Church and Queen, No Conventicle, No Pretender, No Peace without Spain; it appeared to have no specific demands of its own.

But what were these 'parties' to which men gave their allegiance ? Did they bear any resemblance to the late nineteenth- or twentieth-century notion of political parties, as Whig historians from Macaulay to Trevelyan confidently assumed; or were they much closer in type to the miscellany of 'groups', 'factions' or 'interests' with which students of mid-eighteenth-century politics have long been familiar ? Were they in direct line of descent from the parties of the 1670s and early 1680s, Whig and Tory, Court and Country; or did the Revolution so far erase these old distinctions as to bring about basic changes in the political structure ? The structure of post-Revolution politics, even more than its content (though naturally the two aspects cannot be completely divorced from each other), has proved to be our period's chief battleground of scholarly controversy in recent years. Since the present writer has been as closely involved as anyone in the argument, it would be inappropriate for him to elaborate on it in the course of this essay; it would also be superfluous, since a full discussion of the issues is offered later.[33] We cannot be sure that the last shots in the battle have been fired. But most of the smoke has cleared; and the structure revealed seems appreciably nearer in shape to the Macaulay 'model' – with its four main political compartments in William's reign and its two in Anne's[34] – than to the Namier one.

The study of the political history of the years 1689–1714 must surely benefit enormously once these assertive problems of structure have been firmly laid to rest. For the very word 'structure', suggesting as it does a static system, is oddly inappropriate when applied to so dynamic a political world as that of Britain after the Glorious Revolution. After 1688, and even more after 1694, the whole country was shaken and torn by the furious tempest of party. Until 1716 the storm raged almost without abating. And yet within a decade all had changed, and a greater calm than Britain had known for many generations had settled upon the land. This extraordinary transformation has encouraged one distinguished recent contributor to the political history of the period to break completely new ground, by bringing into the foreground of debate not a structural problem but a conceptual one – the problem of political stability.[35]

The Search for Political Stability and the Problem of Scotland

Whatever the rejection of King James II had achieved, it seemed to the post-Revolution generation that in one crucial respect it had failed: it had failed to put an end to the chronic political instability which had beset the two kingdoms since the union of the crowns in 1603. Indeed for thirteen years, at least, after 1688 this malaise of seventeenth-century Britain seemed as stubborn as ever. The reasons why the Revolution brought no immediate cure to the condition, and why in some respects it even aggravated it, provide fruitful matter for speculation and argument. Among the essays which follow, two consider particular aspects of this problem. One of the most obvious legacies of the Glorious Revolution which helped to perpetuate political instability was a foreign king whose character, motives for invading England and accepting its crown,[36] and subsequent policies all made it exceptionally difficult to bring harmony into the new relationship between Crown and Parliament. The extent of his personal responsibility for the conspicuous absence of consistent and acceptable government up to 1694, and again after 1698, is assessed in the later study of 'William III and the Politicians'.[37] In a less obvious and immediate way the Revolution also unleashed a powerful centrifugal force within the political system. This was the force of Scottish nationalism, reinforced by Presbyterian religious feeling, which by the early years of Anne's reign had developed sufficient impetus to threaten the whole island with the prospect of renewed civil war,[38] unless the relations of the two kingdoms could be satisfactorily adjusted. Although King William's recognition of the Kirk as the established Church of Scotland destroyed the flimsy ecclesiastical basis on which the Stuarts had tried to preserve Anglo-Scottish harmony, and his abolition of the 'Lords of the Articles'[39] marked the infusion of a new spirit of independence into the Edinburgh Parliament, Scottish opinion at large was not conspicuously Anglophobe in 1689. But after the Scottish Convention's proposal for a parliamentary union had been cold-shouldered, largely for economic reasons, by its English counterpart, relations between the two countries deteriorated steadily under pressure from a diversity of stresses and provocations.

In his 1965 Ford Lectures J. H. Plumb suggests other reasons, more basic than these, why political stability continued to elude Britain until after 1714. Quite apart from the solution of specific problems, like that of Scotland, he identifies four prerequisites of the achievement of such stability in the eighteenth century: a tamed and eroded electorate; 'single-party government; the legislature firmly under executive control; and a sense of common identity in those who wielded economic, social and political power'.[40] None of these, he argues, could be supplied within the political system of 1689–1714, with its frequent and fierce elections, its 'mixed ministries' thrown up out of the seething cauldron of Whig–Tory conflict, and its Commons' back benches crowded with 'intractable' gentry, inimical as ever to a strong executive. Yet all these conditions had been achieved before 1725 by Sir Robert Walpole. For Plumb, Walpole stands out as the architect and master builder of the monumentally solid Hanoverian political structure, erecting in the space of a few years in the 1720s something which had proved beyond the capacity of any monarch or statesman since the vintage years of Elizabeth I. He did so, however, on foundations partially prepared for him, and using some bricks at least which had been produced out of the furnace of late Stuart struggles.

Of the foundations on which Walpole built, two – the Incorporating Union of England and Scotland concluded in 1707, and the single-party state which resulted from the destruction of the old Tory party – raise causal problems in themselves which are of the greatest interest to any student of post-Revolution Britain: a whole essay will be devoted later to each of them.[41] It can no longer be taken for granted, as once it was, that the death of Queen Anne and the death of the Tory party were more or less coincidental; but most of the roots of the latter's fatal malady can be traced back into the period before 1714, and we shall try to follow them to their points of origin. We shall also look at the tantalising question of why the Edinburgh Parliament agreed to terminate its own existence in 1707 and to bring into being a new state of 'Great Britain' with a common representative assembly meeting at Westminster. Why the English Parliament was so ready during the Spanish Succession war to change its attitude of 1689 is clear enough. But what finally brought the Scots to accept the idea of Union, so soon after a great weight of opinion both in and out of their own Parliament had seemed overwhelmingly against it, remains a fascinating – and at this time highly topical – area for discussion.

Of course the Union did not solve the problem of Anglo-Scottish relations overnight. The bonds tied in 1707 seemed frail enough to many in both countries up to the time of the Jacobite rebellion of 1715, and none-too-secure for a decade or so thereafter. The stresses the Union had to endure in the early years of its life and the reasons why it survived them are scarcely less interesting than the forces which created it, and they have been much less thoroughly explored. The grievances were not all on one side. The Scots, it is true, had good cause to complain of a number of breaches both of the letter and the spirit of the 1707 Act: on judicial and religious issues, on the rights of the Scottish peerage, and finally over taxation – a question which provoked a motion before the House of Lords on 1 June 1713 calling for the dissolution of the Union. But at the same time the English were justifiably concerned at the venality and undue subservience of the sixty-one Scottish representatives in Parliament, especially of the sixteen peers; and hard-pressed squires took it ill when Scotland tried to evade part of her fiscal responsibilities when the war was over in 1713. Should we accept that the only effective cement holding the Union together up to 1715 was a negative one – the fear of Jacobitism and Catholicism? (Certainly the results of the 1713 Election showed how widespread was this fear in Scotland.) Or is this to undervalue the effectiveness of what Dr Riley has called Lord Treasurer Oxford's 'Scottish system' in the years 1710–14, or even the tempting flavour of the first economic fruits enjoyed by the Lowlanders after the breaking down of trade barriers with England in 1707?[42] At all events, more progress had probably been made towards the consolidation of the Union by 1714 than most contemporaries realised; and no problems remained in Anglo-Scottish relations after the failure of the '15 Rebellion which were not capable of being solved by the systematic extension to Scotland of Walpole's patronage system, the scientific distribution of the loaves and fishes among the needy and the deserving.[43]

The example of Scotland may prompt us to ask whether there were other ways in which Walpole's achievement of political stability in the 1720s was assisted, if not anticipated, by post-Revolution developments. And one has but to compare relations between Crown and Commons in the second half of Anne's reign with those which disfigured the early years of William III to realise that progress towards the bridling of the legislature by the executive was by no means delayed until after 1721. Amid all the clamour of the battle between Whig and Tory it is easy to lose sight of the fact that the Whig administration of 1708–10 never lost a significant Commons' division in the course of two sessions, while the Harley administration of 1710–14 suffered only one major defeat in four sessions. The underlying reasons for this greater control are worth considering. Could it be that Godolphin, the Junto and Harley in the years 1708–14 had already grasped the lesson which Walpole so remorselessly applied under George I – that the firmest links which could hold government and Parliament together were those of common party allegiance, reinforced by patronage? Professor Plumb has written memorably of the 'tradition of conspiracy, riot, plot, and revolt among the ruling class that stretched back [from 1688] to the Normans'.[44] But does the evidence of Anne's reign, one wonders – despite the turbulence of party – reveal the seventeenth-century squire and aristocrat as being quite so anarchically-minded, so antipathetic to order and firm government, as the earlier history of the years 1642–60, 1683, 1685 and 1688 would at first sight seem to suggest?

In one further respect Walpole was fortunate. The Britain whose political leadership he assumed in 1721 had experienced since 1689 an extraordinary growth of national self-confidence, a resilient confidence which the bursting of the South Sea Bubble had only temporarily and superficially shaken. Indeed it is well worth pondering how much the growing political stability of the period 1702–63, by contrast with the years from 1603 up to 1701, had to do with the satisfaction of the political nation with successful government and with Britain's high international prestige. The Stuarts had so often brought domestic troubles on their heads by the sheer ineptitude of their rule; and not least by a foreign policy which had only rarely reflected national interests and which had led at times to chronic isolation and humiliation. After 1688, however, and even more after 1701, Britain acquired an international status she had never before possessed. Little wonder that Britons by 1714, despite their internal conflicts, had faith in themselves and in their future. We must next see briefly how this development came about and what problems it poses for the student of the period.

v

Britain in Europe after the Revolution

The Glorious Revolution is the key to this novel position of Britain in her European context. As a constitutional and even as a political landmark its importance may have been exaggerated; but its broad European significance is surely unquestionable. It brought to this island a Dutchman whose knowledge of continental politics and experience of continental diplomacy surpassed by far that of any English king since the

Middle Ages, and whose whole commitment to the Revolution stemmed in the first place from his determination that Britain should no longer evade her European responsibilities. The leader of a nation which, alone perhaps among seventeenth-century states, had formed a true assessment of England's potential capacity, William of Orange was resolved that his new kingdom should play the role for which her growing wealth, her strategic situation, her militant Protestantism, and above all her sea power fitted her. His policies encountered much resistance; they made him for much of his reign so unpopular that at one stage he was on the brink of abdication; but he had the satisfaction of knowing before he died in March 1702 that he had achieved his wish. England, apart from brief interludes of isolationism, would never again contract out of Europe. She had been made conscious of her international responsibilities, and had been brought to accept them.

This momentous change in Britain's relationship to the Continent was largely, therefore, the achievement of one man. But not entirely. William was helped by the rapid development of an informed opinion in England on European issues: and this in turn was stimulated by the Huguenot immigration which followed the revocation of the Edict of Nantes (1685) and by the end of Press censorship (1695). The broadening political education of the post-Revolution generation is strikingly demonstrated in two ways: after 1693, by the gradual adoption of distinctive party standpoints on foreign policy, that of the Whigs outward-looking and in favour of the principle of collective security, that of the Tories xenophobic and advocating disengagement; and again, after 1702, by the success with which the Secretaries of State and other leading statesmen took over from the late king virtually the whole responsibility for fashioning and executing foreign policy.

The major implications of 'the revolution in foreign policy' will be more spaciously discussed elsewhere.[45] Some of the problems it raises have too often in the past been the subject of assertion rather than of reasoned argument. How much genuine substance was there, for instance, in the charges of Tory propagandists that the British alliance was shamelessly abused by her 'friends' on the Continent, notably by the Austrians and the Dutch? And what interests, for that matter, was the new foreign policy designed to serve? It is clear that William III vastly enlarged the scope of policy and gave it a new direction. Was its motivation similarly revolutionised? National security, the Protestant succession, the Balance of Power – these are all vital considerations which from now on loom larger than the personal or dynastic interests of the ruler. But their relative importance, and still more the strength of the economic forces brought to bear on the shaping of policy, remain very much a matter for argument. Perhaps the historian, in his understandable preoccupation with 'principles' of foreign policy in this startling new phase of commitment to Europe, has been too prone to neglect the more mundane and pragmatic influences which from time to time determined its course: in particular, the direct reaction upon it of the shifting pattern of domestic politics. British policy in the years 1710–13, which led to the conclusion of the Treaty of Utrecht, provides us with a perfect case-study of this neglect; and since in other respects, too, the Tory ministry's peacemaking has been misunderstood, we shall bring it into sharper focus in another essay.[46]

Britain at War: the Debate on Strategy

Although serious disputes clouded the making of peace at Utrecht, disputes both within Britain and within the Grand Alliance, the final settlement itself was an international testimonial to Britain's unquestioned arrival as a Great Power. Alone among the major participants in the recent conflict her war-aims were substantially achieved. Yet the burgeoning of national self-confidence by 1714 to which we earlier alluded was more than a reflection of rising European status; above all it was the fruit of success in war. For twenty out of the past twenty-five years the country's resources had been stretched as never before; but not once had they been brought to breaking-point. There had been no serious defeat at sea since 1690. Not since Agincourt had there been military achievements by an English general on continental soil to compare with Marlborough's triumphs of 1704–8. Superficially it may seem strange, therefore, that for most of the war years there raged a great internal debate on strategy: there was a sharp conflict of opinion, first between William III and the Country opposition and later between Whig and Tory, as to the best method of containing or defeating France. Yet this debate seemed entirely valid at the time; and when we recall that nine years of costly attrition between 1689 and 1697 ended in nothing better than stalemate, and that even the Spanish Succession war began badly and ended with three years of bitter frustration, it can be seen that the strategic problem retains its validity for the student also.

Briefly the point at issue is this. The Country and Tory case was that both wars were unnecessarily prolonged and made inordinately expensive by concentrating the bulk of the nation's effort on attacking the enemy's strongest points – his heavily fortified land frontiers – instead of the weak links in his defences – his harbours, sea lanes and colonies.[47] How tenable was this view?

To do justice to either side of the argument would require an essay in itself. All we can do here is to take note of a number of factors which clearly come into the reckoning, but which were sometimes obscured or misunderstood by contemporaries. One concerns the relative size of the army and navy and the relative cost of their operations. Because of the miasma of suspicion which still clung to the idea of a 'standing army', and also because the land forces employed against Louis XIV were the largest any British sovereign had ever put into the field, the notion that these forces were absorbing most of the country's resources took root, though in fact it was quite erroneous. The navy expanded at a furious rate in the 1690s, and between 1688 and 1702 cost £19·9 million, only £2 million less than the army. The 186,000 men serving in the armed forces in the peak year of 1711 included, even nominally, only 67,000 British troops – less than twice the number James II's army had contained in peacetime in 1687.[48] The historian must take care that figures of this kind are not masked by the emotive propaganda put out in King William's day and Queen Anne's by 'blue water' theorists. A second crucial point which such theorists were slow to grasp was that traditional strategic concepts, based on earlier seventeenth-century or even Elizabethan wars, did not automatically hold good now that Britain was pitted against the most formidable military power the world had seen since Imperial Rome. The Dutch Wars of 1652–74 had been fought against a small but highly commercial nation, unusually vulnerable to naval and colonial attack, and to blockade. France's trade and colonies, by contrast, did no more than reinforce the fighting power of a great nation-state, with human and internal economic resources unrivalled in Europe.

Another fact often disregarded at the time, after 1692 at least, was the vulnerability of England, and to some extent of Scotland also, to invasion, and the fact that the first line of defence against this threat was not the fleet but the expeditionary forces of William and Marlborough in Flanders. Even putting the most negative value on their presence there, they prevented Louis releasing perhaps 50,000 troops for an attempt on the largely unfortified British coastline in co-operation with the Jacobite fifth-column. Finally, the critics of large-scale land operations took too little account of the unorthodoxy of French naval tactics after 1692. How could a war be decisively won at sea when the enemy's main battle fleet blandly declined to commit itself to open action and virtually her whole maritime effort was concentrated on commerce-destruction? To eliminate the *corsairs*, which wrought such terrible destruction on British merchantmen in both these wars,[49] and to sustain an effective blockade of the enormous French coastline would possibly have been beyond a navy of twice the size and cost of that actually deployed.

Against such arguments the case for a *purely* maritime strategy may well crumble. But could it not be contended, nonetheless, that after 1702, and still more after 1705–6, the balance in the distribution of resources was wrong; and still more, that these resources were too widely deployed? That Britain was too heavily committed on land and inadequately provided for at sea is suggested by the failure to stop the life-giving flow of silver from the New World mines back to the Bourbon treasuries; by the inability even of Marlborough's genius, in a short campaigning season, to crack wide open the north-eastern fortress defences of France; and not least, by the much more serious recruiting problems which always faced the army, by comparison with the navy.[50] In the final reckoning, however, it was the over-extension of resources, the 'too many irons in the fire' which Lord Treasurer Godolphin was bemoaning as early as 1703, and which he had still more cause to regret after a second front was opened in the Peninsula in 1705, which must seem to most students the most telling criticism of war strategy in the years 1702–11. It was probably this, rather than an excessive faith in land operations as such, which prevented this war of so many successes for British arms ending in unqualified triumph.

War Finance

Still more awesome than the task of conducting the wars against France was the cost of the struggle, which totalled £130 million. As much money was spent on one year of the Spanish Succession war (1710–11) as Charles II's government raised in the first eleven years of his reign. Whereas the Second Dutch War (1665–7) had entailed an average annual expenditure of £1⅔ million, King William's war cost three times as much as this each year, while Queen Anne's cost five times as much. It was in their efforts to find ways and means of footing such colossal bills that the Treasury ministers of William and Anne initiated what has justly been called a 'financial revolution', every whit as far-reaching in its repercussions as the revolution in the constitution or in foreign policy.

Paying for war on credit; waging war without trying to balance the books: these basically were the two reasons why Britain was able to make such an extraordinary effort of arms without the population being milked utterly dry by taxation. Of course kings and ministers before 1688 had paid for their forces at least partly by loans, just as they had allowed expenditure in the course of their wars to outstrip income. But in the wars of 1689–1713 there was a vital difference. Credit finance and deficit finance became for the first time orderly, respectable, a symbol of health rather than frailty.

The most spectacular facet of the financial revolution, the development of a completely new system of public credit, has recently been the subject of a magisterial survey which has resolved most of the problems associated with it.[51] But one can, of course, exaggerate the dependence of post-Revolution governments on credit. Between 1690 and 1700, for instance, net borrowings totalled £11·7 million while fiscal revenue over the same period amounted to close on four times this sum.[52] Taxation remained of prime importance; and the tax changes which took place between 1689 and 1714 were an integral part of the revolution in public finance. For one thing, they saw the end of the age-old distinction between ordinary and extraordinary revenue and of the convention that direct taxes should be levied only to raise the latter; but more important, they created a fiscal structure which was to survive in its essentials for the greater part of the eighteenth century. Although parts of this structure, notably the land tax and the customs system, have been the subject of valuable monographs,[53] large areas are still unexplored. What is more, a number of general questions of great interest raised by the changes in revenue policy after the Revolution deserve to be more thoroughly aired. Thus the equity of post-Revolution impositions as a whole – a highly important factor in the efficiency of any system – remains a matter for debate. Despite the fact that the consumer spending of other sections of the population was progressively tapped as the years went by, through a striking increase in the weight of excise or excise-type duties, many country gentlemen clearly felt that the 'landed interest' was being victimised; and if Gregory King's figures can

what the land tax soon

p.23 line 39:   for 'And yet that a Parliament' read 'And yet a Parliament'.

flower of the Funds'. Perhaps the most pertinent question to be asked about the new tax system of the years 1689–1714 is whether the word 'system' itself is euphemistic. Can any rational principles of policy be discerned through the highly complex web of impositions woven by the end of the Spanish Succession war? Or should we rather accept 'Ways and Means' in this period as a series of improvised, *ad hoc* measures, having no other end in view than the raising of revenue, and taking on at their worst 'more the appearance of bingo than a carefully calculated national policy'?[55] Although some of these problems were briefly discussed more than half a century ago in William Kennedy's stimulating essay,[56] there is need for a thorough, up-to-date assessment.

VI

There were remarkably few facets of the nation's life between 1689 and 1714 which were not touched in some way by the overriding fact of war or the overshadowing fact of the Revolution. If there is occasionally a danger of exaggerating these influences, the risk of their being undervalued, one might think, has generally proved higher. The briefest glance at two fields of national development in this period, those of literature and religion, would certainly suggest so.

Literary Achievement

This was a great age of literary achievement; and few would care to assert that the genius of Swift, Addison, Steele, Defoe or Congreve would not have flowered in any event, even if James II had never been dethroned. Yet would it have enjoyed so much scope, and could it possibly have taken the same forms? Some of the choicest of all Augustan prose is to be found in periodicals like the *Tatler* and the *Examiner*, or the *Spectator* with its sales of 11,500 copies a week in 1711. Such delicacies could never have titillated the connoisseur's palate but for the lifting of Stuart censorship of the Press in 1695, and it is hard to conceive of such freedom being granted under James II's autocracy. Moreover, the wars against France and the safety of the Protestant succession provided the themes of much of the best pamphlet journalism of the day, of Defoe's *True-Born Englishman*, Swift's *Conduct of the Allies*, Steele's *Crisis*; while war and 'Revolution principles' together provided much of the inspiration – if such it can be called – behind the contemporary drama.[57]

Religious Strife: Church and Dissent

The implications of the Glorious Revolution for the religious life of the British people are not so often disregarded. But they are very liable to be oversimplified and misjudged. It is true that the Toleration Act of 1689, an integral part of the Revolution Settlement, has always been rightly recognised as the beginning of a new era in the history of English Protestant Dissent. By allowing freedom of worship for all Trinitarian Protestants who declined to accept the liturgy and government of the official Church, it gave these nonconformists a legally recognised status in the community; and in the next twenty-five years they seemed to the apprehensive eyes of Anglican divines to be gaining ground alarmingly at the expense of the establishment. In 1711, for instance, the Tory House of Commons learned to its consternation that the number of meeting-houses in the London area already outnumbered the churches by two to one. But there are two other sides to the picture. While there were plenty of outward and visible signs of progress – hundreds of monuments in brick and stone, in the shape of Congregational or Baptist chapels or the new academies, raised by the post-Revolution generation to the strength of Dissent – these were not all signs of an inward and spiritual grace. It would be wrong to suggest that the end of the 'great persecution' of 1661–88 was followed by immediate spiritual decline; so long as the Tories were strong enough to attempt to translate their fear of nonconformity into fresh legislation, as they were up to 1714, there was little likelihood of widespread complacency. Yet there is some evidence that even before Anne's death a greater sense of security and its concomitant, growing material prosperity, were slowly beginning to sap some of the old Puritan enthusiasm. Equally important was the fresh impetus the Revolution gave to that remarkable change in the social basis of Dissent which took place between 1660 and 1714. By perpetuating the civil barriers raised against nonconformists under Charles II, the Toleration Act confirmed the gentry in their growing disenchantment with so socially-disabling a religion. By 1714 the sects had become predominantly urban phenomena and overwhelmingly middle class and lower middle class in composition. The descendants of the political revolutionaries of the mid-seventeenth century were in fact to become the industrial revolutionaries of the late eighteenth.

The effects of the 1688 Revolution on the Church of England were even more complex than its influence on Dissent, and they have been more seriously underestimated. It will be apparent when its full implications are explored in a later essay[58] that the Revolution deserves to be recognised as one of the most conspicuous landmarks in the Church's development between the Henrician Reformation of the 1530s and the Ecumenical movement of the 1960s. The Toleration Act, for instance, distorted and weakened the unique link between Church and State in England, forged in 1559 and refashioned in 1660: the Church of England remained the state church 'as by law established'; but it now lost some of the major benefits of establishment without the corresponding gains which would have accrued from total disestablishment. In addition, swearing allegiance to a Calvinist 'usurper' and then seeing the toleration so laxly interpreted in the 1690s undermined the self-confidence of many honest Anglicans, causing them to question the validity of their own position; while it is surely worth pondering how far their sense of insecurity was heightened, not merely by the new intellectual climate of post-Revolution Britain – increasingly rational, sceptical and (under the influence of Locke's political philosophy) permeated by an essentially secular view of man in society – but also by the growing dominance north of the Border after 1689 of an officially countenanced Kirk, self-confident and intolerant.

VII

The Economy at War

The impact of the 1688 Revolution on the British economy is an issue which is rarely discussed. Economic specialists have conspicuously declined to rise to the bait dangled before them by Mr Christopher Hill, who has startlingly claimed – on the strength of evidence which may appear to some insubstantial or fragile, but which ought not to be flatly discounted – that the Revolution was 'no less a turning-point in the economic than in the political and constitutional history of England'.[59] It is rather the effect of war between 1689 and 1713 on the material prosperity of the British people which currently presents the most challenging economic problem to the late Stuart historian. And since it has not proved possible to devote a separate essay to it, it may be useful to conclude our present survey by briefly taking stock of the progress of the debate.[60]

Most of the controversy has centred on the English economy. To Scotland, it is generally agreed, the war brought few benefits and many really serious difficulties.[61] By and large it was only after the Act of 1707 had brought the country within the framework of the Navigation laws that the few advantages Scotland possessed in wartime conditions (for instance, the remoteness of the Clyde approaches from the French privateering bases, and the consequent opportunity for the Glasgow merchants to capture a growing share of the North American tobacco trade) could be properly exploited.

In the case of England the picture is infinitely more variegated and susceptible of widely different interpretations. Moreover, it is not just a separate problem peculiar to the two wars against Louis XIV, but part of a far greater debate involving all the wars of the eighteenth century, up to and including that of American Independence. Reduced to its barest essentials the question in dispute is this: would the economy have advanced more rapidly without war than with it? The foremost modern authority on eighteenth-century economic history postulated that over this century as a whole the prime cause of instability in the economy – of those 'economic fluctuations' which were the subject of his Ford Lectures – was war.[62] It requires no very exhaustive study of the commercial and industrial statistics which have been made available in recent years[63] to convince one that normal economic patterns were disturbed, sometimes quite dramatically, during the five major wars of the years 1689–1783; and T. S. Ashton was surely on firm ground when he claimed that 'there will be few to dispute that, whether for good or ill, the wars of this period tended to accentuate the short-term oscillations of activity'.[64]

But *for good or ill* – this is the intriguing question: the more so since, even when confined to the post-Revolution period, the debate can be conducted at two levels. A limited approach requires, at least, that we consider the evidence bearing on the fortunes of trade, industry and agriculture, and compare the pattern of each in 1689 with that in 1713. But there is also a broader and long-term approach to the problem, which recognises that the years from 1660 to 1800 were years of 'revolutionary' development throughout the whole economy, first in commerce, much later on in agriculture, and finally in industry, and enquires whether these developments were significantly advanced or held back by the trial of strength with Louis XIV.

At both levels the Ashton view adopts a generally pessimistic attitude to the influence of war, seeing it as more damaging than beneficial in the short run and as a retarding factor in the long run. A decade earlier Professor Nef, surveying a far more comprehensive sweep of evidence,

advanced a similar general thesis.[65] Long before this, however, Sir
George Clark had concluded that to English mercantile interests the
Spanish Succession conflict, at least, proved in the end very profitable -
an opinion which he has since reiterated;[66] while among younger
scholars the more optimistic view of eighteenth-century wars has found
a particularly vigorous champion in A. H. John, who has stressed the
stimulus to industry as well as the overall advantages to shipping and
trade.[67] Both schools have claimed their disciples; other leading
authorities have taken up an intermediate position.[68]

Such, very briefly, is the historiographical background to the debate.
What strikes the non-specialist, weighing to the best of his ability the
evidence which the pundits have marshalled, are its many apparent
contradictions. These can be illustrated first by reviewing trade,
industry and agriculture in turn, and taking a few examples within
each field of the very different ways in which war made its impact
felt.

Since the passing of the Navigation Acts in 1651 and 1660 English
shipping had been of crucial importance to English trade. The striking
commercial advances of the reigns of Charles II and James II could
never have been made without a swiftly expanding merchant marine,
whose tonnage by 1686 had reached 340,000. The case against war as a
benefactor of trade would seem to be greatly fortified, therefore, by
estimates of the havoc wrought by French privateers on this fleet
between 1689 and 1697 and again from 1702 up to 1708 or 1709. Over
the whole period the number of English merchantmen sunk or captured
may well have reached 6000, and such losses had a further effect in
inhibiting mercantile enterprise, and therefore new building. It is true
the picture was not as black as it has sometimes been painted. For one
thing, by no means all these ships were genuinely 'lost'; many were
bought back from the French *corsairs* with ransom money. Secondly, a
fair proportion of the remainder were ageing vessels which would soon
have had to be replaced in any event. And thirdly, the depredations
suffered over the period as a whole were at least made good by heavy
captures of enemy prizes (2203 in the second war alone), by extensive
purchases from America, and by the output of home shipyards.
Nevertheless the merchant fleet cannot have been much larger, if indeed
it was any larger, in 1714 than it had been at the time of the Revolution.[69]

On the other hand, the wars against Louis XIV saw useful technical
progress in English shipbuilding. Few of the lessons learned at this

time in those hives of industry, the naval dockyards, seem to have been later adapted to pacific ends. But it was of some importance that English shipowners could no longer rely on the Dutch to satisfy their need for bulk-cargo carriers, the demand for which continued to build up right through the years 1689–1714 as tobacco, sugar, timber, coal and grain entered or left the country in growing quantities. The large, heavily-manned ship in which British yards traditionally specialised had proved quite uneconomical in the seventeenth century for transporting many of these 'bulksom commodities'; but from the 1650s to the 1670s, with such a plentiful supply of Dutch 'flyboats' available, thanks to loopholes in the Navigation Acts, native shipbuilders had lacked the incentive to develop new techniques. It was the shipbuilders of the north-eastern ports – Sunderland, Whitby, Scarborough – who before the end of the century were leading the way with their 'pinks' to a new era of English shipbuilding, in which the 150- to 300-ton ship, with small crew but extensive hold-space, acquired for the first time a recognised place of importance.[70] It would be misleading, however, to suggest that it was the French wars which provided their main incentive. This came rather from the urgent need to replace the Dutch-built ships, many of which came to the end of their natural lives just before or during the war years.

Turning from the means of carrying the goods to the volume of goods carried in this period, and the places to which and from which they were carried, we again find ourselves facing a tangle of evidence which mocks facile generalisation. Take exports, for example. On the whole they held their own remarkably well, especially after the turn of the century. No less than seven times between 1703 and 1713 the value of English products dispatched abroad exceeded that for 1700, a year of peace; and woollen cloth, which had commanded less than 50 per cent of the export market in 1700 compared with about 80 per cent in 1640, was in such demand thereafter that an average of $3\frac{1}{4}$ million pounds' worth a year was exported over the period 1706–15, $£\frac{3}{4}$ million more than between 1697 and 1704. Yet these seemingly healthy figures conceal two very material facts. One is the high proportion of goods sent to the Continent which were paid for by the British taxpayer – arms, uniforms and foodstuffs for the supply of the forces Britain maintained or subsidised there. The other was the sharp decline of the re-export or entrepôt trade, involving mainly colonial or Indian goods. This had been the most revolutionary factor in seventeenth-century commercial progress, multiplying fifteenfold in the sixty years before 1700; but it slumped more spectacularly than any other branch of trade between 1701 and 1713.

The import picture is likewise full of inconsistencies. The overall pattern appears to be one of decline, certainly after 1700;[71] and indeed it proved a blessing in disguise for some youthful native industries that high tariff revenue barriers and the complete prohibition on trade with France cut off or reduced deliveries from many traditional continental suppliers between 1689 and 1713.[72] And yet the very branch of trade which should have been most vulnerable to enemy action – colonial imports into the port of London – actually succeeded for many years in maintaining the electrifying rate of progress which they had developed since the Restoration. Tobacco ships, running the gauntlet of the French privateers, were bringing in nearly half as much again of the Virginian and Maryland leaf by the late 1690s as they had in 1688, while West Indian sugar shipments also showed a significant if not quite so spectacular increase.[73] To judge from the tendency of the main western ports (Bristol, Liverpool, Whitehaven and Glasgow) to gain ground in the post-Revolution period at the expense of London, the flow of goods thither from the New World must also have continued apace after 1689.

The fortunes of English industrialists were no less chequered than those of the merchants. For manufacturing industry at large, twenty testing years of war had a number of basic implications: a few were on the debit side of the ledger; the majority appear on the credit side. The two main adverse trends were the result of war taxation and of interference with certain raw material supplies from abroad, but neither was as serious as is sometimes claimed.[74] A land tax levied at four shillings in the pound should theoretically have damaged industries producing primarily for the better-class home consumer; but many a country squire of Anne's reign preferred to run into debt rather than deny himself the luxuries of life.[75] A few specific industries – brewing was the most notable case in point – were hard hit by excise duties levied to meet the ever-rising bill of war expenditure. But it seems unlikely that industry in general lost more by taxation than it gained, when one remembers the boost to the metalware trades, and to the manufacture of tinplate, paper and silk as a result of the high level of import duties. Nor, on the whole, did raw material shortages impose severe restraints: not at least on the iron-working trades and the paper industry which have been singled out for commiseration.[76] Thus home supplies of linen and woollen rags proved plentiful enough for the needs of paper-making, and the 'Grub Street' war of 1695–1714, with its unprecedented demand for paper from newspaper editors and pamphleteers, did far more to encourage the industry than did the French wars to depress it.[77] By a strange irony the one native industry which was best placed, with its ability to draw on the skills of Huguenot immigrants, to take advantage of wartime windfalls – namely the manufacture of silks – seems to have been prevented from making the very rapid progress with which it is normally credited by falling supplies of raw silk during the war of 1702–13.[78]

There were three major ways in which some sectors of industry quite manifestly benefited, even in the short run, from the stimuli provided by the wars. The most evident was through the direct demands of the armed forces. These gave obvious encouragement to foundries and to the sail-cloth industry, and also to the heavy woollen industry, which had to meet huge orders for uniforms and blankets.[79] The second was through greatly increased home investment, with the heavy transfer of capital in the early 1690s from more risky overseas trading ventures.[80] The third was through the incentive provided to invention and technological change. In the whole century between 1660 and 1760 interest in industrial invention was never as keen as it was in the 1690s: there was nothing comparable in England until the closing years of the Seven Years War. Twice as many patents were issued in the nineties as in any previous decade since the Restoration, sixty-four of them in the years 1691–3; and it would be instructive to know the extent to which this patent-boom was specifically connected with war technology.

In determining the future development of Britain, however, the last year of the Spanish Succession war has a claim to be considered the most important of the whole post-Revolution period. For it was the year 1712 which possibly saw the discovery of a method of using coal in the smelting process in such a way as to produce workable iron from iron ore.[81] Until the successful application of coke at Darby's Coalbrookdale works the blast furnaces of Britain's ironmasters were entirely dependent on dwindling supplies of wood fuel. Even if the lessons of this historic step were only very slowly applied – as late as 1760, for instance, there were still only seventeen coke-fired blast furnaces in Britain[82] – at least they had been learned. To grasp the full significance of this technical breakthrough for the new British iron age of the late eighteenth and nineteenth centuries we need only remember that in 1700 the annual output of English and Welsh coalmines had already reached 3 million tons and was still rising, a level of production which both in absolute terms and per head of the population 'was already of quite a different

order of magnitude from that obtaining on the Continent'.[83] Darby's
discovery, then, together with the development of Newcomen's steam
engine (1705) and its prompt application to pumping, meant that in two
crucial ways Britain had already learned by 1714 how to capitalise
industrially on her richest raw material endowment.

In the third major sector of the economy, agriculture, there are few
signs that twenty years of war inflicted serious damage; but neither is
there much positive evidence to link the wars against Louis XIV,
specifically, with such agrarian progress as late-Stuart England
achieved.[84] Yet there was one way in which these wars made a significant
indirect contribution to the Agricultural Revolution and may have
helped to hasten its coming. Heavy taxation and the difficulty of raising
mortgages in wartime clearly had a great deal to do with that notable
change in the pattern of landownership between 1680 and 1740, first
underlined by Professor Habakkuk,[85] the trend away from the smaller
proprietor in favour of the big landowner and the great estate. It was the
bigger estates (not so much the enormous aristocratic empires sprawling
over several counties as the lands of the go-ahead, well-to-do squirearchy) which were the spearhead of agrarian experiment and 'improvement' in the Hanoverian age.

Often left out of account in the debate on war and the eighteenth-
century economy is the comparative factor: the consideration of
Britain's condition in relation to that of her neighbours. Yet such comparisons are arguably of relevance, and not least when one turns from
the short-term effects of war between 1689 and 1713 to assess their
long-term significance in the broad context of the 'three revolutions'
in the economy during the years from 1660 to 1800.

It is often held that the progress of the 'Commercial Revolution'
which began after 1660 was checked or retarded for a quarter of a
century because of the struggle with France. The controversy on this
point hinges largely on how the long years of fighting affected two of
England's major assets in the field of overseas trade, her shipping and
her markets; and since trade is essentially a competitive business, the
corresponding experience of her two leading trade rivals, France and
Holland, must enter the reckoning. Thus, even if 1714 found the
English merchant marine little if any stronger than it had been in 1689,
it still emerged in far better shape than that of France, which decayed
alarmingly after 1692.[86] Likewise we have to balance the loss or temporary disruption of some of England's former markets, not only against

the new colonial and American markets secured by the Utrecht treaties, but equally against the failure of both the Dutch and the French to make any comparable gains.[87] For the United Provinces, indeed, these two wars spelt the loss of their commercial supremacy to Britain.[88]

Just as comparative evidence has to be borne in mind, so too do factors other than war which adversely affected the English economy in our period. Some of the setbacks the economy met with between 1689 and 1714 would certainly have occurred, and others would very likely have done so, given twenty-five years of unbroken peace. Most of the agrarian troubles, for example, can be ascribed to an exceptional sequence of climatic extremes from the early 1690s down to at least 1710, producing far too many years of alternating scarcity and glut instead of a steady level of production and steady prices.[89] Similarly, after the exceedingly rapid expansion experienced by overseas trade since the Restoration, some decline in the growth rate would have been predictable whatever the political circumstances. This is Ralph Davis's considered view, and he adduces some powerful evidence to back it up.[90] The effects on British trade and exported manufactures of the silver 'famine' and consequent international payments crisis of the late seventeenth century, as well as of the high death rate in many continental countries caused by plague and disastrous harvests, are no less relevant.

T. S. Ashton once expressed the opinion that 'if England had enjoyed unbroken peace the Industrial Revolution might have come earlier'.[91] As far as the wars of our own period are concerned we have already reviewed some of the evidence which raises large question marks against this supposition. But of course we are dealing here fundamentally with a hypothesis in which personal judgement and the individual historian's sense of priorities play so important a part that proving or disproving to everyone's satisfaction becomes an impossible exercise. What caused, or made possible, the Industrial Revolution? If, for instance, we lay heavy stress on the development of transport and communications, then we shall be more sympathetic to Ashton's view. For there is evidence that road building was retarded by diversion of capital during the Augsburg and Spanish Succession wars (though inland waterways made more progress than is sometimes realised and coastal shipping almost certainly expanded).[92] But if, on the other hand, we give greater prominence to any or all of three other major contributors, technological progress, the expansion of markets or the growing sophistication of private financial institutions, the Ashton thesis at once seems less secure.

While weighing the pros and cons of this great economic debate there is one last consideration which, amid all the distractions of conflicting arguments, we might do well to keep in view. Had England chosen to stand aloof from either of the two wars of this period, and especially from the second, she would have stood to pay a heavy economic price. This can best be illustrated from the implications of the Spanish Succession dispute between 1698 and 1702. The consequence of non-intervention would have been, at worst, the closing of Spanish ports to English ships for an indefinite period and the complete dominance of France over Spain's American and West Indian possessions, with grave consequences for English colonists as well as merchants. Even if French influence had extended no further than Spanish territory in the Low Countries and in southern Italy, two leading branches of English trade, with the Flanders and Levant markets, would have been brutally severed. Englishmen in 1701–2 had to set the economic problems of war in the balance against the severe economic penalties of neutrality. The historian of post-Revolution Britain must try to do the same.

NOTES TO INTRODUCTION

1. Scotland probably accounted for just over 1 million. See P. Deane and W. A. Cole, *British Economic Growth 1688–1959*, 2nd ed. (Cambridge, 1967), p. 6, following the calculations of Sir John Sinclair (1825).

2. The older authorities worked backwards from the 1801 census figures on the basis of trends indicated in eighteenth-century parish registers. Ibid. pp. 5–6; cf. D. V. Glass, 'Gregory King's Estimate of the Population of England and Wales, 1695', in *Population Studies*, iii, 4 (1950), 358, who suggests, after a close critical study of King's methods, that a total of 5·2 million would be 'more acceptable'.

3. Cf. Deane and Cole, p. 288, with C. Wilson, *England's Apprenticeship 1603–1760* (1965), pp. 365–6.

4. The latest estimate, by E. A. Wrigley ('A Simple Model of London's importance . . . 1650–1750', in *Past and Present*, July 1967), is considerably lower (575,000) than the usually accepted figure of M. Dorothy George (674,500) in *London Life in the Eighteenth Century* (1925: Penguin ed. 1966), pp. 37, 319.

5. I follow the estimates in Deane and Cole, p. 103.

6. Norfolk, Suffolk and Essex.

7. Deane and Cole, p. 103.

8. i.e. the families of lay peers and baronets, knights, esquires and 'gentlemen'.

9. For a realistic yardstick of professional status see E. Hughes, 'The Professions in the Eighteenth Century', in *Durham Univ. J.*, xliv (1951), 40–55.

10. See pp. 135–54 below, 'Conflict in Society'.

11. See pp. 39–58 below, 'The Revolution and the Constitution'.

12. Ibid.

13. See the bibliographical note on p. 56 below.

14. Two major departments, the Treasury and the Admiralty, have been studied in detail (though only in William's reign), and so have two subordinate ones, the Customs Board and the Salt Office. See S. B. Baxter, *The Development of the Treasury 1660–1702* (1957); J. Ehrman, *The Navy in the War of William III 1689–1697* (Cambridge, 1953); E. E. Hoon, *The Organization of the English Customs System 1696–1786* (New York, 1958); E. Hughes, *Studies in Administration and Finance 1558–1825* (Manchester, 1934). We also know more today than we once did about the recruitment, conditions and organisation of the civil service and diplomatic service, and about the first effects of the Union on the administration of Scottish affairs. See Hughes, op. cit. pp. 167–224, 266–89 *passim*; D. B. Horn, *The British Diplomatic Service 1689–1789* (Oxford, 1961); P. W. J. Riley, *The English Ministers and Scotland 1707–27* (1964).

15. J. M. Beattie, *The English Court in the Reign of George I* (Cambridge, 1967), pp. 17–18.

16. For the Navy Office see Ehrman, op. cit. pp. 185–6, 554, 614.

17. Hughes, in *Durham Univ. J.*, xliv (1951), 54.

18. This was before the revival of the third or Scottish Secretaryship, established after the Union in 1709, but allowed to lapse 1711–13.

19. Baxter, op. cit. p. 256; cf. *The Laws of Honour* (1714), p. 37.

20. Horn, op. cit. pp. 14–35, 44, 81.

21. See R. E. Scouller, *The Armies of Queen Anne* (1966), pp. 42–3; Hughes, in *Durham Univ. J.*, xliv (1951), 217, 222; J. H. Plumb, *The Growth of Political Stability in England 1675–1725* (1967), p. 116.

22. For the most important new committees of all, the Cabinet Council and its offshoot, the Lords of the Committee, see, however, pp. 49–51 below.

23. See G. S. Holmes, 'The Attack on "the Influence of the Crown", 1702–16', in *BIHR* xxxix (1966).

24. See pp. 45, 119–20 below.

25. On the growth of the electorate see J. E. Neale, *The Elizabethan House of Commons* (1949), pp. 140–1; R. L. Bushman, 'English Franchise Reform in the Seventeenth Century', in *JBS* iii (1963); and especially Plumb, op. cit. pp. 27–9, 34–44.

26. For these see Plumb, op. cit. pp. 82–96.

27. Ibid. p. 29; G. S. Holmes, 'The Influence of the Peerage in English Parliamentary Elections, 1702–13' (Oxford, B.Litt. thesis, 1952), folios 11–12, 174–96. The most recent and most authoritative estimate, by W. A. Speck, puts the figure at the end of Anne's reign at 250,700. It will be elaborated in his forthcoming book *Tory and Whig: The Struggle in the Constituencies 1701–1715*.

28. See pp. 80–95 below, 'The Revolution and the People'.

29. e.g. to merchant seamen (see R. Davis, *The Rise of the English Shipping Industry* (1962), pp. 136, 140). It must be stressed that the wage pattern over these twenty-five years showed great regional and industrial as well as chronological variations.

30. For an illuminating account of this activity see Charles Wilson, 'The Other Face of Mercantilism', in *TRHS* 5th ser., ix (1959).

31. See pp. 164–5 below.

32. For a convenient summary of these issues, with illustrations, see *The Divided Society: Party Conflict in England 1694–1716*, ed. G. Holmes and W. A. Speck (1967), pp. 88–131, 138–42; a more extended treatment will be found in Holmes, *British Politics in the Age of Anne* (1967), pp. 51–147.

33. See pp. 96–114 below, 'The Structure of Parliamentary Politics'.

34. Viz. Whig, Tory, Court and Country; Whig and Tory.

35. Plumb, *Growth of Political Stability*.

36. The fullest and best modern discussion of these motives will be found in S. B. Baxter, *William III* (1966), pp. 223–37.

37. See pp. 115–34 below.

38. See pp. 185–6 below.

39. See pp. 178, 179 below.

40. Op. cit. p. xviii.

41. See pp. 176–96 below, 'The Road to Union'; pp. 216–37, 'Harley, St John and the Death of the Tory Party'.

42. Riley, op. cit. pp. 158–255; cf. R. H. Campbell, 'The Anglo-Scottish Union of 1707. II. The Economic Consequences', in *EcHR* xvi (1963–4).

43. Plumb, op. cit. pp. 180–2; Riley, op. cit. pp. 256–94.

44. Op. cit. p. 19.

45. See pp. 59–95 below.

46. See pp. 197–215 below, 'The Road to Peace, 1710–13'.

47. See pp. 123–4 below.

48. Ehrman, *The Navy*, p. xx; Scouller, op. cit. p. 348; Wilson, *England's Apprenticeship*, p. 217; C. T. Atkinson, *Marlborough and the Rise of the British Army* (1921), pp. 27–8. There were, of course, many foreign mercenary regiments in the Queen's pay.

49. J. S. Bromley, 'The French Privateering War', in *Historical Essays 1600–1750*, ed. H. E. Bell and R. L. Ollard (1963).

50. Scouller, op cit. pp. 102–25.

51. P. G. M. Dickson, *The Financial Revolution in England 1688–1756* (1967); see also pp. 47–8, 135–6, 142–5 below.

52. J. K. Horsefield, *English Monetary Experiments 1650–1750* (1960), p. 245.

53. W. R. Ward, *The English Land Tax in the Eighteenth Century* (Oxford, 1953); E. E. Hoon, op. cit.

54. Deane and Cole, pp. 251, 270.

55. Plumb, op. cit. p. 115.

56. *English Taxation 1640–1799* (1913).

57. See J. Loftis, *The Politics of Drama in Augustan England* (1963).

58. See pp. 155–75 below, 'Conflict in the Church'.

59. *The Century of Revolution 1603–1714* (1961), pp. 262 ff; cf. Hill, *Reformation to Industrial Revolution* (1967), pp. 133, 135, 139.

60. In writing this section I have been helped by salutary criticism and valuable suggestions from Dr T. C. Smout.

61. See pp. 184, 187–8 below.

62. T. S. Ashton, *Economic Fluctuations in England 1700–1800* (Oxford, 1959), p. 56.

63. e.g. Deane and Cole, op. cit.; E. B. Schumpeter, *English Overseas Trade Statistics 1697–1808*, ed. T. S. Ashton (1960).

64. Op. cit. p. 83.

65. J. U. Nef, *War and Human Progress* (Harvard, 1950), esp. pp. 219–25.

66. G. N. Clark, 'War Trade and Trade War, 1701–13', in *EcHR* i (1927–8); cf. *The Later Stuarts*, 2nd ed. (Oxford, 1955), p. 252: 'At last the British merchants had done what they had so often attempted in vain: they had enriched themselves by war.'

67. A. H. John, 'War and the English Economy, 1700–63', in *EcHR* 2nd ser., vii (1955).

68. For Charles Wilson's balanced review of the controversy and comments upon it see *England's Apprenticeship*, pp. 276–81. Professor Davis pleads con-

vincingly that war was only one among a number of factors – and not necessarily the most important – applying the brakes to commercial progress by the beginning of the eighteenth century. See, *passim*, R. Davis, *The Rise of the English Shipping Industry*; 'English Foreign Trade, 1660–1700' and 'English Foreign Trade, 1700–1774', in *EcHR* 2nd ser., vii (1954), xv (1962); *A Commercial Revolution* (Hist. Assn Pamphlet, 1967).

69. Davis, *English Shipping Industry*, pp. 22, 67–9, 316–17, 403; 'Merchant Shipping in the Economy of the Late Seventeenth Century', in *EcHR* 2nd ser., ix (1956), 70–2; Ashton, op. cit. p. 141.

70. Davis, op. cit. pp. 45, 48–50, 52, 57, 62–3.

71. It was 1717 before total import values again equalled those of 1700.

72. See R. Davis, 'The Rise of Protection in England, 1689–1786', in *EcHR* 2nd ser., xix (1966).

73. I am indebted to Professor Ralph Davis for clarifying this point for me.

74. Cf. Ashton, op. cit. p. 64.

75. See p. 138 below.

76. Ashton, op. cit. pp. 71, 80.

77. D. C. Coleman, *The British Paper Industry 1495–1860* (1958); for details of sustained bar-iron imports from Sweden see Deane and Cole, p. 51.

78. See import figures, 1695–1719, ibid. pp. 51, 53, 59.

79. Hence the prosperity of the Yorkshire cloth towns in this period, especially in Anne's reign, while Devon, which generally produced lighter and finer cloths, enjoyed more mixed fortunes.

80. See p. 141 below. This development, it must be said, was not necessarily of benefit to the economy as a whole.

81. See M. W. Flinn, 'Abraham Darby and the Coke-smelting process', in *Economica*, NS xxvi (1959), for the serious doubts raised against the traditionally accepted date of 1709 for Darby's discovery.

82. H. R. Schubert, *History of the British Iron and Steel Industry* (1957), pp. 331–3.

83. E. A. Wrigley, 'The Supply of Raw Materials in the Industrial Revolution', in *EcHR* 2nd ser., xv (1962–3), 4.

84. e.g. the rise in corn production, which owed far more to the abolition of export duties on grain after the Revolution.

85. See p. 152 below.

86. Davis, *English Shipping Industry*, p. 69.

87. Pressure of space compels us to beg the vital and contentious question of whether the profitability of colonies to the home economy has not been greatly exaggerated. For a recent view, which would seem to reinforce Adam Smith's doubts of the eighteenth century, see R. P. Thomas, 'The Sugar Colonies of the Old Empire: Profit or Loss for Great Britain?', in *EcHR* 2nd ser., xxi (1968).

88. P. Geyl, *The Netherlands in the Seventeenth Century: II 1648–1715* (1964), p. 341; C. Wilson, *Anglo-Dutch Commerce and Finance in the Eighteenth Century* (1941).

89. See Ashton, op. cit. pp. 16–17, 26, for the effect on bread prices of the climatic freaks of Anne's reign and the contrast with the levels of the next twenty-five years.

90. See *English Shipping Industry*, pp. 22–3, 29; *A Commercial Revolution*, pp. 15–17.

91. Op. cit. p. 83.

92. See T. S. Willan, *River Navigation in England 1600–1750* (Oxford, 1936); *The English Coastal Trade 1600–1750* (Manchester, 1938).

1. The Revolution and the Constitution

JENNIFER CARTER

For the British constitution the years between the Bill of Rights (1689) and the Act of Settlement (1701) were as formative as the Glorious Revolution itself. These were years when the constitutional implications of what had happened at the Revolution were worked out in an atmosphere of continuing tension between Crown and Parliament. They saw the constitution diverge further than ever from the contemporary continental type at a time when, paradoxically, William of Orange's presence on the throne was ensuring closer involvement of Britain in European affairs than at any time in the seventeenth century. So far-reaching were the developments of the 1690s, together with those further steps anticipated by the Act of Settlement, that one may ask whether they were intended by the revolutionaries of 1688? Again, how many of these changes were embodied in the legislative structure of the Revolution settlement (legislation which, it can be argued, looked backwards as much as forwards), and how many were simply practical solutions devised to meet new problems as these arose, particularly under the stress of a major war? It is with questions of this nature in mind that we must try to assess the effects of the Revolution on the constitution.[1]

Whig apologists of the Revolution traditionally maintain that it replaced the arbitrariness of royal rule by a constitutional monarchy responsible to Parliament. 'The nature of our constitution is that of a limited monarchy', declared one of the managers of the case against Dr Sacheverell in 1710, and he quoted with approval the words of the Scottish Claim of Right (1689), that James II 'did invade the fundamental constitution . . . and altered it from a legal limited monarchy, to an arbitrary despotic power'.[2] But the 'limited monarchy' to which Lechmere referred in 1710 was the product of what happened at the Revolution, and even more perhaps of what happened afterwards.

Indeed, modern historians have questioned the motives of those who made the 'Glorious Revolution', and have asked whether they were concerned with establishing a limited monarchy and a parliamentary constitution, or with protecting the rights of property and a privileged ruling class against an active central government? Some historians see the Revolution as an aristocratic plot, others as a conspiracy by William of Orange to obtain the throne. Many have emphasised the constitutional continuity through 1688-9; and some suggest that the Revolution settlement allowed the political instability of the seventeenth century to continue until 1716 or even 1725.[3]

The key question about 1689 is whether it established a new king on the throne, or a new type of monarchy? From the later eighteenth century Burke looked back a hundred years and saw the Revolution as but 'a small and a temporary deviation from the strict order of a regular hereditary succession'.[4] It is true that some contemporaries thought they were changing the constitution, not just the monarch. We are to decide 'whether we shall be governed by Popery and arbitrary government, or whether we shall be rid of both', Sir George Treby told the House of Commons on 28 January 1689.[5] Yet the revolutionary content of 1689 is to be found less in direct limitations on the monarch's power, and the banning of Roman Catholicism as the royal religion, than in the fact that the normal order of succession was overridden when the crown was offered to William and Mary. Debates in the English Convention show how reluctantly Parliament interfered with the divine right succession. The Commons' resolution against a Popish prince was readily adopted by the whole Convention, but the Lords were not so willing to endorse the 'contract' theory and accept that the throne was vacant after James II's flight. In the end Parliament had to compromise: the contract was left out of the Declaration, but it retained the convenient fiction that James II had abdicated and the throne was therefore vacant.

Although the 'contract' had been dropped, the offer of the crown to William and Mary, immediately after the public reading of the Declaration of Rights, was an implied contract. The new King and Queen had not succeeded to the throne in the natural order of events, but because the Convention Parliament put them there. The only implication that ultimately could be drawn from this was that England had a monarch depending on a parliamentary title, and a constitution based on law. The changed position of the Crown was emphasised by the new form of coronation oath devised for William and Mary, in which the monarch swore to govern 'according to the statutes in Parliament agreed on', whereas previously the oath had contained no reference to Parliament and the King promised to keep the laws and customs granted by his predecessors.

Yet the revolutionary moment in 1689, when the Declaration of Rights and the new coronation oath were drafted, was but a temporary consensus of the governing classes. It had been necessary to replace James II. It was harder for some to acknowledge the logic of what they had done. The debates of January and February 1689 had already demonstrated this, and Tory hesitation then had not been attributable only to the hope that if Mary succeeded to the throne she might be more amenable to management than William – Tories hesitated because they felt a conscientious revulsion against altering the succession. Danby maintained that William and Mary were now undoubtedly King and Queen, 'yet no man could affirm they were rightfully so by the constitution'; and in 1710 he was still defending this point when he voted against the impeachment of Sacheverell.[6] For twelve years after 1689 there was intermittent dispute about the royal title and the oath of allegiance.

The oath of allegiance was framed to omit the normal acknowledgement of the monarch as 'rightful and lawful'. Whigs resented so much immunity for Tory consciences and attempted to force a recognition *de jure*. The Act for Confirmation of William and Mary and the Convention Parliament contained the phrase, 'we do recognise and acknowledge your Majesties were, are and of right ought to be by the laws of this realm our sovereign liege lord and lady King and Queen', but it prescribed no new form of oath. Attempts to impose new oaths failed in 1690, 1692 and 1693. It was not until after the assassination plot of 1696 that a majority of the Commons were prepared to sign an Association pledging themselves to uphold William as 'rightful and lawful' king, and most of the Lords signed a similar declaration. Even then, genuine scruples prevented some hundred Tory M.P.s from signing, and the Lords' abstentions numbered about twenty, though the formula they devised avoided the phrase 'rightful and lawful'. Not until 1702, after Louis XIV's quixotic recognition of the Pretender as James III, were all office-holders, ecclesiastics, members of university colleges, schoolmasters, dissenting ministers, and members of Parliament obliged to take an oath of allegiance acknowledging William as 'lawful and rightful' king, and an oath abjuring the Pretender.

Even now the struggle was not really over. The Tories continued to try to minimise, and the Whigs to exploit the alteration of the succession at the Revolution. But by the end of William's reign the situation had changed in at least two important respects. First, practical necessity had once more prevailed to force supporters of the hereditary succession to tamper with it again in the Act of Settlement. Secondly, attitudes and objectives in both parties had shifted. Within the Anglican Church a divine right justification might be found for the Revolution itself,[7] while Country party Tories by the late 1690s were strongly attacking the prerogative and promoting Place bills to curb the influence of the Crown over Parliament. This campaign of the Country interests 'culminated in the Act of Settlement, that great and authentic back-bench victory'.[8] Although it was partly relegated from the world of day-to-day politics, however, the change in the succession was the cardinal constitutional fact of 1689. By comparison, the balance of power between King and Parliament was comparatively little influenced by limitations deliberately imposed on the Crown in the Revolution settlement.

The Declaration of Rights stands apart from the rest of the Settlement as a precedent condition of William and Mary's accession. Considered as a summary of the terms upon which they were offered the crown it does not seem harsh to the monarch, and, in contrast to the Act of Settlement, the Bill of Rights hardly tried to anticipate future constitutional problems, but concentrated on points that had been troublesome in the past. In effect it gave the crown to William and Mary on condition that they did not behave like James II: the exercise of their powers and prerogatives was otherwise little curtailed. This seems generous if it is conceded that James II, and Charles II too in the later years of his reign, while keeping within the limits of the constitution, certainly stretched its meaning pretty far. For example, King James had not used the dispensing power extensively before testing its validity at law; but was not the verdict in Hales's case obtained by packing the Bench,[9] and how far could the issue of individual dispensations go before amounting to a virtual suspension of certain laws? Similarly, there was technical justification for the Ecclesiastical Commission, but its composition and activities were hardly consonant with the position of the Established Church.[10] A significant set of clauses in the Bill of Rights dealt with the misuse of legal processes, and here again it can be argued that the Bill is concerned to assert the best interpretation of the constitution, as against recent practices.[11] To say that the Bill of Rights made minimal changes in the powers of the Crown is not to minimise its importance. Several of the clauses have permanent value as statements of constitutional principle, as for instance, 'elections of Members of Parliament ought to be free' or, 'excessive bail ought not to be required, nor excessive fines imposed, nor cruel and unusual punishments inflicted'. Yet none of this defined very narrowly the powers of the monarch.

Moreover, the Declaration of Rights failed to include various provisions discussed in committee, which, if included, would have imposed further limitations on the prerogative. For instance, the drafting committee had discussed a clause concerning the tenure of judges, and another for restricting the royal pardon. Neither clause was enacted in 1689, though both got into the Act of Settlement. Nor does barring a Roman Catholic from the throne seem a great innovation. In seventeenth-century terms it was incongruous for the head of Church and State not to share the established faith. Experience of James II convinced the influential majority of his subjects that the religion of the ruler could not be Roman Catholic. It remained for the Act of Settlement to lay down 'that whosoever shall hereinafter come to the possession of the crown shall join in communion with the Church of England'. The Revolution left the Church of England still firmly supporting the State, and the policy of limited toleration followed in William's reign denied dissenters full civil rights. The old theory that political and religious allegiance were co-extensive was dented, but not yet demolished.[12]

Perhaps the one feature of the Bill of Rights which did seriously attempt to narrow the power of the Crown was the clause stating, as if it had been existing law in James's reign, that 'the raising or keeping of a standing army within this kingdom in time of peace unless it be with consent of Parliament is against the law'. Even this change was to work out in an unforeseen way. Its meaning was not effectively tested until after the Treaty of Ryswick (1697), when the question of whether to continue a standing army in peacetime was hotly disputed in Parliament. A hard-pressed government used circumlocutions – such as 'guards and garrisons' – to avoid the unpopular term 'army'; passed off three regiments of foot as 'marines' chargeable on the naval establishments; and transferred soldiers to Scotland and Ireland to keep them out of sight and off the English establishment. The Whig ministers felt bound to reverse their earlier attitudes and argue that there should be an adequate force for national defence, but could not decide whether to go all out to keep a sufficient army, or put most emphasis on the retention of foreign troops. This vacillation helped them to lose on both counts, and William's personal appeal to the Commons to be allowed to keep the Dutch foot-guards 'resulted in the most hostile demonstration against the Crown since the Revolution'.[13] The Disbanding Act of 1699 fixed the number of troops to be kept on establishment, and in this negative sense legalised a peacetime standing army. No Mutiny Act was passed from 1697 to 1702; which disposes of the notion that this Act – authorising a code of military discipline that was convenient but not essential – could legalise a standing army, still less force the monarch to call Parliament every year for the purpose of passing it. The Crown was forced to meet Parliament annually after 1689 to get money, not to pass the Mutiny Act.

Disputes about the standing army illustrate the continuing strain between Crown and Parliament after the Revolution, and show that the Bill of Rights was not a final constitutional settlement. From time to time Parliament thought to impose further checks on the prerogative. For instance, after William III had vetoed a Place bill in 1694 the Commons sent him an address claiming that this power had not customarily been used to block bills designed to remedy grievances. William returned a noncommittal answer and the Commons let the matter rest.[14]

Further evidence that it was not so much the legislation of 1689 as subsequent parliamentary activity that sought to impose important limitations on the Crown is supplied by the Triennial Act of 1694 and the Act of Settlement of 1701 – albeit the latter's sharpest edges were filed away before taking effect. If the financial situation had been otherwise, the implications of the Revolution might have worked out quite differently. As it was, the financial controls which the Commons fumbled for in 1689 were put into its hands by the wartime needs of government, and consequently learning to live with Parliament was the greatest change the monarchy had to face after 1689. Since 1688 there has never been a year without a meeting of Parliament, and the longest gap between parliamentary sessions in William's reign was the ten months from 5 January to 22 October 1691. The Revolution had not impaired the royal right to summon, prorogue and dissolve Parliaments, and the Declaration of Rights had done no more than declare frequent Parliaments desirable – it did not lay down how often Parliament should meet, nor provide a means for its assembly if the King refused to issue writs. The Triennial Act of 1664 was still on the statute-book, though it had been ignored by Charles II at the end of his reign. Much controversy intervened, including a royal veto on a bill passed by Parliament in 1693, before the Triennial Act of 1694 became law. This Act reiterated that Parliament should meet at least once every three years – a somewhat empty demand in wartime when annual supply meant annual sessions – but it also laid down that no Parliament should last longer than three years. From 1694 Britain entered a period of sharpening political conflict and increasing party commitment that lasted until the Septennial Act of 1716. The unusual number of General Elections kept political excitement running high throughout William's reign and Anne's, and the frequency of elections meant both that government influence in the Commons could not easily be built up, and that local and national lines of party division hardened.

The Triennial Act should be seen in the general political context of post-Revolutionary disenchantment with William III and fierce parliamentary attacks on his ministers, and in the specific constitutional context of Place bills designed to limit the influence of the Crown. The Place bill campaign reached a climax (though a false one) in the Act of Settlement. Four bills aimed at excluding all placemen from the Commons failed between December 1692 and early 1700, but Acts passed in 1694, 1700 and 1701 excluded from the House the Collectors of Land Tax, and the Commissioners of the Salt Duty, and of Customs and Excise. The place clause in the Act of Settlement provided that after the death of Anne 'no person who has an office shall be capable of serving as a member of the House of Commons'. Mr Holmes has shown how the very completeness of the anticipated victory spelled its impermanence – the Court interests were prepared to allow the clause to go through in 1701 and set about revising it afterwards – and the concession could be allowed to the Tories as a sop for their acquiescence in the much more important business of settling the succession. An opportunity to modify the place clause came with the Regency Act of 1706 (re-enacted in 1708 after the Union with Scotland), which allowed certain categories of placemen to remain in the Commons. The impact of anti-placemen legislation was further dulled because so few failed to secure re-election when they faced their constituents under the terms of the 1706 rule, and because the law did not touch the House of Lords.[15] While it remained a lively issue in eighteenth-century politics, legislation against placemen must be rated a qualified success as a constitutional device for limiting the growth of the Crown's influence in the House of Commons.

Other parts of the Act of Settlement besides the placemen clause reveal Tory animus, and patriotic reaction against William III. It laid down that a foreign king could not take the country into war for the defence of his foreign dominions without consent of Parliament; that the monarch should not leave the British Isles without permission from Parliament; that after the Hanoverian succession no foreigners should be appointed to the Privy Council, nor to any office, nor given lands, nor allowed to sit in Parliament. The impeachments of the Junto lords in 1701 lent topicality to the clause 'That no pardon under the Great Seal of England be pleadable to an impeachment by the Commons in Parliament'; while the Partition Treaties affair[16] doubtless underlay the clause which attempted to fix responsibility for advising the King upon the Privy Council.

It would be unfair to William III's record in judicial matters to argue that any fault of his accounted for the inclusion in the Act of Settlement of another clause which had failed to get into the Declaration of Rights – the clause stating 'Judges' commissions be made *quam diu se bene gesserint* and their salaries ascertained and established, but upon the address of both Houses of Parliament it may be lawful to remove them'. Greater security of tenure for judges was undoubtedly a constitutional gain, but it was against Charles II and James II that an accusation of tampering with the judiciary for political ends could be brought home,[17] not against William III who had voluntarily appointed all his judges 'during good behaviour'. After 1701 judges could be removed when the monarch who had appointed them died, but William's restraint, in refraining from removing judges for political reasons before the Act of Settlement passed, was reinforced by Lord Chancellor Cowper recommending only a few changes at the accession of George I. For its part, Parliament never took advantage of the power to address the monarch for the removal of an English judge.

The Act of Settlement was entitled 'An Act for the further limitation of the Crown and better securing the Rights and Liberties of the Subject'. It went a good deal further in this respect than the Bill of Rights – and the Tories were now foremost in pressing for limits which the Whigs would hardly have dared suggest in 1689, especially limitations designed to take effect after Anne's death. Yet these sections of the Act, including the place clause, have a somewhat unreal quality. It seems almost as if the significant constitutional adjustments in the relative positions of Crown and Parliament had been made between 1689 and 1701: now the Act of Settlement capped the sober structure of the new relationship with a few flourishes, some of which related to a future hypothetical situation and were altered before they took effect. The two salient features of the post-Revolution constitution were, first, that however much it was disguised a parliamentary monarchy had replaced divine right monarchy; and, secondly, that since 1689 the monarch had learned somehow to live with Parliament. The necessity of living with Parliament was imposed by financial stringency; the means of doing so was painfully arrived at through management and the gradual acceptance of party politics.

The financial settlement made in 1689 allowed the King an ordinary revenue too small for his needs, and at first even this was not voted him for life. Whether this was a clumsy attempt to control the Crown by means of Parliament's purse strings, and how such an initial attitude would have developed in peacetime are immaterial, as the question of ordinary revenue was immediately overtaken by extraordinary demands for war purposes. Within two days of the Committee of the Whole House resolving that the annual revenue should be £1,200,000, a Grand Committee voted special supplies for the Irish campaign.[18] In the course of the reign the distinction between ordinary and extraordinary supply was tacitly abandoned, and Parliament came to accept that the costs of government would have to be paid for year by year. Parliament took full responsibility for the land forces in the session of 1690–1, and in each war year thereafter voted money for a specific number of troops for the coming year's campaign. In 1698 the financial position was further clarified when Parliament assumed responsibility for the public debt and the peacetime cost of the armed forces, while voting to the Crown a Civil List, granted for life and estimated to yield £700,000 a year. Thus the principle of parliamentary supply was asserted, while the Crown retained enough independence to satisfy eighteenth-century notions of a balanced constitution.[19] Civil List expenditures remained a sensitive subject because this money could be used to influence Parliament, but in comparison with the total national expenditure, especially in wartime, the Civil List was but a small amount.

The scale of finance needed for William's war was unprecedented. To raise the sums required taxes had to be strained to the utmost and new methods of public borrowing evolved. After giving up the Hearth Tax as a popular gesture in 1689 William's government tried many experimental taxes. The great bulk of tax revenue came, however, from three sources: Customs yielded £13·2 million; Excise £13·6 million; and the new Land Taxes £19·2 million in the course of the reign.[20] Much could be said of the difficulty of administering these taxes, even when civil servants rather than tax farmers were doing the job, but the system's resilience is testified by the fact that it remained unchanged until the introduction of Income Tax in 1799. But the costs of war could not be met from taxes alone – tax revenue fell short of expenditure by almost £1 million a year; there was a debt carried over from previous reigns; and much money was needed to anticipate tax returns.

Government had to borrow to cover the gap between revenue and expenditure in the 1690s, and the methods then adopted had far-reaching consequences. Dr P. G. M. Dickson has explained how in William's reign government learned to float long-term loans and Parliament accepted the need to underwrite them by appropriating the yield of specific taxes for the payment of investors' interest. In 1694 the Bank of England was launched to raise £1·2 million for the government at 8 per cent. The money was immediately forthcoming, and thanks to it William scored his only big military success with the capture of Namur in 1695. The eventual benefits to government were even more spectacular – with the Bank as its principal creditor money became available for loans at more favourable rates, and always on a parliamentary basis, as the Bank was forbidden to lend without Parliament's approval. It would be hard to over-estimate the significance of the 'financial revolution' that began in the 1690s. Britain paid for two wars, and came out of them in better financial trim than her allies and enemies. The economy benefited from new financial techniques and new opportunities for investment. An ever-increasing number of citizens were bound to the regime by financial pledges. The government no longer had to resort to desperate expedients like the 1672 Stop of the Exchequer, and could even feel its way towards annual budgets – William caused an estimate of the requirements of the armed forces to be laid before Parliament in 1689, and in 1690 the Commons asked for an estimate of war expenditure. Parliament had found the way to make itself an indispensable and not intolerable partner in government. In his final Speech from the Throne William III adjured Members 'to take care of the public credit, which cannot be preserved but by keeping sacred that maxim, that they shall never be losers, who trust to a Parliamentary security'.[21]

All these happy consequences of the new system of public finance did not, of course, accrue at once. Initially there were mistakes and clumsiness, on the part of both government and Parliament. The Commons habitually over-estimated the yield of taxes, leaving government struggling when the expected supplies failed to materialise. The loans were sometimes flops, while the re-coinage of 1696 almost shipwrecked the Bank of England.[22] M.P.s often displayed a carping and grudging spirit about finance, and the Commissioners of Public Accounts appointed between 1691 and 1697 did not have a particularly constructive record.[23] Nevertheless, it is further evidence of the stabilisation of the financial system that William's government accepted successive commissions with good grace, thus admitting the principle of parliamentary audit; while the Commons quickly mastered the techniques of appropriating supplies to particular purposes. Several duels fought between the two Houses served to confirm the Commons' exclusive right to introduce money bills, and the House of Commons exploited its advantage by tacking unrelated clauses to money bills – a practice which was discredited by the unsuccessful attempt to tack the Occasional Conformity Bill in 1704 rather than by the Lords' protest that tacking was 'highly dangerous' and their hopeful resolution that it was 'unparliamentary'.[24]

The successful hammering out of the new financial relationship between Crown and Parliament in William's reign was a painful process, partly because Parliament had yet to learn self-discipline and the King and his ministers had still to perfect the techniques of parliamentary management. How William III came to terms with the politicians in an almost continual struggle to achieve stable government is the subject of a separate essay in this book. Professor Clayton Roberts sees the post-Revolution period as one of interaction between parliamentary management and 'undertaking'. Professor Plumb has argued that the Revolution settlement so weakened the monarchy that stability was impossible until the executive re-established its predominance over the legislature by means of patronage and the acceptance of single-party government. Clearly the working out of these tendencies took longer than William's time. Yet in William's reign much had already been settled, and there was good progress towards defining the respective roles of monarch and Parliament, and reconciling them in the Cabinet.

The greatest constitutional significance attaches to the emergence of a Cabinet system as the link between Crown and Parliament, but the stages by which it evolved were complex. Plumb reminds us that the large Cabinets of William's reign and of Anne's, numbering nine to sixteen members, did not necessarily promote harmony between the politicians,[25] nor were they always successful intermediaries between the monarch and Parliament. Within its limits, though, the Cabinet did provide a means of sustaining government activity, with some sense of direction and a growing degree of competence, despite personal and party rivalries. Wars were fought and Parliament persuaded to pay for them. The leading politicians strove to get into, and if possible to dominate, the Cabinet. They were convinced 'that a coalition-scheme is impracticable',[26] and there were obvious advantages for the Crown too during those comparatively brief periods in William's reign and Anne's when an almost homogeneous Cabinet matched a clear majority in Parliament. Despite these advantages neither William nor Anne wished to let the party men gain the upper hand, and with the help of the great political managers – Sunderland, Shrewsbury, Godolphin, Marlborough, Harley – they kept control of the composition of Cabinets, so that their membership continued to include men who did belong to the dominant political group in Parliament.

Not only the membership of the Cabinet, but that of the Privy Council too could be of constitutional significance.[27] The Privy Council still advised the monarch on the dissolution of Parliament and the making of peace and war, and politically vital debates on these topics took place in the post-Revolutionary period, though the chances of upsetting a Cabinet decision diminished. For instance, the last-ditch stand of Whig Privy Councillors against the Treaty of Utrecht failed, and when on 7 April 1713 Cholmondeley asked for the matter to be considered further at another meeting he was told that the treaties must be ratified at once, and punished for his temerity by dismissal from his office as Treasurer of the Household. The Privy Council came briefly into its own again at the time of Anne's final illness, when it was the centre of government, and the Whig lords who were excluded from the Tory Cabinet appeared there to safeguard the Protestant succession.

The development of the Cabinet system in the 1690s owed nothing to the Revolution as such. It was the response to certain practical problems that presented themselves subsequently – the problem posed by King William's frequent absences from the country; the need for Queen Mary to have systematic advice while she was nominally ruling in Britain; the urgent necessity for co-ordinated wartime planning. William's ability to retain personal control of the membership of the Cabinet may have helped reconcile him to a system he would otherwise have found objectionable. Initially he was against Cabinets and seems to have done without one for a year, but when he was about to go abroad for the first time he 'agreed the necessity of a Cabinet Council', and said 'that there must be a Council to govern in his absence, and that the Queen is not to meddle'.[28] The clause of the Bill of Rights entrusting the exercise of regal power to William alone was reversed in 1690, but Mary and nine advisers were instructed that, 'All things (without exception) are to be debated in this cabinet-council before the Queen, during the King's absence.'[29] Similar arrangements were made in succeeding years, even in 1694 when 'a real Cabinet without the name'[30] met during William's absence, although he had intended not to allow this. As Shrewsbury explained in a mollifying letter, 'accidents will arise upon which orders can never, in your Majesty's absence, be given unless some people do meet to take the lead'.[31] In December 1694 Queen Mary died, and from 1695 to 1701 Lords Justices were appointed to conduct government business in Britain while the King was away. They were in effect the members of the Cabinet meeting in a more formal guise.[32] Perhaps this new constitutional status of its members helped to confirm the Cabinet habit, or perhaps William's objections to it had diminished – at any rate meetings of the Cabinet during the winter months while the King was in England, which had been fairly rare up to 1694, became pretty regular from 1695 onwards. The practice of Cabinet meetings, both with and without the monarch, was thus well established before Queen Anne came to the throne.

William III remained master of his Cabinet, and kept the conduct of military and diplomatic affairs in his own hands. Professor Baxter has emphasised how detailed was the King's control of all aspects of government business, and how often this is underestimated by British historians who do not read Dutch.[33] When he first left England, in 1690, King William instructed Mary and her advisers, 'All business that will admit delay must be sent to the King that his pleasure may be known upon it.'[34] Queen Anne too was active in the day-to-day work of government, although her capacity was less than William's because of her smaller experience and intelligence, and the disadvantages of her age, sex and ill-health. The old myth that George I was a mere cipher of his ministers has now been quite discredited. Clearly the survival of the Cabinet after the Revolution did not necessarily mean a devolution of power from the Crown to ministers. Equally clearly, though, it could lead to that, and this might possibly be linked with the post-Revolution tendency to depersonalise the monarchy – several Acts of Parliament, including Queen Anne's Regency Act, treat the Crown almost like any other executive office.[35]

The Cabinet's role as co-ordinator of the increasingly complex tasks government undertook was made necessary by the war. Raising men for the armed forces; controlling the movements of shipping; planning expeditions; organising home defence; containing disaffection; trying to keep in balance economic policy, trade, the coinage, food supplies, and all other aspects of the war economy – these things required constant efforts at co-ordination, which could only be made effectively at a meeting of the chief ministers and advisers of the King, who were heads of the most important government departments, and also members of Parliament. The success they achieved was not complete, but at least the war was carried on, and the growing executive kept under the King's control. It was not a foregone conclusion that William would retain full control of the executive, and some sharp skirmishes were fought between Crown and Parliament on this point – a further illustration of the continuing tension between them after 1689. Thomson suggested that the proposed Council of Trade, the parliamentary Commissioners for Wool, statutory Commissioners of Public Accounts, and the debates of 1691 about command of the forces together constitute a pattern of attempts 'to develop an entirely new type of executive'.[36] These moves were paralleled by Parliament appointing trustees to supervise the redistribution of Irish lands in accordance with the terms of the Act of Resumption of 1700.[37] Burnet said at the time of the abortive parliamentary Council of Trade, 'Here was a debate plainly in a point of prerogative, how far the government should continue on its ancient bottom of monarchy, as to the executive part.'[38]

William headed off the parliamentary demand for a Council of Trade by establishing his own Board of Trade in 1696. It can be taken to exemplify government's increasing interest in widening spheres of administrative activity. Admittedly there had been a series of previous Councils and Committees for Trade and Plantations, but the Board of Trade was a new departure in terms of expertise and systematic attempts to collect information as the basis of policy decisions.[39] Simultaneously other government departments were showing signs of increasing administrative efficiency. The Treasury began to keep annual accounts of income and expenditure in William's reign.[40] In the Admiralty there was considerable departmental progress as the Royal Navy expanded to fulfil its wartime task.[41] Control of the army remained more personally with the King, though the office of Secretary-at-War gained in stature, and the other departments through which the army was administered also increased their activity.

In William III's reign there was a 'revolution in government', associated perhaps with the contemporaneous rise of the professional and business classes which provoked such dislike among the landed interest, and the careers of many individual civil servants illustrate the trend towards a more powerful and active executive. Among the outstanding administrators of William's reign were William Blathwayt and William Bridgeman, both of whose official lives spanned the Revolution. Blathwayt was a Clerk of the Privy Council from 1686; Secretary to the Lords of Trade and Plantations, Surveyor and Auditor-General of Plantation Revenues, and a member of the Board of Trade (1696–1707); Under-Secretary of State (1681–3); Secretary at War (1683–8 and 1690–1704); and personal secretary to the King in Flanders (1692–1701), when he 'in a comparatively subordinate office, had greater power than any minister'.[42] Bridgeman, among other appointments, was probably the first Under-Secretary of State. In 1694 he became Secretary to the Admiralty where he showed great organising ability.[43] The Revolution allowed such men as these to push ahead with administrative expansion and improvement, because now the aims of government were approved by the established political classes – whereas before 1689 royal policies had been suspect, and government activity more than usually unwelcome.

Perhaps nothing done in the 1680s by Charles II and James II caused so much reaction against them as their interference with local privilege and the accustomed pattern of existing hierarchies – in counties, in corporations, or in university colleges. After the Revolution there was a distinct, though not complete, withdrawal of central authority from controlling local affairs, and the typical eighteenth-century situation of gentry and aristocratic independence in the localities took shape. Significantly, one of James II's last gestures of conciliation had been to issue a proclamation restoring the borough charters forfeited under *quo warranto* proceedings. The reversal of the legal proceedings of forfeiture and the restoration of the 'rights and privileges' of London were confirmed by an early Act of William and Mary's reign.[45] No similar action was taken in the case of other cities and boroughs, and great confusion remained in many places. For example, in a case of 1692 the judges were asked 'Whether there be any Corporation now subsisting in Nottingham?'[46] But if crude interference with borough charters ceased, and the Revolution was not made the opportunity for a great purge of minor office-holders,[47] William's government and Anne's continued the previous practice of reviewing the commissions of the peace and lieutenancy and making changes for political reasons. After the assassination plot J.P.s and deputy-lieutenants who had not taken the voluntary Association were removed.[48] Activity of this sort returned to what might be called a normal level, after the exceptional level caused by James II's frantic search for amenable officials.

It is difficult to strike the right balance when describing central government activity as it effected the localities. Since the Revolution, not only had direct interference with charters stopped, and the re-modelling of appointments diminished, but the new religious policy meant fewer orders about controlling the activity of dissenters. On the other hand, there were now more frequent directions to local authorities concerning wartime problems, and a continuing concern for keeping the peace.[49] Perhaps the best way to describe what was happening is to suggest that there was a progressive change in the quality, rather than the quantity, of central government involvement at the local level. Whereas in the earlier seventeenth century government still applied real sanctions, by means of Star Chamber and High Commission, after the Restoration these devices were not available; and after the Revolution the magnates of local society were more on their dignity than before and government less willing to upset them.

In the sense of making the world safer than ever for gentlemen, the Revolution can be thought of as substituting a divine right of property-owners for the divine right of kings.[50] Property remained the basis of political status and the keynote of English law.[51] For example, it was in 1704 that the House of Lords confirmed in *Ashby v. White* that the right to vote was a piece of property, and a man had a remedy at law if he was denied it. Equally, as Mr Christopher Hill remarks, 'From 1688 onwards England was, for the propertied class, an exceptionally free society by contemporary European standards.'[52] This freedom owed much to the constitutional changes of the later seventeenth century, and to a series of legal reforms tending towards one of the most admired characteristics of the eighteenth-century constitution – its respect for the legal rights of the individual. Among the most important of these legal reforms were improvements in the law of treason in 1696, 1703 and 1709; and the more precise definition of riot contained in the Riot Act of 1715. The benefit of this was not confined to the propertied class. On the other hand, the process of attainder was used – though admittedly for the last time – to procure Fenwick's execution in 1696. Some personal freedoms were still interpreted erratically. The Bill of Rights had safeguarded the right of subjects to petition the King, but in 1701 the Commons itself imprisoned the five Kentish petitioners whose petition to the House was politically unwelcome. The Habeas Corpus Act was suspended for the first time in 1689, and important precedents were then evolved which meant that this could be done only with the concurrence of Parliament.[53] The Licensing Act lapsed after 1695, a victory for the freedom of the Press, though this came about for no very liberal reasons, and journalists were still subject to severe libel laws and treated with suspicion by governments. Still, the gain in Press freedom could be counted an indirect benefit to all citizens. Likewise, the degree of religious toleration established in William's reign transcended social class barriers and property advantage.

The profit and loss account of the Revolution is finely balanced, and may to some extent be adjusted according to taste. Whigs from the seventeenth century to our own day have emphasised the progressive features of the Revolution settlement. Revisionists have pointed out that the revolutionaries' aims were not altruistic and the Revolution's results were in many ways limited. The inconclusiveness of the Revolution is reflected in William III's style of kingship. He was certainly not inclined by nature to be a constitutional monarch. His temper was autocratic; he kept important areas of decision to himself; and he chose his principal advisers with little tenderness for British susceptibilities. From the moment William let it be known he would not be his wife's gentleman usher, it was clear that he meant to rule to the full extent of his powers. Yet William was not an unthinking autocrat. He had experience in Holland of dealing with difficult subjects, and he knew how to work with the grain of a system instead of against it. He was not needlessly revengeful, and he must take a good share of personal credit for two of the most attractive aspects of the reign – partial religious toleration and the gradual improvement of the legal system.

It has been the main argument of this essay that the Revolution's results were no foregone conclusion. The basis of the monarchy was changed in 1689 by the substitution of a parliamentary for a divine right title. From that point onwards the constitution could have developed in different ways; and the legislation of 1689 did not set stringent limits on the monarch's power and prerogatives. In the 1690s the circumstances of the war gave Parliament an unexpected advantage over the Crown because the government needed money, and the political climate suggested to members of Parliament that they impose various limits on the powers of the Crown not contemplated in 1689. At the same time, however, the demands of wartime administration were tending to strengthen the executive. By the time the Act of Settlement was passed, a series of practical adjustments had been made in the constitutional relationship of Crown and Parliament that prepared the way for the 'balanced' constitution of the eighteenth century. Meanwhile, Britain under its Dutch King had found the way to a system of government as efficient as the much-admired continental monarchies, without resorting to their methods of centralisation and absolutism.

BIBLIOGRAPHICAL NOTE

Among source books, E. N. Williams, *The Eighteenth Century Constitution* (Cambridge, 1960) is recommended for its choice of documents and its editorial comment. A good collection without commentary is W. C. Costin and J. S. Watson, *The Law and Working of the Constitution*, vol. i, *1660–1783* (1952). Valuable constitutional material appears in *English Historical Documents 1660– 1714*, ed. A. Browning (1953), and in *The Divided Society: Party Conflict in England 1694–1716*, ed. G. Holmes and W. A. Speck (1967).

The Whig view of the Revolution is elegantly presented in G. M. Trevelyan, *The English Revolution 1688–1689* (1938), and a modified Whig case by D. Ogg, *England in the Reigns of James II and William III* (Oxford, 1955) – a distinguished and broad-ranging study. The revisionist who has attracted most notice – by no means all favourable – is L. Pinkham, *William III and the Respectable Revolution* (Cambridge, Mass., 1954); but more helpful than the 'conspiracy theory' in explaining the consequences of 1688 are: G. L. Cherry, 'The Legal and Philosophical Position of the Jacobites, 1688–89', in *J. Mod. Hist.*, xxii (1950); J. P. Kenyon, *The Nobility in the Revolution of 1688* (Hull, 1963); P. Laslett, 'The English Revolution and Locke's "Two Treatises of Government"', in *Camb. H.J.*, xii (1956); C. F. Mullet, 'Religion, Politics and Oaths in the Glorious Revolution', in *Review of Politics*, x (1948).

The most important recent works bearing on the constitution are C. Roberts, *The Growth of Responsible Government in Stuart England* (Cambridge, 1966), and J. H. Plumb, *The Growth of Political Stability in England 1675–1725* (1967). Two older books of continuing value are K. Feiling, *History of the Tory Party 1640–1714* (1924), and M. A. Thomson, *A Constitutional History of England 1642 to 1801* (1938). Monographs and articles on aspects of government and administration include the works of Baxter and Ehrman on the Treasury and the Navy (see p. 58, notes 40–1); J. Carter, 'Cabinet Records for the Reign of William III', in *EHR* lxxviii (1963); J. H. Plumb, 'The Organization of the Cabinet in the Reign of Queen Anne', in *TRHS* 5th ser., vii (1957); M. A. Thomson, *The Secretaries of State 1681–1782* (Oxford, 1932).

NOTES

1. I am most grateful to the editor for helpful guidance; to Dr Doreen Milne, for reading a draft of this chapter; and to Dr I. F. Burton, who answered enquiries about the army.
2. *State Trials*, ed. T. B. Howell (1812), xv, 61; J. Halliday, 'The Club and the Revolution in Scotland, 1689–90', in *SHR* xlv (1966).

3. A brief conspectus of views is *The Revolution of 1688 – Whig Triumph or Palace Revolution?*, ed. G. M. Straka (Boston, 1963). See bibliographical note for other titles.

4. *Reflections on the Revolution in France* (1790), p. 23.

5. Anchitell Grey, *Debates of the House of Commons* (1769), ix, 12–13.

6. A. Browning, *Thomas Osborne, Earl of Danby* (Glasgow, 1951), i, 432, quoting Bodl. MS Ballard 45, fo. 27a; J. P. Kenyon, *The Nobility in the Revolution of 1688* (Hull, 1963), p. 3.

7. G. M. Straka, 'The Final Phase of Divine Right Theory in England, 1688–1702', in *EHR* lxxvii (1962).

8. G. E. Aylmer, 'Place Bills and the Separation of Powers: some seventeenth-century origins of the "Non-political" Civil Service', in *TRHS* 5th ser., xv (1965), 63.

9. A. F. Havinghurst, 'James II and the Twelve Men in Scarlet', in *Law Quarterly Rev.*, lxix (1953), 531–6.

10. D. Ogg, *England in the Reigns of James II and William III* (Oxford, 1955), pp. 175–9; R. Beddard, 'The Commissioners for Ecclesiastical Promotions, 1681–84: An Instrument of Tory Reaction', in *HJ* x (1967).

11. Cf. D. J. Milne, 'The Results of the Rye House Plot and their Influence upon the Revolution of 1688', in *TRHS* 5th ser., i (1950).

12. F. G. James, 'The Bishops in Politics, 1688–1714', in *Conflict in Stuart England*, ed. W. A. Aitken and B. D. Henning (1960), pp. 232–3.

13. I. F. Burton, 'The Secretary at War and the Administration of the Army during the War of the Spanish Succession' (London Ph.D. thesis, 1960), folios 6, 66, 69, 73; J. R. Western, *The English Militia in the Eighteenth Century* (1965), pp. 85–103.

14. *CJ* xi, 72: 27 Jan 1694; M. A. Thomson, *A Constitutional History of England 1642 to 1801* (1938), p. 198.

15. G. S. Holmes, 'The Attack on "the Influence of the Crown", 1702–1716', in *BIHR* xxxix (1966).

16. See pp. 70–1 below.

17. Havinghurst, in *Law Quarterly Rev.*, lxix (1953), 531–2, and 'The Judiciary and Politics in the Reign of Charles II', in ibid. lxvi (1950). Cf. G. W. Keeton, 'The Judiciary and the Constitutional Struggle, 1660–88', in *J. of Public Teachers of Law*, vii (1963), 59, 67.

18. *Parl. Hist.*, v, 193, 195–6.

19. E. Reitan, 'The Civil List in Eighteenth-century British Politics', in *HJ* ix (1966), esp. p. 318 n 2, p. 319.

20. P. G. M. Dickson, *The Financial Revolution* (1967), p. 47.

21. *Parl. Hist.*, v, 1330.

22. The recoinage cost some £3 m. M-H. Li, *The Great Recoinage* (1963), p. 140.

23. Thomson, op. cit. p. 208.

24. *LJ* xvi, 569: 4 April 1700; xvii, 185: 9 Dec 1702.

25. J. H. Plumb, *The Growth of Political Stability in England 1675–1725* (1967), pp. 101–6; J. Carter, 'Cabinet Records for the Reign of William III', in *EHR* lxxviii (1963).

26. *The Divided Society: Party Conflict in England 1694–1716*, ed. G. Holmes and W. A. Speck (1967), p. 168, quoting Finch MSS P.P. 150 (xii).

27. Ibid. pp. 168–9; J. Carter, 'The Administrative Work of the English Privy Council, 1679–1714' (London Ph.D. thesis, 1958).

28. H. C. Foxcroft, *Life and Letters of . . . Halifax* (1898), ii, 244, 246.

29. 2 Will & Mar, sess. I, c.6; HMC *Finch MSS* iii, 378.

30. SP 8/15, fo. 35.

31. W. Coxe, *Correspondence of Charles Talbot, Duke of Shrewsbury* (1821), p. 35.

32. E. R. Turner, 'The Lords Justices of England', in *EHR* xxix (1914).

33. S. B. Baxter, 'Recent Writings on William III', in *J. Mod. Hist.* xxxviii (1966), esp. p. 264.

34. HMC *Finch MSS* iii, 378.

35. Thomson, op. cit. p. 182 n 1.

36. Ibid. pp. 241–4; R. M. Lees, 'The Constitutional Importance of the "Commissioners for Wool" of 1689', in *Economica*, xiii (1933).

37. J. G. Simms, *The Williamite Confiscation in Ireland 1690–1703* (1956), p. 119.

38. *History of My Own Time* (Oxford, 1833), iv, 287.

39. P. Laslett, 'John Locke, the Great Recoinage, and the Origins of the Board of Trade: 1695–1698', in *William and Mary Q.* 3rd ser., xiv (1957); R. M. Lees, 'Parliament and the Proposal for a Council of Trade, 1695–96', in *EHR* liv (1939).

40. Dickson, op. cit. p. 46; S. B. Baxter, *The Development of the Treasury 1660–1702* (1957), pp. 49, 53, 56–7, 262.

41. J. Ehrman, *The Navy in the War of William III* (Cambridge, 1955).

42. G. N. Clark, *The Dutch Alliance and the War Against French Trade, 1688–1697* (Manchester, 1923), p. 144. See also G. A. Jacobsen, *William Blathwayt* (New Haven, 1932).

43. Ehrman, op. cit. p. 559.

44. R. H. George, 'A Note on the Bill of Rights: Municipal Liberties and the Freedom of Parliamentary Elections', in *American Hist. Rev.*, xlii (1937); 'The Charters Granted to English Parliamentary Corporations in 1688', in *EHR* lv (1940).

45. 2 Will & Mar, c.8.

46. PRO P.C. 2/74, pp. 332, 367.

47. Browning, op. cit. i, 440; R. Steele, *Tudor and Stuart Proclamations* (Oxford, 1910), p. 477.

48. PRO P.C. 2/76, p. 417; 2/78, pp. 4, 13, 16, 17–19.

49. e.g. ibid. 2/73, pp. 339, 499; 2/74, pp. 101, 162; 2/75, p. 146; 2/76, p. 345.

50. Ogg, op. cit. p. 546.

51. A. Harding, *A Social History of English Law* (1966), pp. 296, 498.

52. C. Hill, *Reformation to Industrial Revolution* (1967), p. 113.

53. Thomson, op. cit. pp. 284, 285–8; *CJ* xiii, 518: 8 May 1701.

2. The Revolution in Foreign Policy

G. C. GIBBS

THAT the accession of William III was an event of European significance which would inevitably transform Britain's relations with the powers of Europe was at once apparent to William's English contemporaries; and what was apparent – at least in part – at the time, has long since become a commonplace of historical writing on the subject. The impact, indeed, of William's accession upon the prevailing tendencies and assumptions of British foreign policy, upon its longer-term objectives and priorities, and ultimately upon the manner and the context in which that foreign policy was formulated and conducted, was both profound and enduring – so profound and so enduring that it may be claimed to constitute a revolution no less remarkable than the corresponding changes which occurred during the same period in domestic politics and in the constitution. It is the object of this essay to consider this claim in the light of some of the outstanding developments in foreign affairs during the period 1689–1718.

I

The immediate consequence of William III's accession so far as foreign policy was concerned was a war against France declared in May 1689 and waged as a principal member of the European coalition already formed against Louis XIV. In retrospect this can be seen to have established a pattern of enmity towards France and of military involvement in wartime in the continent of Europe that was to persist, almost without a break, throughout the next hundred years and more. In an exact sense, however, this was less a revolution than a counter-revolution, a return, as was noted at the time, to an earlier medieval tradition.[1] Yet while it is true that some notions are so old that they often appear revolutionary, in the context of the seventeenth century and, in particular, of what was done and what was not done by Charles II and James II, William's actions in 1689 marked a sharp reversal in the then prevailing tendencies of British foreign policy.

Under Charles II and James II British foreign policy had been characterised by a fundamental unconcern for French advance in Europe. Charles II from the beginning of his reign had striven for an alliance with France, and had achieved it ultimately in the Treaty of Dover of 1670. From the worst consequences of that alliance Charles II was saved by his own miscalculations – by the unexpected obduracy of Dutch resistance to France – and by enforced withdrawal from the war against the Dutch in 1674. Such maritime and commercial gains, therefore, as subsequently accrued to England, from her freedom to exploit at the expense of the Dutch the benefits of neutrality in the years 1674 to 1678, accrued fortuitously. They were also paid for at a heavy national price, counted in terms of the surrender of an independent British foreign policy and of a permanent breach between the Crown, on the one hand, and, on the other, Parliament and public opinion, which from 1674 at least had identified in Louis XIV the personification of Popery and arbitrary power, and even before 1674 had discovered some of the maritime, commercial and colonial dangers implicit in unchecked French expansion.[2] Charles II's foreign policy was thus afflicted during the last decade or so of his reign with what amounted to diplomatic lock-jaw, and the reign of James II brought no relief. It is arguable, indeed, that James II had no foreign policy, or that if he had a foreign policy it has certainly remained a mystery to historians. Granted that he was not a puppet of Louis XIV (he had no financial need to be, for the most part, and had no wish to be), the effect of his preoccupation with domestic policies – symbolised perhaps in a contraction of the diplomatic service during his reign[3] – and of the contentious nature of those domestic policies, was to paralyse English initiative in Europe as effectively as if he had been Louis XIV's puppet. In their separate ways, therefore, both Charles II and James II turned away from Europe, and in doing so frustrated the establishment of an effective European alliance against Louis XIV.

It was William's chief concern in invading England in 1688 to reverse this state of affairs; and the achievement of the English throne, made possible and made necessary by James II's totally unexpected flight, was valued by William principally as a means of bringing England into full and active membership of the European coalition against France.[4] Indeed, he is supposed to have remarked to confidants that the day on which Parliament pledged its support for war against France was for him the true beginning of his reign; and, whether or not he uttered the remark, the sentiment it expresses is indisputably authentic.

William's overriding life purpose, unattainable without English support, was to curb and to contain French power, which in 1672 had come close to destroying the independence of the Dutch republic, and it may be asserted at once that any account of William's actions in 1688 which fails to take proper account of this fundamental fact must necessarily be hopelessly out of focus.[5] To say, however, that William III's foreign policy was anti-French, and to leave it at that, would also be seriously misleading, and would render quite inexplicable the final chapter of William's life which was concerned to achieve with French co-operation a settlement of the various European problems created by the imminent prospect of the death of Charles II of Spain. At times, especially in the 1680s, it is true, William's struggle against France appeared to him almost as a holy war between the forces of light and the forces of darkness, and he waged it with a sort of Messianic fervour which rendered him oblivious to, or contemptuous of, the great risks and the intolerable burdens his policies sometimes imposed upon the Dutch republic. 'Our cause is just', he once remarked, 'our conscience is clear; therefore we await with patience and resolve what God has decided for us.'[6] Yet the passion that thus moved him was not hatred of France, nor even hatred of Louis XIV, but concern for the peace, liberties and well-being of Europe, and consequently for the equilibrium of Europe, which happened during his life-time to be threatened by overgrown French power, and after 1697 haunted by the prospect – in reality the chimera – of a union of the French and Spanish thrones on the death of Charles II of Spain. If a similar threat to the European equilibrium had arisen from overgrown Habsburg power, then, as William said to Sir William Temple in 1675, he would have been 'as much a Frenchman as he was now a Spaniard'.[7]

For William III, then, Europe existed as a reality, and the frequency with which in his personal correspondence as well as in his public pronouncements he referred to its well-being and its liberties bears testimony to what was in fact a constant political pursuit.[8] Ultimately, as in the negotiations with Louis XIV over the Partition Treaties of 1698 and 1700, his European sense conquered or transcended even his enmity against France, and found its final embodiment in what has been described with little exaggeration as a policy of collective security for Western and Central Europe.[9]

The policies that William III championed were thus neither specifically English nor specifically Dutch, but European, a fact that, in a rather odd way, Louis XIV acknowledged when upon William's death

he confidently expected great changes in the foreign policies of both
England and the United Provinces. However, if William's policies were
neither specifically Dutch nor specifically English, it does not follow
that they ignored fundamental English and Dutch interests, only that
these were weighed in a scale of priorities that was European. The
achievement of a balance of power in Europe, which to William, it is
clear, meant essentially an equality of power between France and the
Habsburgs, and necessitated the perpetual separation of the crowns of
France and Spain, was an objective of fundamental concern to both
England and the United Provinces. That this was so, and for the most
part was recognised at the time to be so, is strikingly evidenced by the
fact that William's policies outlived him and were pursued after his
death irrespective of party differences in both countries. Thus, although
the English Tories were in general much more insular and xenophobic
than the Whigs, it was a Tory-dominated House of Commons which
committed England to a war in defence of a balance of power in 1701,
just as it was a Tory ministry which sought to guarantee that balance in
its peace negotiations after 1710 by insisting on the permanent separation of the French and Spanish crowns, and which justifiably criticised
the Whig opposition for threatening to 'destroy the balance' by continuing to advocate a policy of 'no peace without Spain' after the death
of the Emperor Joseph in April 1711.[10]

Moreover, since, as the *Craftsman* later argued, the enemy was
wherever the present flow of power appeared,[11] it followed that concern
for the equilibrium of Europe required permanent British involvement
in the affairs of Europe. The notion, indeed, that Britain was part of
Europe and had a role to play in the European power system was
William's principal contribution to the subsequent course of British
foreign policy, at least as it developed under the first two Hanoverians;
even so persistent and generally so isolationist a critic of government
policies as the *Craftsman*, for example, admitted in its more responsible
moments that the balance of power was one of 'the original, everlasting
principles of British politics', and that the tranquillity of Europe was 'so
essential a circumstance to the prosperity of a trading island, that . . . it
ought to be the constant endeavour of a British ministry to preserve it
themselves, and to restore it, when broken or disturbed by others'.[12]
The accession of the Hanoverians, whose duties to their German
electorate created for British statesmen problems of conflicting loyalties
in the conduct of foreign policy similar to those created in 1689 by the
accession of a Dutchman to the English throne, necessarily strengthened

this sense of permanent involvement in European affairs. After 1714, therefore, as before under William and Anne, the need to maintain a balance of power in Europe, especially in Western and Southern Europe, was a guiding principle of British foreign policy,[13] and was pursued largely within a system of alliances with the Emperor and the United Provinces – known to contemporaries as the 'old system' – which William had created. In this respect, indeed, William's policies came to be followed too slavishly, repeated parrot-wise in a situation in which, with the emergence of Prussia in 1740 as a major European power, the 'old system' had ceased to correspond to the realities of the European power structure.

Even when, in the Diplomatic Revolution of 1756, the realities were faced at last and Britain abandoned the old system in favour of a new continental alliance with Prussia, that alliance was defended in terms that had a distinctly Williamite ring about them,[14] and spelt continued British involvement in Europe during the Seven Years War. The Seven Years War, however, finally dissolved the simplicities of the Williamite balance, until, that is, the French Revolutionary wars recombined them. The rise of Prussia, the strengthening of the Habsburg Empire consequent upon its defeat by Prussia, the steady growth of Russia and the diminution in the power and prestige of France moved the centre of gravity of European politics to Eastern Europe after 1763, and created for British foreign policy problems of adjustment that were new and perplexing, the more perplexing, perhaps, because Britain had been accustomed for so long to see Europe as William had seen it.

William III, however, did more than make Britain a European power; he also stamped upon British foreign policy a particular order of priorities in foreign affairs that was both his own order of priorities and was a necessary consequence of the very nature of his position as a monarch who had gained his crown by revolution.

For William the first concern of both England and the United Provinces was security, a concept which in his mind – as distinct from the mind of, say, Louis XIV – was essentially defensive and non-expansive. It was more important to him than trade. Trade, he once acknowledged, referring to the Dutch republic, was the pillar of the state, but he would not risk the state for trade, and if the state was lost, commerce would also be lost.[15] For a Dutchman, indeed, William cared relatively little about trade, and readily admitted that he knew less of English trading interests than he did of Dutch.[16] The negotiations concerning the Partition Treaties (1698–1700), for example, give the impression of someone who needed constantly to be primed about commercial questions. Moreover, his knowledge of even the geography of Spanish America was decidedly scanty, as scanty it would seem as that of Nottingham, who, when William's Secretary of State, apparently needed to be reminded of the whereabouts of French Guiana, while even in Europe William experienced some similar difficulties – the Tuscan ports, which figured so prominently in the many exchange projects discussed during the negotiations for the Partition Treaties, being almost as much a mystery to him as they are to most students today.[17] For all that, William was capable of arguing to a brief, and, since security and trade were not always opposite poles of endeavour, the quest for security sometimes brought incidental trading advantages. The Partition Treaties are a case in point. Whatever arrangements William made he realised that he was bound to incur criticism from some quarter, for whatever arrangements were made they were bound in some degree to strengthen Louis XIV. It was a question of achieving the least injurious settlement. This William did; he was forced to concede Naples and Sicily to France,[18] which imperilled, as William well realised, the highly prestigious trade with the Levant, but he excluded the Bourbons from Spain, the Indies and the Spanish Netherlands, which safeguarded even more important English trading interests.

If, however, William's concept of security embraced vital English economic interests, it meant above all, in English terms, the security of the Revolution settlement – that is the preservation of the constitution, of the Protestant religion and of national independence, all of which were threatened by a return of James II 'with Popery at his heels and the French king riding on his back'.[19] More specifically, security was embodied first of all in a demand by William for the *de facto* recognition by Louis XIV of his title as King of England, which was conceded by Louis XIV at the Peace of Ryswick in 1697. Subsequently, upon Louis' recognition in September 1701 of the Old Pretender as James III, security prompted a demand for international recognition, to be made jointly and severally by the powers of Europe, of the Protestant succession as established by the Act of Settlement in 1701 – an objective that was only fully achieved in the Treaty of Quadruple Alliance of 1718.

In its origins, therefore, the War of Spanish Succession was for England a war for the Protestant succession, as well as, and more than, a war for markets. Subsequently, however, commercial considerations came more to the fore, profoundly affecting both English strategy and English war aims. The Cadiz expedition of 1702, for example, which anticipated the allied conversion in the Methuen treaties of the following year from the notion of a war to partition the Spanish empire to a war for securing to the Habsburg Archduke Charles the entire Spanish empire,[20] was attractive in part because Cadiz was the port from which direct trade with the Spanish colonies was customarily conducted. Moreover, one of the consequences of attempting to place the Archduke Charles upon the Spanish throne, if not one of the reasons for deciding to do so, was a secret agreement by Charles, concluded in 1708, to allow Britain a limited right to trade with the Spanish colonies. Again, commercial considerations weighed heavily with English negotiators during the discussions leading up to the conclusion of separate peace preliminaries with France in 1711, while at the Peace of Utrecht a rich harvest of commercial concessions was gathered – the *asiento*, or the monopoly of carrying slaves to the Spanish colonies, together with a limited direct trade with Spanish America via an annual permission ship, most-favoured nation treatment for British trade with Spain itself and, in North America, the acquisition of Newfoundland – with some restrictions allowing the French the right to dry their fish along a limited portion of the coast – Acadia and Hudson Bay. And although some of these gains proved upon closer examination to be more apparent than real, they were immensely significant, and, from an English point of view, they were much better than the arrangements William had been obliged to accept in the Partition Treaties. For at Utrecht the French were kept out of Naples and Sicily which were placed in the hands of the Emperor and the duke of Savoy, two powers which, while they possessed or developed maritime pretensions, were much less of a maritime danger than France.

In the light of these developments, and in view also of the upsurge of French colonial commerce in the late seventeenth century and of the importance attached to commercial matters by some of Louis XIV's advisers,[21] it is not surprising that to some observers and statesmen at the time the war appeared to have been fought mainly for economic reasons – fundamentally for the riches of the Indies.[22] But for England at least, the chief motor of foreign policy was the security of the Protestant succession. And from the point of view of an understanding of the priorities of British foreign policy, what is significant about, say, the negotiations leading up to the conclusion of separate peace preliminaries with France is less what was haggled over than what was not haggled over; without French recognition of the Protestant succession there could have been no negotiations and no peace. Furthermore, as long as Jacobitism remained an active political force in Britain, and as long as other European powers were prepared to countenance Jacobite aspirations, the Protestant succession continued to be threatened. Given the slowness of eighteenth-century communications, the fact that Britain's standing army was small and dispersed, and that its militia was totally inadequate, a relatively small Jacobite force, once landed, could create a degree of confusion and danger out of all proportion to its size, as was demonstrated in 1715 and 1745. In the decade after 1715, indeed, the security of the Protestant succession was the foremost concern of British statesmen; and it remained a permanent concern of British statesmen until the defeat of the Jacobite rebellion of 1745 finally laid the danger to rest.

II

The changes wrought upon the direction, priorities and underlying assumptions of British foreign policy by William's accession had been immediate, as well as profound, and, on William's part, they had been changes freely and deliberately made. The changes that took place after 1689 in respect of the manner and the context in which that policy was formulated were not immediate, and, in so far as they were controlled by William at all, they were not made quite freely.

Nowhere, indeed, had the conservatism of the revolution of 1689 been more apparent than in its treatment, or, to be more accurate, its lack of treatment of the executive power of the Crown. William had been admitted on conditions, but these conditions had not limited the Crown's executive power. The King was expected to rule as well as to reign and, in particular, he was expected personally to formulate and to execute foreign policy. Admittedly, he was also expected to execute certain acts through his ministers, and, in the case of foreign affairs, through the two Secretaries of State for the Northern and Southern departments, who, as their titles suggest, divided between them correspondence with Europe on a geographical basis. Further, the King was supposed to ask for advice on important matters. But he was not bound to ask advice of any particular person or body of persons, even less was he bound to accept such advice. Parliament, it is true, could scarcely be prevented from offering advice, if it chose to do so, but its necessary contact with foreign policy was confined strictly speaking to the receiving of subsidy treaties, treaties altering domestic tariffs and also, it was argued, treaties of cession which involved the surrender of territories formally annexed to the Crown.[23]

The control of foreign policy thus lay, and was agreed to lie, unambiguously in the Crown. It was, indeed, the fairest jewel in the Crown's prerogative; without it, argued Charles II in 1676, the king would be reduced to 'the empty sound of a king'.[24] Subsequently, it is true, in the Act of Settlement of 1701, which is almost a history in miniature of William's reign, a restriction was placed upon the Crown's future prerogative in foreign affairs. It was declared that upon the accession of the House of Hanover, Britain would not be obliged to engage in any war for the defence of the Crown's foreign possessions without the consent of Parliament. Very properly this clause in the Act of Settlement has been saluted as the first statutory limitation upon the Crown's prerogative in foreign affairs; it was also, perhaps, an undeserved rebuke, directed at William for having, it seemed, used British power to advance specifically Dutch interests. In practical terms, however, it imposed no restriction that did not already exist; long before 1689 it had become clear that if the Crown wished to wage war at the public expense – and it could wage war in no other way – it would have to get the consent of Parliament.

In theory, therefore, William enjoyed in 1689 virtually complete freedom to make war, to declare peace and to conclude treaties, and the practice of his reign conformed closely to the theory, at least until the crisis engendered by the Partition Treaties. William acted as his own foreign minister, a role which his own strongly authoritarian instincts and his own highly developed sense of princely power naturally led him to assume, and which his vast experience of foreign affairs well equipped him to perform. The most secret and the most important matters in foreign policy he handled himself with the aid of a few Dutchmen and, in particular, with the aid of his close friend from childhood, Bentinck, naturalised and created earl of Portland. His English ministers were mere clerks, not even confidential clerks, and for the most part were content to be treated as clerks, deferring to William's superior knowledge where they were not silenced by the fear of incurring his wrath.[25] Thus the treaty of Grand Alliance of 1689 was signed by William himself, not by his English ministers, and apparently had still not been communicated to any of his ministers several years after it had been signed, while English ministers were admitted to the negotiations relating to the first Partition Treaty of 1698 only at a stage when, as Portland admitted, their sole function was to say yes or no to terms already agreed between William and Louis XIV.[26]

Moreover if, until nearly the end of his reign, William's English ministers were not effectively consulted about foreign policy, Parliament was scarcely even informed. No more information was divulged than was necessary to secure supply, which meant in practice an annual exhortation to greater effort in the Speech from the Throne, the laying before the Commons of subsidy treaties, and little else. Neither the treaty of Grand Alliance of 1689, for example, nor the Peace of Ryswick in 1697 was laid before Parliament after signature for its information or approval.[27] For the most part Parliament tolerated the ignorance in which it was kept. In part this was because, as a critic of government admitted in 1689, 'war and peace we meddle not with; we are only to supply it';[28] in part it was because the objects for which war had been begun in 1689 seemed so clear, and so clearly desirable, as to make the war, in William's words to Parliament in April 1689, 'not so properly an act of choice as an inevitable necessity in our defence'.[29] Criticism, therefore, was levelled at the way in which the war was being waged, but not at the war as such. Further, what William did not see fit to divulge, members of Parliament could not easily discover for themselves in 1689. Some coverage of European news was available in the *London Gazette*, the official, and indeed only, newspaper in 1689, and the *Gazette*, it seems, was encouraged by William after 1689 to report news of the campaigns in the Low Countries during the war. The amount of space, however, which could be devoted to such news was necessarily limited in a newspaper which practised a virtual monopoly in the reportage of particular categories of domestic news, and its choice of foreign news was also limited by the nature of its position as the official government organ for the dissemination of news – its news might be accurate, but it would naturally be concerned to avoid matters that could cause offence or injury to the government, or excite criticism of its policies.[30]

Thus, respect for the prerogative of the Crown, belief that the Crown's policies were consonant with fundamental English interests and the difficulties confronting members of Parliament who wished to acquire precise knowledge of what was happening in Western Europe combined to give William, until near the end of his reign, a degree of freedom in the conduct of English foreign policy that would have been the envy of Charles II and James II. Ignorance, however, ceased to be bliss when the King sensed dangers to which Parliament appeared insensitive and when it appeared to Parliament that English interests were being disregarded by the King. Such a situation arose during the period 1698 to 1701 when William came to see very clearly the serious, humiliating, even crippling weaknesses attached to policies inspired and conducted without regard to Parliament, and to accept that an informed Parliament might be more easily persuaded of the efficacy of royal policies than an uninformed Parliament.[31]

Briefly, the background to the crisis was in the first place a general mood of isolationism and pacifism – what Lord Chancellor Somers described in 1698 as 'a deadness and want of spirit in the nation universally'[32] – which arose naturally in the aftermath of a long war that had imposed upon England unprecedented burdens and that appeared to have achieved its main objective in the acceptance by France of the Revolution settlement. For William, however, the peace meant no relaxation in vigilance; having, as he said to Parliament, rescued England's religion, laws and liberties, he was determined to preserve them entire and leave them to posterity. And in William's view this could not happen unless some European agreement could be reached about what was to happen upon the long-expected and now imminently expected death of Charles II of Spain. It was to the achievement of such an agreement that William immediately directed his diplomatic efforts after the Peace of Ryswick.

Accordingly, after 1697, Parliament and Crown moved steadily away from each other; Parliament seeking withdrawal from Europe, William seeking continued and closer involvement. The sense of estrangement was sharpened by an upsurge of anti-Dutch feelings. Even during the war irritation with and distrust of the Dutch had not been silenced; it would have been surprising if it had, for wartime coalitions, by definition almost, impose upon those who join them some sacrifice of individual interests for the common good. But in the case of England and the United Provinces there was more to the problem than the inevitable frictions of wartime coalition. Deep-seated trading rivalries existed and drew constant nourishment from the prevalent economic doctrine that in matters of trade profit to one nation must mean loss to another – 'trade being to . . . nations what a mistress is unto lovers'.[33] In the war the expression of such rivalries had been somewhat muted by a realisation of the need to co-ordinate resources against the common enemy. Peace removed this restraint, and William, as a Dutchman and as the appointed chief servant of the United Provinces, drew upon himself after 1697 the traditional odium felt for the Dutch as trading rivals.

And William's own actions and behaviour did not improve matters. His public manner was cold, stiff and withdrawn; and when he relaxed, he relaxed ostentatiously in the company of his Dutch favourites, whose services, it seemed to English eyes, were extravagantly rewarded from the royal bounty at the expense of English subjects. Further, he made long annual trips to the Dutch republic, which were viewed with hostility and suspicion in England, and he did not conceal the pleasure such trips gave him; he felt on such occasions, he said, like a fish returning to water.[34] To this natural feeling of homesickness for the land of his birth was added after 1697 a sense of exasperation, so desperate that at times it verged on defeatism, caused by what appeared to William as English blindness and stupidity, indifference and parochialism, in the face of an approaching European war upon the death of Charles II of Spain. It was, indeed, true that William observed what English opinion did not observe, that the Spanish succession was a vital concern for England; what he seems to have been unaware of, however, was that he had been partly responsible for this situation by conducting foreign policy as if Parliament did not exist. The Partition Treaties of 1698 and 1700, as has been said previously, were his own work, achieved without consulting ministers or informing Parliament. When the contents of the treaties became known in the summer of 1700 and the spring of 1701 they aroused much hostile comment, outside and inside Parliament, from Whigs as well as Tories, directed not only at the terms of the treaties, which threatened important trading interests at a time when the state of English trade in general was causing some anxiety,[35] but also at the manner in which they had been concluded.

Things became worse before they became better. On 1 November 1700 Charles II of Spain died and his will, drawn up shortly before his death, appointed Louis' second grandson, Philip, duke of Anjou, as successor to the entire Spanish empire. On 16 November Louis accepted the will, and his decision was welcomed by the mass of opinion in England. The will, it was argued, was a better guarantee of peace than the Partition Treaties, which would require a war to enforce them, better for English trading interests, since it did not relinquish important territory to France, as the Partition Treaties had done with Naples and Sicily, and a better safeguard of future security, since Philip would become a Spaniard – as, in fact, he did in time become – and consequently would produce no change in Spanish policy. When, therefore, in February 1701, the first session began of a new Parliament with a Tory majority in the Lower House, the mood was firmly pacific. Yet by June 1701 Parliament was ready to envisage war against France.

For this transformation in English opinion Louis XIV was largely responsible. His acceptance of the will was followed by a series of acts which convinced Englishmen that their country's security was in danger. Thus Louis announced that Philip V's succession to the Spanish crown did not invalidate his claim to the French crown, forcibly removed Dutch garrisons from certain towns in the Spanish Netherlands, assumed for a French company the *asiento* and imposed restrictions upon English trade with France which were paralleled by restrictions upon English trade to Spain. Historians have not found it easy to explain these acts and have found it impossible to establish an agreed explanation for them. The most recent and the most sophisticated treatment of the problem argues that Louis' actions were the product neither of pride nor stupidity, but that they were, in Louis' eyes, essentially defensive measures designed to convince Spain of Philip V's determination and capacity to maintain the indivisibility of the Spanish empire, and betoken a failure of nerve.[36] The argument is convincing, though it is arguable that, in a sense, pride and stupidity had been kicked out of the front door only to reappear at the back: for if Louis believed in the light of his past record that his actions could be regarded as essentially defensive, then he was capable of a degree of myopia or self-deception to be found only in a man who was either very stupid, which Louis was not, or possessed of an habitual and inordinate sense of self-esteem, which Louis certainly was. And whatever the explanation of Louis' acts, they appeared to the rest of Europe as a clear expression both of his determination to uphold the will of Charles II, whatever the consequences, and of his determination to profit from it. As such they convinced opinion in England that English security and vital trading interests were in danger, and that the danger must be met.

Louis' actions spoke for themselves, but in England their impact was deepened by the use William made of the opportunity they created. In Parliament William skilfully exploited the procedural device of royal messages, which by convention Parliament was required to answer by addresses, to establish a continuous dialogue between Crown and Parliament, as a result of which Parliament was led gradually to the point of accepting the need for a strong foreign policy. The dialogue was also to some extent public, for the Crown's messages to the Commons, and the addresses of the Commons in reply, were published and circulated widely, in an abbreviated version of the journals of the House known as the *Votes* of the Commons, published by the authority of the Commons daily throughout the session. It was in this way possible to bring public pressure to bear upon Parliament, and the pressure was increased by a vigorous propaganda campaign, in which the talents of Defoe were enlisted.[37] That William may have inspired this campaign to some extent seems likely; he was not always choosy about his methods, and the intimidatory tone of the Kentish Petition and the Legion Letter of May 1701 are reminiscent of his earlier essays in the art of intimidation practised against opponents in the United Provinces.[38]

In the short run the session of 1701 was a victory for the Crown. Yet, even in the short run, it was a victory which to some extent Parliament had shared, at least to the extent of obliging William to acknowledge its right to be informed about foreign policy and of censuring – through the impeachments of ministers – the manner in which the Partition Treaties had been concluded. In the long run, however, the victory went to Parliament for having weakened permanently the Crown's prerogative in foreign affairs. What William had been forced to concede, Anne was unable to refuse, especially since engagement in a long and expensive war necessarily made foreign affairs a permanent and important concern of Parliament. Henceforth the Speech from the Throne came to contain a passage at least relating to foreign affairs. In thus announcing policy in very broad but nevertheless carefully drawn outline, the Crown was providing Parliament with an essential lead to its deliberations and was seeking to elicit from Parliament, in the form of the customary addresses of thanks of the two Houses, expressions of support for that policy. And, since such support had to be won and could not be commanded, and once won had to be kept, it also became usual for ministers and others to expound foreign policy in Parliament and to lay treaties and papers before Parliament, either at its request or upon the initiative of the Crown.

Special circumstances might also necessitate special measures designed to ensure that individual members of Parliament were prepared for the direction government policy was intended to take in the session and were thoroughly conversant with its case before the debates in Parliament had begun.[39] A celebrated example of such measures in Anne's reign was Swift's great pamphlet *The Conduct of the Allies* (1711), commissioned by prime minister Harley, composed with ministerial assistance and 'planned to be ready on the first day of the new session of Parliament'.[40] In subsequent years the practice of preceding the parliamentary battle by a preliminary propaganda barrage became so common that to the contemporary journalist Abel Boyer, the compiler of the extremely informative monthly periodical, the *Political State of Great Britain*, it seemed that 'scarce anything is ever debated in Parliament that is not first canvassed without doors',[41] while to another and later observer, William Pulteney, writing in 1730, the appearance at or near the opening of Parliament of a government-inspired pamphlet constituted an annual custom.

Of course Parliament was not told the whole truth, nor did it expect to be told the whole truth, for it was recognised that prudence or courtesy, of which the King was admitted to be the best judge, might require strict secrecy, especially if negotiations were incomplete – on the anvil, in the contemporary phrase. Sometimes, too, Parliament was deliberately misled, as, for example, in the announcement from the throne in the Queen's Speech of 7 December 1711 that the Dutch had readily concurred in the arrangements for a peace conference. What is significant about that announcement, however, is less its falsity than the reasons which made such deception necessary and the reaction of Parliament to it. The peace that Anne's Tory ministers designed to make involved the repudiation of aims to which Parliament had repeatedly and publicly committed itself; to win parliamentary appro-bation of the peace, therefore, it was necessary to deceive opinion in England by suggesting that the moves made towards peace com-manded the support of her European allies and, alternatively and simul-taneously, that her allies by their alleged military slackness deserved to be deserted.[42] However, neither deception nor concealment were as easy as they had been in 1689, as is strikingly illustrated in the reaction of members to the Crown's assertion about the attitude of the Dutch just referred to. This was challenged immediately in the Commons; the government, said Sir Peter King, must take them for children to make such a declaration.[43]

What made such challenges possible in the first place was that Parliament was no longer dependent upon the Crown for its information about foreign affairs. In this context the breakthrough had come with the lapsing of the Licensing Act in 1695. Independent newspapers then appeared again, and thereafter multiplied rapidly, until by 1700 the reading of newspapers had become a settled habit in England, as it had elsewhere in Europe at that time, and in England the habit was not confined to a ruling minority. Most of the news in the independent newspapers was foreign news, from choice and from necessity.[44] This appears to have consisted largely of extracts from foreign newspapers, especially Dutch newspapers whose gazetteers made a point of maintaining regular, direct correspondence with the personnel of Dutch embassies abroad, and also profited from the virtual impossibility in the Dutch republic of keeping secret the conduct of foreign policy under a constitution which gave to every province the right to ask for copies of nearly all secret documents. Much of the foreign news in contemporary newspapers, therefore, in so far as such news related to current diplomatic negotiations, was probably diplomatic gossip, but it was also often informed diplomatic gossip – a useful supplement to the intelligence services of the great powers, and for English M.P.s the only continuous contact with British foreign policy during the parliamentary recess, and a valuable source of additional information while Parliament was sitting. For example, the first public knowledge in England of the existence of the second Partition Treaty of 1700 came via the *London Post* under a heading 'The Hague', which cited the news as having come from Spain (the leak, in fact, can be traced to Louis XIV).[45] Or again, the first partial revelation to Englishmen of the existence of peace negotiations with France came via the *Daily Courant* of 13 October 1711, leaked to the Press by the Imperial envoy a few days after the news had been privately communicated to the representatives of the allies in London for the information of their governments. And this partial revelation immediately forced the British government to further revelations, made this time via the government-inspired *Post Boy*.

These incidents illustrate not only the value of newspapers as purveyors of foreign news, but also the role played in the dissemination of foreign news in England by foreign governments and their envoys in London, who, either because they felt the need to convince a body of opinion of their own at home, or because they sought to influence opinion, especially parliamentary opinion in England, often made public facts or arguments that an English government would have preferred not to be made public. To appeal openly to the nation against the sovereign was – to quote words used by the *Craftsman* in 1727 to describe a celebrated example of such an appeal, involving the Imperial resident, Palm – a practice that 'was indecent between gentlemen and is much more so between crown heads'.[46] Nevertheless it was a not uncommon form of indecency. The Spanish ambassador was expelled in 1699 for a public statement, considered seditious, which confirmed both the existence of the Partition Treaty of 1698 and the fact that negotiations were in progress for the second, while in 1712 both the Imperial and Hanoverian ministers in London were forbidden the Court of Anne for having joined forces with the Whigs in opposing publicly the peace negotiations with France.[47] Contacts between members of Parliament, especially members of the Opposition in Parliament, and foreign envoys were, indeed, common form, and had been long before 1689, regardless of a Commons' standing order of 1643 forbidding such contacts. Wratislaw, the Emperor's ambassador to London, for example, was assiduous in 1701 in priming members of Parliament about the dangers embodied in Louis XIV's acceptance of the will, even assisting in the actual wording of the Lords' address of 17 February 1701.[48]

None of this should be taken to imply the existence of open diplomacy. The Crown could still keep its secrets. The existence of the Barrier Treaty of 1709, for example, was not publicly revealed until August 1710, characteristically in a newspaper, and its actual provisions were not known outside ministerial circles for more than a year. And secrecy as such was generally accepted as perfectly proper. Nevertheless the knowledge that members of Parliament were no longer dependent upon the Crown for information about foreign affairs, or no longer as dependent as they had been before 1695, inevitably exercised a considerable influence upon the Crown's conduct of foreign policy. In the circumstances the Crown usually deemed it sensible to take Parliament into account, and to some extent even into its confidence, in the actual formulation of foreign policy; when it did not, it was obliged to learn sense the hard way, as George I was in 1717, when he received a sharp reminder of the dangers and weaknesses of a personal diplomacy formulated and pursued without sufficient regard to the views of Parliament.[49] And the effects of this sharing of the Crown's prerogative power with Parliament were not confined to the formulation of foreign policy: English negotiators, at times of protracted crisis, were placed at a considerable disadvantage *vis-à-vis* their European counterparts, who, not having a Parliament at their backs, were able to negotiate in a freer, less hurried way. The advent of a parliamentary foreign policy, therefore, added an element of instability, as well as inflexibility, to a system which already appeared in European eyes to be chronically unstable. The English, remarked the French ambassador in 1717, would crucify Christ again if he returned to govern England.[50]

Constitutional theory in these matters, however, remained unchanged, and largely unquestioned. What the Crown saw fit to divulge continued by contemporaries to be ascribed to its 'wise and gracious condescension'. The word 'condescension' captured exactly the essence of the theoretical relationship between Crown and Parliament in questions of foreign policy, but it was scarcely an accurate description of a process which in practice had been begun not quite voluntarily and which had not been prompted by mere politeness; it was, indeed, a characteristic English constitutional euphemism. In normal circumstances Parliament continued to follow the Crown's lead in foreign policy, but the Crown had to provide a lead, and had to show that it was pursuing policies substantially in harmony with the general view of British interests. The provisos were important, and in practice nothing could safely be taken for granted.

BIBLIOGRAPHICAL NOTE

Recommendations for reading have been confined to works in English; it will be obvious, however, that no student of foreign policy will get far who is not prepared to read European languages.

Two books useful in situating the events of the years 1689 to 1718 are J. R. Jones, *Britain and Europe in the Seventeenth Century* (1966), and D. B. Horn, *Great Britain and Europe in the Eighteenth Century* (Oxford, 1967). On the period itself the most outstanding recent contributions have come from the late Professor Mark A. Thomson whose various essays have been conveniently collected in *William III and Louis XIV. Essays by and for Mark A. Thomson*, ed. R. Hatton and J. S. Bromley (Liverpool, 1968). What I owe to these essays will be apparent at once to the reader of them. I have attempted to pursue some of Thomson's themes in 'Parliament and Foreign Policy in the Age of Stanhope and Walpole', in *EHR* lxxvii (1962); 'Parliament and the Treaty of Quadruple Alliance', in *William III and Louis XIV. Essays* . . . pp. 287–305; and 'Newspapers, Parliament, and Foreign Policy in the Age of Stanhope and Walpole', in *Mélanges offerts à G. Jacquemyns* (Brussels, 1968), pp. 293–315. For William III the best biography in English is S. B. Baxter, *William III* (1966), although its understanding of Dutch politics and society has been seriously criticised by Dutch historians, and it is sometimes uncertain in its handling of international relations.

William's foreign policy, however, is best studied through his correspondence, and, in English, for the period 1697 to 1702 there is a useful selection in *Letters of William III and Louis XIV*, ed. P. Grimblot (1848). Some of the basic documents of British foreign policy are available in *British Diplomatic Instructions 1689–1789: ii, France, 1689–1721*, ed. L. G. Wickham Legg (Camden Society, xxxv, 1925); its introduction, however, must be read alongside J. G. Stork-Penning, 'The Ordeal of the States' (see p. 78 n 42 below). G. M. Trevelyan, *England under Queen Anne*, 3 vols (1930–4), is still indispensable, though it displays a lack of understanding of Habsburg aims and policies.

NOTES

1. Lord Somers, *A Vindication of the Proceedings of the Late Parliament* [1689], printed in *Parl. Hist.* v, app. iv, p. xx.

2. For a brief but judicious reassessment of Charles II's foreign policy see K. H. D. Haley, *Charles II* (Hist. Assn Pamph. 1966), pp. 15–21.

3. P. S. Lachs, *The Diplomatic Corps under Charles II and James II* (New Jersey, Rutgers U.P., 1965), p. 14.

4. See p. 36 n 36 above. William's ambitions upon and reasons for wanting the English throne are discussed by R. Fruin, 'Prins Willem III en zijn verhouding tot Engeland', in *Verspreide Geschriften* (1900–5), v, 1–193; P. Geyl, 'Willem III, de Stadhouder – Koning', in *Studies en Strijdschriften* (Groningen, 1958), pp. 145–67.

5. Cf. L. Pinkham, *William III and the Respectable Revolution* (1954), esp. p. 91.

6. M. A. M. Franken, *Coenraad van Beuningen's Politieke en Diplomatieke Aktiviteiten in de jaren 1667–1684* (Groningen, 1966), p. 236.

7. I am grateful to Dr Ragnhild Hatton for drawing my attention to this remark which is quoted in her 'Louis XIV and his fellow monarchs', to appear in *Louis XIV: The Craft of Kingship*, ed. J. C. Rule.

8. For a recent discussion of the manner in which the Dutch came to identify the interest of the Republic with the wider interest of Europe, and in particular of the way their attitudes were shaped by the desperate situation which faced them *c.* 1672, see J. W. Smit, 'The Netherlands and Europe in the Seventeenth and Eighteenth Centuries', in *Britain and the Netherlands in Europe and Asia*, ed. J. S. Bromley and E. H. Kossmann (1968), esp. pp. 31–2.

9. M. A. Thomson, 'English and French Policy, 1689–1718', in *William III and Louis XIV. Essays 1680–1720 by and for Mark A. Thomson*, ed. R. Hatton and J. S. Bromley (Liverpool, 1968), p. 276.

10. BM Loan 29/36: Lord Oxford's 'Meditation in the Tower'.

11. *Craftsman*, 6 March 1727 (1731–7 edn., i, 155–6).

12. Ibid. 25 May 1728, 17 June 1727 (iii, 95; ii, 34).

13. Even the alliance with France in 1717 expressed this felt need, for the longer-term objective of the alliance was to complete the Utrecht settlement and to provide reciprocal guarantees for the successions in Britain, France and the Habsburg dynasty in Austria.

14. M. Schlenke, *England und das friderizianische Preussen 1740–1763* (Munich, 1963), pp. 218–25.

15. N. Japikse, *Prins Willem III, De Stadhouder-Koning* (Amsterdam, 1930–3), ii, 177.

16. See, for example, *Letters of William III and Louis XIV*, ed. P. Grimblot (1848), i, 426.

17. Japikse, ii, 401; Grimblot, i, 462, ii, 23; HMC *Finch MSS* iv, 521.

18. The assertion by S. B. Baxter, *William III* (1966), p. 372, that the Partition Treaty of 1700 contained a secret clause under which the duke of Savoy was to exchange his own homeland for Naples and Sicily is based on a misreading of the treaty. The secret clause (for which see Grimblot, op. cit. ii, 504–6) says nothing about Naples and Sicily, and describes various exchange projects concerning Milan. The Savoy exchange proposal was discussed only after the ratification of the treaty, as Prior makes plain in his private journal (BM Loan 29/335, *sub* Nov 1700).

19. *Parl. Hist.*, v, 407.

20. See G. M. Trevelyan, *England under Queen Anne*, i (1930), p. 265.

21. See P. Goubert, *Louis XIV et vingt millions de Français* (Paris, 1966), pp. 141–2, 172–9; J. Delumeau, 'Le commerce extérieur français au XVIIe siècle', in *Le XVIIe Siècle. Aspects de l'economie française au XVIIe siècle* (Paris, 1966), pp. 95–100.

22. Delumeau, op. cit. p. 102 (quoting Louis XIV and de Torcy to that effect).

23. The notion that the cession of such territories required Parliament's consent was raised in regard to Dunkirk (1662) and the prospective sale of Tangier (1679).

24. *CJ* ix, 426.

25. G. Davies, 'The control of British foreign policy by William III', in *Essays on the Later Stuarts* (1958); M. A. Thomson, *The Secretaries of State 1681–1782* (Oxford, 1932), pp. 7–12. See also HMC *Finch MSS* iv, 30, 340, 425.

26. *Correspondentie van Willem III en van Hans Willem Bentinck*, ed. N. Japikse (The Hague, 1927–37), ii, 99.

27. They were laid before Parliament for the first time in 1701. *LJ* xvi, 619; *CJ* xiii, 484.

28. *Parl. Hist.* v, 137.

29. *CJ* x, 104.

30. M. A. Thomson, *Some Developments in English Historiography during the Eighteenth Century* (Inaugural Lecture, University College, London, 1956), p. 5; E. S. De Beer, 'The English Newspapers from 1695 to 1702', in *William III and Louis XIV. Essays* . . . pp. 118–19.

31. The best short account of these developments is in Thomson, 'Parliament and Foreign Policy, 1689–1714', in *William III and Louis XIV. Essays* . . . pp. 131–5.

32. *Parl. Hist.* v, 1247.

33. Franken, op. cit. p. 12.

34. Geyl, loc. cit. p. 162.

35. See *CJ* xiii, 298–9.

36. Thomson, 'Louis XIV and the Origins of the War of the Spanish Succession', in *William III and Louis XIV. Essays* . . . pp. 140–61.

37. J. Sutherland, *Defoe* (1937), pp. 63–9.

38. See, for example, Geyl, loc. cit. pp. 154, 156–7; Japikse, *Willem III*, i, 253; J. K. Oudendijk, *William III Stadhouder van Holland, Koning van Engeland* (Amsterdam, 1954), pp. 69–73.

39. Thomson, in *William III and Louis XIV. Essays* . . . pp. 135–9. See also G. C. Gibbs, 'Parliament and Foreign Policy in the Age of Stanhope and Walpole', in *EHR* lxxvii (1962).

40. Jonathan Swift, *Political Tracts 1711–1713*, ed. H. Davis (Oxford, 1951), p. viii.

41. *The Political State of Great Britain*, 60 vols (1711–40), xiii, 111.

42. There is an effective repudiation of the charges of military slackness levelled against the Dutch in J. G. Stork-Penning, 'The Ordeal of the States – some remarks on Dutch politics during the war of the Spanish Succession', in *Acta Historiae Neerlandica*, ii (1967).

43. Quoted in D. Coombs, *The Conduct of the Dutch* (The Hague, 1958), p. 284.

44. Gibbs, 'Newspapers, Parliament, and Foreign Policy in the Age of Stanhope and Walpole', in *Mélanges offerts à G. Jacquemyns* (Brussels, 1968), pp. 296–304; De Beer, in *William III and Louis XIV. Essays* . . . p. 124.

45. *London Post*, 31 May/3 June 1700.

46. *Craftsman*, 13/16 March 1727.

47. Grimblot, op. cit. ii, 351–6; G. Brauer, *Die hannoversch-englischen Sub-sidienverträge 1702–1748* (Aalen, 1962), pp. 76–7.

48. O. Klopp, *Der Fall des Hauses Stuart* (Vienna, 1875–88), ix, 157.

49. Gibbs, in *EHR* lxxvii (1962), 29–30.

50. Archives Etrangères, Angleterre, t 291 : D'Iberville, 7 Jan 1717, quoting an anonymous English bishop.

I wish to thank Professor Ragnhild Hatton for reading this essay in typescript and for making a number of valuable suggestions.

3. The Revolution and the People

ANGUS McINNES

And some were damned to scythes and spades,
And all those hard laborious trades;
Where willing wretches daily sweat,
And wear out strength and limbs to eat.

B. Mandeville, *The Grumbling Hive* (1705)

THIS essay is concerned with the man in the street – the domestic servant, the agricultural labourer, the industrial worker, the craftsman, the pedlar, the vagabond; all those, in fact, who were known at the time by the collective term 'the labouring poor'. To these we shall add two other categories of somewhat more exalted rank – the small tenant farmer and the owner-occupier possessing some twenty or thirty acres of land. Although these last two groups would have been looked on by contemporaries as falling within 'the middling sort of mankind', since their way of life was substantially the same as that of their more humble brethren, and since they employed very little help but earned their bread largely by the sweat of their own brows and the labour of their own hands, we shall include them within our survey. Taken together these ordinary men and women comprised around 80 per cent of England's 5½ million inhabitants. What was the place of these, the common people, in the England of 1689–1714? How did they view their lot? And what effects, if any, did the Glorious Revolution have on their lives?

A first clue to the standing of the ordinary Englishman is provided by the actual words used by the people of the day. Most revolutions have their battle cries. One thinks, for example, of the stirring phrase 'liberty, equality, fraternity' shouted through the streets of Paris at the time of the French Revolution. The Glorious Revolution was no exception to this general rule. A glance at the reports of the debates in the Convention, or at the flood of pamphlet literature which poured from the presses after James II's departure clearly shows that when contemporaries wished to express the spirit of the Revolution three words came most readily to their lips. William's coming, supporters of the Revolution proclaimed over and over again, had secured the cause of 'liberty', 'property' and 'religion', 'all which', as the invitation to the Prince of Orange put it, 'have been greatly invaded'.[1]

On the surface these three words may well seem to have little in common. But in fact they all boiled down to one and the same thing. All of them denoted that the Revolution had been set in train chiefly to ensure the dominance and to foster the influence of a propertied and privileged minority. 'Property', of course, was obviously the concern of the property-owning few rather than of the unpropertied many. But so also were the ideas expressed by property's two companion words. Take 'liberty', for example. In the seventeenth century 'freedom' did not mean what it does today. When we use the words 'freedom' or 'liberty' we mean the absence of restraints, the chance to do what we want to do without hindrance from others. In William III's day the meaning of 'freedom' was very different from this. It implied privilege and exclusiveness. The freeman of a town, for instance, possessed certain privileges from which lesser mortals were excluded. Again, the free-holder claimed exclusive rights in his own freehold. The 'liberties' of Parliament in the seventeenth century consisted of a number of special privileges, such as freedom from arrest during parliamentary sittings, which were enjoyed by M.P.s and their families and by no one else. To be free of all vice indicated not blameless virtue, but a hearty indulgence in immorality. Freedom, in short, conveyed the notion of possession, not the absence of something. Hence in nailing their colours to the banner of 'liberty' the men of 1689 were rallying to the cause of privilege.

What is true of 'liberty' is true also of 'religion'. There were many sorts of Catholicism in the seventeenth century, just as there were many sorts of Puritanism. Daniel Defoe, a keen observer and one of the most skilled journalists of the period, stumbled on one type of Popery when he visited Durham on one of his journeys round England. 'The town,' he recorded, 'is well built but old, full of Roman Catholics who live peaceably and disturb nobody, and nobody them; for we being there on a holiday, saw them going as publicly to mass as the dissenters did on other days to their meeting house.'[2] This sleepy, dust-laden kind of Catholicism was characteristic of much of northern England at the close of the seventeenth century. It could be found in the fastnesses of

Yorkshire and Lancashire as well as in Durham. It was part of an age-old way of life that was slow-moving, traditional and paternalistic, and it owed very little to the rigours of the Jesuit order or the Counter Reformation. Vastly different was the kind of Popery rampant in Louis XIV's France. Louis looked upon religion as a weapon of state, something to cow his subjects, to bind them beneath the sway of his untrammelled will. It was this more political, more abrasive brand of Catholicism which James II attempted to import into England and which did so much to hasten the Revolution. James's policy alarmed people of all shades of opinion. Even many of the Catholics of the north opposed him, just as their forebears had opposed the introduction of the papal archpriest George Blackwell into England in the reign of Elizabeth. But the men who more than any others were alarmed by what James was doing were the property-owners. They saw in James's political Catholicism, his 'ecclesiastic tyranny' as they called it,[3] a threat to their position in society and a blow to their estates. 'Frenchified popish' monarchy, they were acutely aware, was incompatible with the rule of a privileged oligarchy. 'Popish councils and councillors', exclaimed Abel Boyer, are sworn enemies of privilege, of 'rights and liberties'. Tyranny, echoed Defoe, is 'an oppression of property'.[4] In crying 'religion', therefore, the apologists of the Glorious Revolution were, as often as not, intoning 'privilege' at one remove. 'Liberty', 'property' and 'religion' were thus all part of a single syndrome.

This impression, conveyed by the language of 1689, that the England of the Glorious Revolution was a country dominated by the 'free', a land in which ordinary men and women occupied a very subordinate place, is confirmed by what happened in Parliament once William was securely on the throne. Gradually, in the course of the 1690s, the Whigs shed their radical, opposition cloak. By 1694 the younger Whig leaders, Somers, Wharton, Montague and Russell had all been absorbed into the ministry and become pillars of the establishment, and for much of the remainder of William's reign they were to render sterling service to the King. It was, for example, the financial genius of Charles Montague, the godfather of the Bank of England and of the system of deficit finance which grew up after the Revolution, which made it possible for William to meet his military commitments. The growing respectability of the Whigs meant that the most radical group in the House of Commons was now the Country party led by Thomas Clarges, Paul Foley and Robert Harley. But even the Country party was a party of the landed gentry. Country members kept up a continuous dirge of complaint against high taxation which hit the gentry badly, against government corruption which bled the honest squire to feed the greedy courtier, and against the granting of English estates to foreign favourites such as William Bentinck, duke of Portland. Perhaps the most characteristic project of the Country party during these years was Harley's abortive Land Bank scheme. The Land Bank was rather like a modern building society. The idea was that the bank should issue loans on the security of mortgages, and it was planned to have branches dotted around the countryside. The whole thing was designed to appeal to the typical backwoods squire, firstly by offering him a ready source of cash, and secondly by threatening to knock out the City-dominated Bank of England. Thus even the most radical of the groups inside Parliament after the Revolution was a party of property-owners. Political disputes in the reigns of William and Anne were essentially disputes between different kinds of propertied men. Politics in other words were monopolised by a narrow *élite*. They did not concern ordinary people.[5]

The stranglehold which the privileged few had on society at this time is brought out with still greater force if we turn from political squabbles to the sort of laws which actually reached the statute-book. The legislation relating to the grain trade is a case in point. In the early part of the seventeenth century strenuous efforts were made to protect the grain consumer. The activities of corn merchants, for example, were closely scrutinised, attempts were made to eliminate speculators and hoarders, the export of grain was restricted, and little was done to stop its import. After the Restoration, however, the interests of the consumer slid more and more into the background. Practically all the restrictions on the activities of the internal corn trader were dismantled, high duties were placed on imported grain, and in 1689 a law went through offering bounties on the export of wheat, rye, barley and malt. In Anne's reign the bounty system was extended to cover beer and oatmeal. All this reflected the tightening grip of the producer and the distributor, the propertied men, upon society.

But perhaps even more revealing than the corn laws is the criminal legislation of the period. At the time of the Glorious Revolution the number of crimes punishable by death was around 50. After 1689 this number shot up, and before the eighteenth century was out it had exceeded 200. The great majority of these capital offences were crimes against property. You could be hanged for stealing a horse, for setting fire to a heap of hay, or for breaking and entering. Picking a pocket to the value of one shilling incurred the same penalty. For a person even to appear to be a potential threat to property was regarded as a serious offence. A poor man or woman caught begging could be 'stripped naked from the middle upwards and openly whipped until his or her body be bloody'.[6] A penniless girl who had the misfortune to bear an illegitimate child and who might therefore become a charge upon the rates or, worse still, be reduced to stealing, was treated with equal savagery. The borough records of Nottingham record the following incident:

> It is ordered by the court that Susanna Tute, Ruth Blackston and Mary Beresford who have lately been delivered of bastard children now chargeable to the parish of St Mary in this town shall on Wednesday next be tied in the ducking stool at St Mary's workhouse after they shall have been whipped at the house of correction and drawn from thence along Stoney Street, the High Pavement, Bridlesmith Gate and round the Malt Cross and then to the workhouse again.[7]

A propertyless person needed a pass from the authorities before he could travel from place to place without fear of molestation. John Locke, the philosopher of the Revolution, was enraged by the fact that poor people sometimes tried to forge these passes. In 1697 he advised the government to introduce legislation which would ensure 'that whoever shall counterfeit a pass shall lose his ears for the forgery the first time that he is found guilty thereof, and the second time that he shall be transported to the plantations, as in case of felony'.[8] In the reign of Anne a bill went through Parliament legalising the pressing of the unemployed into the army. By an Act which reached the statute-book in the reign of her predecessor the man in receipt of poor relief was made to wear a large Roman 'P' and the first letter of the parish to which he belonged on the right sleeve of his coat so that his degradation would be plain for all to see. No humiliation was considered too much if it served to pin down or keep out of harm's way those who seemed to offer a threat to the safety of property.

The political vocabulary of the Revolution, then, the quarrels inside Parliament, and the laws enacted during the period all show that from 1689 to 1714 England was firmly under the thumb of the well-to-do. Ordinary men and women, the vast majority of the population, had little control over their own destinies. They were second-class citizens, the worker bees of the hive, whose lot was to labour and obey. 'The poorer and meaner people', declared the duke of Albemarle in 1671, 'have no interest in the commonweal but the use of breath.'[9] The statement was even truer after 1689.

But what was the reaction of the common people to all this? How did they regard their degraded and underprivileged position? Oddly enough, most ordinary men and women seem to have been largely unworried by the discrimination shown against them. The labouring man might curse his stars from time to time, or drown his sorrows at the local alehouse. But that generally was as far as criticism went. There was no Leveller movement under William and Anne, no swell of revolution from below. As Bernard Mandeville astutely observed those 'damned to scythes and spades' were not just wretches but 'willing wretches'.[10] They accepted their low standing with a stoicism that would have amazed later generations.

Admittedly in times of especial hardship the lower orders were liable to take the law into their own hands. A series of bad harvests in the 1690s, for instance, produced a rash of corn riots in various parts of the country. Again, when prices rocketed during the harsh winter of 1709–10, the London mob seized upon the wave of resentment caused by the Whig ministry's decision to impeach the High Church champion Henry Sacheverell to surge through the streets of the City rioting and pillaging. Even violent outbursts of this sort, however, were strangely conservative in character. Their aim was to prevent change rather than to initiate it. The insurgents were not attempting to alter the system, but merely to rid it of abuse and hence render it more viable. At Northampton in October 1693, when the poorer inhabitants of the town seized sacks of wheat from the carts of local corn dealers, they did not keep the grain but sold it in the market at what they judged a fair price – five shillings a bushel. Their aim was to stop unjust profiteering, not to do away with merchants. In the spring of 1710 the Sacheverell rioters did not burn and destroy indiscriminately. They attacked the houses of the Whigs and pulled down the chapels of the Whigs' dissenting allies, but they left the Tories unmolested. The crowd was protesting not against the exercise of power by the propertied classes, but against what it regarded as the Whigs' abuse of power in unnecessarily prolonging the war and thereby driving up prices. Like motor mechanics the people intervened occasionally to make the machine function more smoothly, but they never attempted to scrap the old vehicle entirely and replace it with a new model.

What makes their political torpor particularly surprising is that political discrimination was accompanied by huge economic inequalities.

For the men at the top, life was almost unbelievably sumptuous. Every year tens of thousands of pounds were poured by the well-to-do into houses and statuary, pictures and furniture, woods and gardens. It was not unknown for a nobleman's park to measure fifty miles in circumference. The stables at Woburn Abbey, the home of the duke of Bedford, were the size of a small village. Blenheim Palace cost a quarter of a million pounds without the furnishings. Entertainment too was on a gigantic scale. There were 365 rooms at Knole in Kent to accommodate all the servants and guests. James Brydges, duke of Chandos, Queen Anne's Paymaster-General, maintained a private orchestra of twenty-seven players to amuse his visitors. It cost him £1000 a year (multiply by twelve for the modern equivalent) over and above board and lodging. No obstacle, however intractable, was allowed to stand in the way of aristocratic self-indulgence. So that he could lay out the grounds of Houghton Hall, his Norfolk house, to his satisfaction, Sir Robert Walpole had the local village knocked down and moved further away. When the outbreak of Queen Anne's War put a stop to trade with France, Robert Harley had his favourite claret run over duty free by a smuggler disguised as a secret service agent. Walpole went one better. After his appointment as a member of the Lord High Admiral's Council in 1706 he used an Admiralty barge to smuggle in his French wines.

The contrast between such princely living and the lot of ordinary persons was total. In 1696 the statistician Gregory King estimated that over half the population of England and Wales was 'decreasing the wealth of the kingdom'[11] – in other words, earning insufficient to hold body and soul together without recourse to poor relief or private charity. All over the north of England, averred Roger North, working people went barefoot. Child labour was commonplace. Without it many families could not have survived; but it was also, among the well-to-do, a source of pride. Defoe was delighted to find that around Halifax 'hardly anything above four years old' was unemployed. John Locke, advocating the establishment of parish work schools for the offspring of labouring people 'above three years old', thought it a scandal that such children should be 'maintained in idleness' in their infancy, and thus their labour 'lost to the public till they are twelve or fourteen years old'.[12]

Among the breadwinners, the landless farm-worker was particularly badly hit for his work tended to be only seasonal. At harvest time he could make a reasonable living for himself and his family, but in winter he was frequently laid off for long stretches. Defoe had this at the back of his mind when he described the purely agrarian areas of England as the 'unemployed counties'.[13] But it was not just the labourers who suffered. Every year more and more of the small owner-occupiers, victims of the land tax and dwindling profit margins, went under. They simply could not scrape together sufficient capital to adopt the new farming techniques which were coming into vogue.[14] Nor was the lot of the small tenant farmer a particularly happy one. Husbandmen, wrote Richard Baxter movingly in 1691, 'are usually so poor that they cannot have time to read a chapter in the Bible or to pray in their families. They come in weary from their labour, so that they are fitter to sleep than to read or pray.'[15] The men who fared best were those who succeeded in combining both agricultural and industrial work. Even here, however, things were by no means all milk and honey. Defoe came across one of these hybrid workmen when he visited Derbyshire – a lead miner who also worked his own plot of land. His home, declared Defoe, was 'clean and neat'. There were 'shelves with earthenware and some pewter and brass'. A whole side of bacon hung in the chimney corner 'and by it a good piece of another'. There were 'a sow and pigs running about at the door, and a little lean cow feeding upon a green place' just outside. A field of 'good barley' plus five small children, 'plump and fat, ruddy and wholesome', completed the scene. But even Defoe, the prince of optimists, had to admit that there was a darker side. The home, for all its neatness, was a cave cut into the side of the mountain. The miner himself was a hideous spectacle 'lean as a skeleton, pale as a dead corpse, his hair and beard a deep black, his flesh lank'. When Defoe gave the man's wife a small sum of money 'at most something within a crown' she broke down and wept at the magnitude of the gift, for the most her husband could earn was five pence a day 'if he had good luck'.[16]

Why then, if all this is true, did the man in the street knuckle under so easily? What made him so politically quiescent under such heavy provocation? One reason was undoubtedly the hard facts of his existence. Many aspects of the physical situation in which the ordinary man found himself militated against his becoming a political animal. The vast majority of working men and women, for instance, were largely uneducated. An examination of village records shows that even local officials – churchwardens, overseers of the poor and so on – were often too illiterate even to write their own names. Again, the average man's work was so exhausting and his hours of labour so long that even if he managed to acquire some knowledge of reading he had little energy left at the end of the day to think, plan or organise. Locke recognised this when in his *Reasonableness of Christianity*, published in 1695, he advocated the drawing up of a simplified form of Christianity for those who 'labour and travail' since their daily toil meant that they 'have not eisure for learning and logic'.[17]

Equally important was the isolation of the working man. Bad roads and the attitude of the authorities to the wanderings of the propertyless ruled out travel for many people. England at this time was, to quote Mr Laslett, 'a federation of segments',[18] a mosaic of isolated village communities. The word 'country', it is interesting to note, was rarely used to signify the nation as a whole. It denoted rather the local community, the market town with its cluster of villages. Under such conditions it was impossible for anything like a nation-wide working-class consciousness to develop. Then there was the harshness of everyday life. Dirt and disease were rife everywhere. Even the correspondence of the pampered and the affluent is strewn with references to smallpox, rheumatism, fevers and agues of all sorts. Medical treatment was often excruciating. To have a tooth out in the eighteenth century was no mean ordeal. The amputation of a limb without anaesthetic involved unthinkable pain. Everywhere one turned life seemed raw and cruel. Even the sports and pastimes of the period were streaked with blood – cock-throwing,[19] bear-baiting, goose-riding.[20] The most popular of them all were the hangings at Tyburn. Seats with a good view of the gallows were sought after as avidly as Cup Final tickets are today. Some of the scenes which took place at these public executions were terrible. At this time the drop was not used. Consequently the victim's neck was not broken straight away. Instead the prisoner was strangled to death in a slow agony. Frequently the friends and relatives of the dying man were forced to pull him by the legs or beat his breast so as to end his torment. In the midst of so much barbarism the cross of the ordinary man became bearable. His grim heritage did not seem a property-owning plot. Harshness was the way of the world. It was inevitable.

But the physical world in which he lived, though important, was by no means the sole reason for the common man's inaction. Just as significant was the mental climate of the day. In the Middle Ages men believed that God had created the universe in a series of layers, a great ordered hierarchy of being stretching down from the Almighty at the top through the angels and men to the brute beasts and the inanimate earth. Within this hierarchy every creature and every thing had its own appointed place and function. Degree, priority and place were the very essence of the thing. 'Take but degree away', warned Shakespeare's Ulysses in *Troilus and Cressida*, 'untune that string, and hark, what discord follows!' It was the job of the labourer to labour, and of the ruler to rule. Each had an appropriate way of living commensurate with the heaviness or lightness of his responsibilities. If anyone tried to alter this then:

> the bounded waters
> Should lift their bosoms higher than the shores,
> And make a sop of all this solid globe.

In short, primeval chaos would ensue.

This essentially medieval notion that the world functioned in a series of layers was still the basic belief of Englishmen in the reigns of William and Anne, and it continued so for a long time afterwards, as the writings of Paley, Blackstone, Soame Jenyns and even Burke all show in their differing ways. It is true, of course, that many of the props of the theory had been knocked away over the years. The earth-centred universe with its succession of concentric spheres had gone; much of the magic of the Thomist synthesis had faded too. But as the old supports snapped new ones appeared to shore up the structure. There was, for example, the Puritan idea of calling, which stressed that every voyager to the Heavenly City had been assigned by Providence a particular task in which he had to labour to God's greater glory. Again, the theory of mixed monarchy, popularised by Locke in his *Two Treatises of Government*, saw society as an amalgam of differing units, each making its distinctive contribution to the good of the whole.

Perhaps one can best illustrate the continuing vitality of the tradition by examining the educational theory of the period. Schooling was not looked upon as a means of developing the individual, but rather as a way of fitting a person for the particular role in life to which he had been born. The numerous charity schools for the education of poor children, for instance, which were springing up in various parts of the country in the years after the Revolution, were designed not to turn out educated men and women, but to fit their pupils 'for service or the meaner trades and labours of life'.[21] Accordingly the duties of diligence and obedience to social superiors were constantly dinned into the children. It is 'especially requisite', stated one teaching manual published in 1707, 'that all children who are bred in charity schools for service and apprenticeships should be strictly obliged to practice here that subjection to their teachers which they must afterwards pay to their masters according to the flesh, with fear and trembling in singleness of heart, as unto Christ'. 'Make me dutiful and obedient to my benefactors, and charitable to my enemies', ran the opening prayer of the girls' charity school in Sheffield. 'Make me temperate and chaste, meek and patient, true in all my dealings and content and industrious in my station.'[22] So that they might be 'sufficiently distinguished from children of better rank', the pupils had to wear a uniform 'of the coarsest kind and of the plainest form'.[23]

The curriculum of the schools was of the simplest – just a basic grounding in reading, penmanship and elementary arithmetic calculation. Anything more than this, it was feared, might give the inmates ideas above their station. Games were permitted, but not for the pupils' enjoyment, 'only as a necessary relaxation to their mind and body'. Music was frowned upon. Fine singing, like fine writing and fine needlework, asserted Edmund Gibson, bishop of London, tended to make charity-school children value themselves too highly. 'And therefore', he concluded, 'all these things should be carefully kept out of our charity schools.'[24] The whole ethos of these schools was fundamentally at variance with any modern concept of education. Their basic character was neatly caught by the Reverend Isaac Watts in his *Essay towards the Encouragement of Charity Schools*:

> The Great God has wisely ordained in the course of His Providence in all ages, that among mankind there should be some rich and some poor. And the same Providence hath allotted to the poor the meaner services, and hath given to the rich the superior and more honourable business of life. Nor is it possible according to the present course of nature and human affairs to alter this constitution of things, nor is it our design to attempt anything so unreasonable.[25]

The age of Newton, no less than the era of Thomas Aquinas, saw the world as a fixed hierarchy, an immutable, divinely-appointed series of inequalities. In such an intellectual climate it was scarcely conceivable for the ruled to claim parity with the ruler.

Together, then, the physical and mental environment of the common man go a long way towards explaining his acceptance of the *status quo*. In addition, however, it is possible to isolate a third major reason for his inertia. English society after 1689 was studded with safety valves, outlets to channel off undesirable political emotions. The most common of these was the tavern. The London gin-drinking orgies, so terrifyingly portrayed by Hogarth, were still as yet some years away in the future. But even under William and Anne it was commonplace for the working man to seek oblivion in intoxicating liquor. Defoe, indeed, saw imbibing as the chief recreation of the labouring poor:

> Good drunken company is their delight;
> And what they get by day, they spend by night.
> Dull thinking seldom does their heads engage,
> But drink their youth away, and hurry on old age.[26]

And if the bottle did not do the trick there were other palliatives. Many of the fairs held periodically up and down the country were scenes of debauchery and wild behaviour. Bartholomew Fair in London became so notorious that in the 1690s the authorities made several spirited, though only partially successful, efforts to curb its activities. Rioting has already been mentioned. The stage was another prophylactic. Theatrical performances, argued John Dennis in 1698, by giving delight diverted men's minds from thoughts of rebellion or disobedience.[27] Then again there were the parliamentary elections held every three years after the passing of the Triennial Act in 1694. In the counties and also in the more open boroughs many quite humble people had the vote. Even those who did not enjoy the franchise could participate in the tumults which often raged about the hustings. The kind of laws which reached the statute-book suggest that the actual influence wielded by these ordinary people was probably very slight; the power of the landed squire to tyrannise over his village was too great for the common man to indulge his political fancy too freely.[28] But this was largely unimportant. What mattered was the sense of participation which electoral activity brought. Along with the alehouse and the food riot it was one of society's safety valves. It helped to ensure that if, on occasion, the physical and mental universe did not entirely subdue the unfree, the remaining spark of political desire could satisfactorily be sublimated.

In finance, in foreign policy, in the constitutional field the Glorious Revolution was an event of much significance. But for the man in the street it did not mark a parting of the ways. Only a century later, with the coming together of large numbers of people in the mushroom towns of the industrial north, with improved education, with the influx of Jacobin ideas from France, and above all with the onset of romanticism did the day of the common man begin to dawn. In England the romantic movement was spearheaded by William Blake, poet, painter, engraver and visionary, one of the greatest Englishmen who has ever walked the earth. Blake led a lifelong crusade against the eighteenth-century tendency to generalise and pigeon hole, to place things in groups and categories. He painted a picture of Isaac Newton sitting at the bottom of the ocean, describing a circle with a pair of compasses and gazing into it. Newton, Blake argued, had by his laws and his generalising reduced the world to a geometrical figure sunk in unfathomable darkness. He had cut out whole realms of human experience. It was the uniqueness and individuality of things, not their sameness, asserted Blake, that constituted the glory and the wonder of the earth. Blake was incensed by Reynolds's attempt to draw up general laws of perspective for the painter. Every creature and every thing, he maintained, had its own form and its own perspective that was unique and unrepeatable. The wild beast of the jungle blazed forth its strength in every sinew; the lamb was the quintessence of its own gentleness.[29] Blake's passionate belief in the infinite variety of creation enabled him to take a totally different view of the common man from that adopted by the men of the Revolution. His attitude to pauper children, for instance, was totally at variance with theirs. For him the indigent child was not a potential vagrant whose spirit had to be broken. The penniless infant was, like all of us, a child of God, deserving of mercy and compassion:

> Is this a holy thing to see
> In a rich and fruitful land,
> Babes reduc'd to misery,
> Fed with cold and usurous hand?
>
> Is that trembling cry a song?
> Can it be a song of joy?
> And so many children poor?
> It is a land of poverty!
>
> And their sun does never shine,
> And their fields are bleak and bare,
> And their ways are filled with thorns:
> It is eternal winter there.[30]

Blake insisted that even the most humble, most begrimed, most illiterate person was an immortal soul as unique and as precious as the duke among his rolling acres or the bishop in his palace. Only when men realised this, proclaimed the poet, only when they understood that the world was a collection of individual and irreplaceable particles and not a fixed hierarchy of layers, only then would 'the countenance divine shine forth upon our clouded hills' and Jerusalem be 'builded here among these dark satanic mills'.[31] The men of 1689 were innocent of Blake's vision, and it was, more than anything, because of this that the Revolution was not a triumph for the people.

However, it would be wrong to end upon a note of gloom. One of the most striking consequences of the Revolution was that it led to the firm establishment of the rule of law. In his various political writings John Locke set out to render the arbitrary use of royal power intellectually indefensible. At the same time the Bill of Rights declared against the use of the prerogative as an instrument to suspend or dispense with legislation. This was followed by a clause in the Act of Settlement of 1701 putting an end to the arbitrary dismissal of judges. Since after 1689 the substantial property-owners were, to all intents and purposes, the real law-givers, all this aided them in their drive for power. But incorruptibility is a dangerous thing, and when, in the age of Paine and Blake, ordinary people began to advance political claims, they too found protection under the umbrella of the law. Radicals like Alderman Sawbridge, for example, were able to invoke 'Revolution principles' in their protests against the use of the military to quell civil disturbances. Similarly the Bill of Rights Society was able to raise an outcry against arbitrary arrests and the neglect of Habeas Corpus. Again, when men such as John Thelwall and William Hone were brought before the courts by the government, they were triumphantly acquitted, for after 1689 the authorities found it well-nigh impossible to pack juries. The Revolution was not a watershed for the common man. His lot was as hard after the great upheaval as it had been before. Even so, when in the fullness of time the voice of the humble came to be raised, the events of 1689 did at least help to oil the wheels of political action. Hence the coming of King William is not entirely without significance in the story of ordinary men and women.

BIBLIOGRAPHICAL NOTE

In the nineteenth and early twentieth centuries historians tended to see the Revolution as a victory for representative government and hence as a great step forward for all Englishmen. A fine example of this 'Whig interpretation' is G. M. Trevelyan's *The English Revolution 1688–1689* (1938). The more modern view of 1689 – the view adopted in this essay – accepts much of the Whig case, but stresses that for the common man the triumph of 'representative' institutions only meant exchanging one master for another. This view is set out in three general surveys: D. Ogg's subtle and learned *England in the Reigns of James II and William III* (1955); D. Marshall's unjustly neglected *English People in the Eighteenth Century* (1956); and C. Hill's brilliant *The Century of Revolution* (1961). It also underlies a number of more specific studies: M. Beloff, *Public Order and Popular Disturbances 1660–1714* (1938); M. G. Jones, *The Charity School Movement: A Study of Eighteenth-Century Puritanism in action* (1938); L. Radzinowicz, *A History of English Criminal Law* (1948), vol. i; and C. B. Macpherson, *The Political Theory of Possessive Individualism* (1962), with its exciting reassessment (ch. 5) of the work of John Locke as advocate of the rule of a propertied minority.

A number of exceptionally valuable local studies, e.g. M. D. George, *London Life in the Eighteenth Century*, 3rd ed. (1951), and J. D. Chambers, *Nottinghamshire in the Eighteenth Century*, 2nd ed. (1966), have contributed to our understanding of the sub-political nation. So have the new ways of looking at society and the tapping of new kinds of source material illustrated in the work of G. Rudé, *The Crowd in History 1730–1848* (1964), and P. Laslett, *The World We Have Lost* (1965). Perhaps the best way, however, to appreciate the conditions in which the common people lived out their lives after 1689 is to spend an afternoon in the nearest County Record Office poring over the Quarter Sessions records. These papers serve also as a reminder that, ultimately, the historian does not build up his picture of the past from the writings of other scholars but from the fragments which people long dead have left behind them.

NOTES

1. *English Historical Documents 1660–1714*, ed. A. Browning (1953), p. 120: Shrewsbury *et al.* to William of Orange, 30 June 1688.

2. D. Defoe, *A Tour Through England and Wales* (1928), ii, 249.

3. e.g. Defoe, *The True-Born Englishman* (1701):

> And of all the plagues with which mankind is cursed,
> Ecclesiastic tyranny's the worst.

4. W. Kennett, *The Wisdom of Looking Backward* (1715), pp. 153–4; Boyer, *The Reign of King William III* (1702–3), ii, 15; Defoe, *The Shortest Way with Dissenters and Other Pamphlets* (1927), p. 158.

5. But see n 28 below.

6. 39 Eliz I c.4. This Act of 1597 was still being actively enforced in our period. For example, in July 1699 the Staffordshire justices issued a 'general order' charging all high constables in the county to direct their petty constables to 'seize and duly punish all vagrants and beggars as the law directs'. Staffs RO, Q/S Me 1: Quarter Sessions Minute Book, July 1699; Q/S O 10: Quarter Sessions Order Book, July 1699.

7. *Records of the Borough of Nottingham*, ed. W. H. Stevenson *et al.* (1882–1956), vi, 126: Sessions Record Book, 9 Oct 1729. Cf. ibid. p. 57 for a similar incident in 1713.

8. Locke's 'Report on the Poor', printed in H. R. Fox Bourne, *The Life of John Locke* (1876), ii, 380.

9. *Observations upon Military and Political Affairs* (1671), p. 146.

10. B. Mandeville, *The Grumbling Hive* (1705), lines 41 and 43. See the epigraph to this essay.

11. 'Natural and Political Observations . . . upon the State and Condition of England, 1696', printed in G. Chalmers, *Estimate of the Comparative Strength of Great Britain* (1804), app. pp. 48–9.

12. Defoe, *Tour*, ii, 95; Locke, 'Report on the Poor' (1697), loc. cit. pp. 383–5.

13. *A Plan of the English Commerce* (1927), p. 67.

14. There is a summary of recent findings on agrarian improvement in seventeenth-century England in G. E. Mingay, 'The "Agricultural Revolution" in English History: a reconsideration', in *Agrarian Conditions in Modern European History*, ed. C. K. Warner (1966), pp. 60–79. For H. J. Habakkuk's important work on the triumph of the large landowner over the small man see p. 152 below; also 'La Disparition du Paysan Anglais', in *Annales ESC* xx (1965), 649–63.

15. F. J. Powicke (ed.), 'The Reverend Richard Baxter's Last Treatise', in *Bulletin John Rylands Lib.* x (1926), 181.

16. *Tour*, ii, 161–4.

17. *The Works of John Locke* (1714), p. 540.

18. P. Laslett, *The World we have lost* (1965), p. 185.

19. The object in cock-throwing was to impale live cocks, thrown with their legs tied, on sharp stakes.

20. A live goose was hung up by its feet, and its head and neck were greased. The participants then attempted to pull off the bird's head while riding by at a gallop.

21. I. Watts, *An Essay towards the Encouragement of Charity Schools* (1728), p. i. One of the arguments advanced by the archdeacon of Huntingdon in 1706 in favour of the establishment of charity schools was that the kind of education offered in the grammar schools was 'too high' for those 'born to the spade and to the plough'. W. Kennett, *The Charity of Schools for Poor Children Recommended* (1706), p. 12.

22. J. Talbott, *The Christian Schoolmaster* (1707), p. 42; 'The Poor Girls' Primer', quoted in C. Birchenough, *History of Elementary Education in England and Wales* (1920), p. 190.

23. Watts, op. cit. p. 42.

24. Talbott, op. cit. p. 65; *Directions given by Edmund Lord Bishop of London to the Masters and Mistresses of the Charity Schools within the . . . Diocese of London* (1724), p. 5.

25. Op. cit. p. 14.

26. *True-Born Englishman*, pt ii, lines 27–30.

27. J. Dennis, *The Usefulness of the Stage* (1698).

28. This is a contentious point. Some authorities argue that the humble voter played a more meaningful and positive political role. See esp. J. H. Plumb, *The Growth of Political Stability in England 1675–1725* (1967), pp. 27–9, 34–47; *The Divided Society: Party Conflict in England 1694–1716*, ed. G. Holmes and W. A. Speck (1967), pp. 1, 77–82. For a viewpoint which parallels the stand taken in this essay see J. D. Chambers, *Nottinghamshire in the Eighteenth Century*, 2nd ed. (1966), esp. pp. 3–75.

29. W. Blake, *Songs of Innocence* (1789): 'The Lamb'; *Songs of Experience* (1794): 'The Tyger', lines 1–4:

Tyger! Tyger! burning bright
In the forests of the night,
What immortal hand or eye
Could frame thy fearful symmetry?

30. *Songs of Experience*: 'Holy Thursday', lines 1–12.

31. W. Blake, *Milton* (c. 1808), preface.

4. The Structure of Parliamentary Politics

HENRY HORWITZ

FOR the past four decades, students of early modern English political history – under the spell of the late Sir Lewis Namier's analyses of mid-eighteenth-century politics – have been engaged less with narrating and explicating the political *events* of this period and more with investigating and reconstituting the very *structure* of politics. Traditional assumptions have been thrust aside, new interpretations asserted, and in turn the work of the 'Namierite' revisionists has itself been called into question. And perhaps nowhere, outside the mid-eighteenth century, has there been more controversy or confusion over the character of politics and the nature of political divisions than in the days of King William and Queen Anne, at least since the appearance in 1956 of Robert Walcott's major venture in revision, *English Politics in the Early Eighteenth Century*. The object of this essay, then, is twofold: first, to review the background, course and current state of this debate over the structure of politics in the post-Revolution years; and second, to grapple with the chief issue in dispute – the question of whether politics at Westminster during this period was carried on within a two-party or a multi-party framework.

I

The view that parliamentary politics between 1689 and 1714 revolved around the conflict of the Whig and Tory parties is deeply rooted in the historiography of this period.[1] And in the years just before and immediately after the publication in 1929 of Namier's *The Structure of Politics at the Accession of George III*, this interpretation was given renewed and most knowledgeable statement in W. T. Morgan's *English Political Parties and Leaders in the Reign of Queen Anne* (1920), K. Feiling's *History of the Tory Party* (1924) and G. M. Trevelyan's *England under Queen Anne* (1930–4). Yet each of these scholars, while giving pride of place to the Whig–Tory struggle, also drew attention to other elements on the political scene which tended to divert and sometimes even to blunt the thrust of party – the important part played by the monarch (not only William, but even Anne), the continuing role of the Court and the placemen as a third force within the Houses, and (as Feiling particularly stressed) the persistence after 1689 of the older conflict between Court and Country. Moreover they recognised the existence, at times, of substantial divisions within the two parties, while Feiling – dealing with the entire period – also emphasised the significance of the partisan realignment of the 1690s.

The 1920s and early 1930s, then, saw the formulation of some important modifications to the two-party interpretation as expounded by the 'Whig' historians of the nineteenth century, but in the event these proved to be only the preliminaries to Walcott's frontal assault. As early as 1941, Walcott – taking aim particularly against Trevelyan's earlier works and the tradition they epitomised – advanced the argument that 'the description of party organization under William and Anne which Trevelyan suggested in his Romanes Lecture [of 1926] on the two-party system is less applicable to our period than the detailed picture of eighteenth-century politics which emerges from Professor Namier's volumes on the age of Newcastle'.[2] Walcott's invocation of Namier's studies was, indeed, a notable testimony to the growing influence of the methods of structural analysis and collective biography – with their concentration on the personal background, electoral circumstances and political record of every individual M.P. – that Sir Lewis had so skilfully exploited. And in his full-dress work of reinterpretation of 1956, Walcott once again acknowledged the inspiration of Namier's researches.

However, as one reviews Walcott's contributions to the study of the political history of William's and Anne's reigns, it becomes evident that his indebtedness to Sir Lewis extended beyond the approach he adopted to the substantive conclusions at which he arrived. As W. R. Fryer rightly observed, Walcott's 'view might be summed up as the interpretation of Sir Lewis Namier, extended backwards to this earlier period'.[3] Above all, just as Sir Lewis had maintained that 'the political life' of the mid-eighteenth century 'could be fully described without ever using a party denomination',[4] so Walcott denied the validity of a two-party interpretation of post-Revolution politics, whether in its traditional form or in the modified versions of Morgan, Feiling and Trevelyan.

Walcott based this contention on two main grounds: (1) the voting behaviour of M.P.s during the period as a whole; and (2) the parliamentary alignments of a single session. On the one hand, in surveying the twelve division lists from these years of which he knew, Walcott asserted that a substantial proportion of members did not vote as consistent Whigs or Tories. As he put it, 'on each of these issues there was theoretically a "Whig" and a "Tory" position, and Members should have voted consistently on one side or the other time after time. Unfortunately, the lists do not square with this theory. The "Tory" side in any one division inevitably includes many who at other times voted "Whig" and vice versa.'[5] On the other hand, in a detailed examination of the parliamentary session of 1707–8 Walcott laid bare this sort of inconsistency in the behaviour of the supposedly united Whig and Tory parties. On some questions he found Whigs and Tories outside the ministry combining to oppose the administration, while at the same time he discovered the head of the ministry, Godolphin, mustering a body of 'Lord Treasurer's Whigs' in his efforts to push through the government's measures. Moreover, in tracing the outcome of this bitterly fought session and the General Election which followed in the summer of 1708, Walcott suggested that the eventual outcome was not the formation of a strictly Whig ministry, as some of his predecessors had supposed. Rather, the ministerial changes of 1708 were, at least at first, made in favour of the 'Lord Treasurer's Whigs'. Thus, in Walcott's view, the evidence about group alignments and individual voting in Parliament could hardly be fitted within the confines of a two-party framework; instead, it revealed the need to formulate a new interpretation which would consort better with the facts of political behaviour.

When Walcott turned from the work of destruction to the task of reconstruction he again followed closely in Namier's footsteps. For one thing, he suggested that the really important distinction among M.P.s of this period was not that of party, but that of 'type', and that the three leading types of members were essentially the same as those of the mid-eighteenth century – the courtiers and placemen, the 'politicians' under their various leaders, and the independent country gentlemen. Furthermore, Walcott maintained that the chief form of organisation among the politicians (the most numerous type of member) was, as in the 1760s, the connexion – linked together by ties of kinship, neighbourhood, dependency and interest. He then went on to isolate each of these connexions and to identify their members in the Parliament of 1701–2, basing his findings on electoral, biographical and genealogical data. Altogether he reckoned there were seven such connexions, which, though they might at times merge into two opposed bodies, nonetheless preserved their separate identities and often acted independently in pursuit of their principal goal – the attainment and enjoyment of office. Hence, while some of these connexions could be considered 'Whig' and others 'Tory' in outlook, they neither constituted two united parties nor did they consistently act in accord with their supposed political principles.

In any case, these connexions did not act in isolation, for though together they comprised the largest single segment of the Commons (an average of 218 in the Houses of 1701–2, 1702–5 and 1705–8), the 'organised' government interest along with other courtiers and place-men numbered 142 members and the country gentlemen 146 members on average in these three Parliaments.[6] Walcott maintained that the courtiers and placemen supported the ministry in power almost auto-matically, while the more active segment of the country gentlemen opposed the current administration with almost equal consistency, regardless of either their own or the ministers' party labels. In fact, these two types of M.P.s might be said to personify the persistence of the old Court–Country split.

Walcott's reconstitution of the structure of parliamentary politics between 1689 and 1714 might, then, be summed up in the following fashion. While on such great issues as the Church and the succession there was a Whig and a Tory position in the country at large, within the Houses were to be found a series of shifting alignments between the rival political connexions on one hand and the court and country elements on the other, instead of two united parties in conflict with one another. Each administration was made up of a combination of courtiers and members of one or more of the connexions; each opposition was similarly composed of a combination of country gentlemen and members of those connexions not in office. Thus, in place of a two-party interpre-tation Walcott advanced a multi-party one, with the various connexions and unorganised elements within Parliament being ranged schematically around the perimeter of a circle on which Court and Country figured as the north and south 'co-ordinates' with Whig and Tory as the east and west 'co-ordinates'; it is then possible 'to read the roster of party groups as though we were boxing the compass: courtiers, Court Tories, Churchill Tories, Harley Tories, Rochester Tories, Nottingham Tories, October Club Tories, Country Tories, Country Members, Country Whigs, Junto Whigs, Walpole–Townshend Whigs, Court Whigs, and so back to the Courtiers'.[7]

II

When Walcott's arguments were first rehearsed in print in 1941 they attracted only brief notice. But by the time his book appeared in 1956 they had gained wide currency, so much so that one reviewer could remark that his main findings 'have generally been accepted'.[8] On the whole this work – in which Walcott's earlier hypotheses were now advanced in more definitive form – was well received by students of the eighteenth century. Not all were as enthusiastic as J. W. Wilkes, who proclaimed that 'the vast and erroneous generalizations about eighteenth-century political life in England, begun by the Whig historians of the nineteenth century, have suffered yet another blow'.[9] Yet many were prepared to cite his conclusions without demur, whether in their reviews or in their own writings.[10]

From the outset, however, other scholars – and particularly specialists in the 1689–1714 period – were more dubious about their validity. While ready to acknowledge the extent of Walcott's labours, they were also quick to observe that 'studies such as [this] cannot tell us all we need to know, if we are to understand English politics'.[11] What is more, their reservations about Walcott's findings and his methods were confirmed and extended as the results of other researchers' explorations in the newly-accessible wealth of manuscript materials for this period began to appear in articles and dissertations in the early and mid-1960s. And even more recently, the 'Walcott interpretation' has suffered new setbacks from J. H. Plumb in his suggestive survey of English political developments from 1675 to 1725 and from Geoffrey Holmes in his detailed analysis of politics in Anne's reign.

The grounds of the reservations and criticisms voiced by these scholars might be summed up under two principal heads: (1) evidence and methodology; and (2) specific conclusions. First of all, some of Walcott's examples and certain of his procedures have been sharply challenged. On the one hand, it has been observed that in choosing to focus on the 1707–8 session he selected a most unusual example, for the conjunction of 'high Whig' and 'high Tory' during the early months of that session astonished contemporaries, while the session as a whole was certainly the most chaotic of Anne's reign.[12] On the other hand, his method of isolating the political connexions and identifying their members has come under heavy fire for loose use of what electoral and parliamentary data he did invoke and especially for his heavy reliance on genealogical evidence. It has been calculated that of the 212 M.P.s whom he placed in one or other of the connexions in the 1701–2 Commons, no less than ninety-six were so allocated seemingly on the sole basis of kinship.[13]

Now, to be sure, Walcott did recognise that almost any two aristocratic families of the period will be found to be related; nonetheless, his efforts to demonstrate the political significance of the family groups which he did identify as the bases of his seven political connexions are strewn with pitfalls. Take, for instance, the case of the 'Finch connexion' headed by the second earl of Nottingham and chiefly composed, on Walcott's reckoning, of the nominees and clients of that earl's noble kinsmen. Walcott, it is true, did not include all Nottingham's relations and their associates in this group, but only those who seemed to take the same general political stand in Parliament as did the Tory earl himself. But even after removing some of the potential members of this connexion because of evidence about their political behaviour, to suppose that the residue constituted an effective parliamentary grouping can be very misleading. Indeed, a closer look at the available evidence reveals that some of Nottingham's *Tory* kinsmen were estranged from him by personal enmities, that others had no personal dealings with him, that some of the supposed nominees of his titled relations were not chiefly dependent on those kinsmen for their elections, and that others allocated to his connexion were in practice more closely associated with such political leaders as Rochester.[14] Nor is the Finch connexion the only instance in which Walcott's procedures appear to have led him astray; similar strictures have been levelled against the construction of his 'Newcastle–Pelham–Townshend–Walpole' and 'Hyde–Granville–Gower–Seymour' connexions.[15] In short, as W. A. Speck has put it, 'the slender branches of the family trees, so carefully cultivated by Walcott, will not bear the weight of the political fruit which he seeks to graft upon them'.[16]

Secondly, Walcott's critics have contended that his atypical 'examples' and faulty use of Namierite techniques have skewed his conclusions in several vital respects. For one thing, it has been suggested that the connexions must be conceived in broader terms than those in which he presented them. In particular, it would appear that they attracted into their orbits not merely the professional politicians *per se*, but also other M.P.s including many country gentlemen who, if not ambitious for office, were wont to follow the lead of men such as Rochester or Nottingham, Harley or the Junto. For another, it has been argued that political attitudes and issues had a considerable impact on parliamentary alignments. Many of the political leaders of the day were bent on gaining office not merely for its material rewards, but mainly for the influence which it offered, and great politicians such as Rochester and Wharton did refuse, or resign from, office when they felt their views would not carry due weight in the royal councils. Similarly their followers were linked to them not simply by ties of family, proximity, dependency and interest, but also (and in some cases chiefly) by the bonds generated by common convictions. The result was that many, perhaps even most, of a leading politician's adherents might refuse to stand by him should he appear to deviate from the policies or principles he had previously upheld: the Junto suffered many desertions when it backed a standing army in 1698–9, while Nottingham's following almost melted away after he chose to oppose the peace in 1711–12 in conjunction with the Whigs. Finally it has been maintained that Walcott's concentration on the rather unusual alignments of the 1707–8 session, coupled with his distortion of the composition and character of the followings of the chief political leaders, has obscured the ample evidence for the subsumption of these groupings under the two parties, Whig and Tory, and for the magnetic attraction and repulsion of intra-party loyalties and inter-party differences.

For the most part Walcott has suffered these and other criticisms in silence, but in 1962 he did briefly and obliquely respond to his early challengers. There were, he agreed, a few controversial issues which stirred M.P.s during these years, but after making this concession he went on to reiterate his main conclusion: 'within the walls of Parliament as it concerned itself with the day-to-day work of government in the intervals between controversy over the great issues (most of them religious), the apparent division into two national parties dissolves into the multi-party structure normally associated only with the reign of George III'.[17]

But despite Walcott's restatement, the discovery of new division lists for the period has thrown further doubt on his analysis by suggesting that the broad division between Whigs and Tories in the country as a whole 'was carried over into Parliament' not only on religious questions, but also on those 'which involved no principle' – questions such as the vote on Harley's South Sea scheme in May 1711 or the contest for the Speakership in November 1705.[18] Neither of these votes involved a direct clash of ideas, but rather opposition to or support of the current administration. Yet what is striking about the voting behaviour of the individual members, as recorded on these lists and correlated with other extant ones, is 'the small number whose voting habits were irregular' and the 'considerable number of members who voted consistently along party lines'.[19]

III

The cycle of scholarly opinion from the 1920s to the 1960s has now been traced in brief. What remains to be considered, given the grave flaws of the 'Walcott interpretation' even in its most recent formulation, is how to describe and explain the structure of parliamentary groupings during the period from 1689 to 1714. And here it would appear, in the light of both scholarly controversy and the findings of recent research, that there are sufficient grounds to advance three main contentions: (1) that the two parties did have an effective existence and that their rivalry was a prime feature of parliamentary politics; (2) that throughout this period contemporary political conditions both limited the role of the parties and distorted the conflict between Whig and Tory; and (3) that the structure of parliamentary politics during these years was not altogether stable and was especially fluid during William's reign.

The most telling evidence for the existence and importance of the two parties within Parliament may be easily marshalled. To begin with, close analysis of the extant Commons' division lists for both reigns reveals that most M.P.s who participated in more than one of these recorded divisions voted consistently as Whigs or Tories. For William's reign, some eight division lists have now been found, two giving the names of both supporters and opponents of the contested questions and the remainder listing only one side.[20] When correlated with one another, they yield the names of some 437 members who voted on two or more of these eight questions, of whom only 65 (or 15·1 per cent) voted on both the Tory and Whig sides.[21] A similar analysis, made by W. A. Speck, of nine of the ten surviving division lists from Anne's reign produces even more striking results. Four of these lists give the names of both supporters and opponents of the question in contention, and altogether they yield a total of some 1064 M.P.s who voted twice or more on these nine issues, of whom only 130 (or 12·2 per cent) wavered in their party allegiances.[22]

The results of such tabulations, to be sure, must be treated with caution. For one thing, the tenth extant division list from Anne's reign – giving the names of the supporters of the Court in one of the votes on the place clause of the Regency bill of 1706 – reflects a Court–Country, rather than a Whig–Tory split. For another the surviving lists are both few and incomplete. Undoubtedly our tabulations would be substantially altered were the lists of the supporters of the disbanding bill of 1699 or the opponents of the Tack of 1704 to be found, for each of these majorities included a notable proportion of deserters – disaffected Whigs in the former instance, moderate Tories in the latter. Yet when all due qualifications are made, what remains is a record of notable consistency along party lines in the voting behaviour of the members of the Commons.

And what is true of the Commons also appears to hold in large measure for the Lords, according to Holmes's computations of the peers' voting records between 1701 and 1714.[23] Moreover, when the twenty-two division lists from both Houses between 1689 and 1714 are brought together, what emerges is that no less than seventeen of the specific questions that prompted these divisions had no direct connexion with religious issues.[24] Thus, not only do the surviving division lists furnish a record of consistent party voting by the great majority of active commoners and peers, but also this consistency appears to extend over a considerable range of issues.

Side by side with the surviving division lists must be placed the evidence of the *Commons' Journal* and the Lords' Proxy Book. The *Journal* supplies the names of the two tellers on each side in every division in the full House. And from a study of the tellers, correlated with the appropriate division figures, it has been deduced that voting on most public business in Anne's reign proceeded along party lines.[25] The Proxy Book supplies the names of those peers entrusted with proxies by absent members of the Upper House. And what its entries disclose is that the great majority of absent peers assigned their proxies to lords of like views and affiliations. For example, the proxy arrangements recorded for the 1695–8 Parliament attest to the existence of two separate networks of peers whose members exchanged proxies only among one another – a Tory group numbering 39 (counting both recipients and givers) and a Whig–Court group of 37. Again, out of a total of 111 entries in the Proxy book between 1704 and 1707, there are only five instances of a Whig peer leaving his proxy with a Tory or vice versa.

Impressive as is the evidence of the division, teller and proxy lists, it can be supplemented by other data. It is, of course, well known that partisan antagonisms did much at times to inflame relations between the two Houses. In fact, it may be said that most of the prominent disputes between the Lords and the Commons during this period, while debated chiefly in terms of the rights and privileges of each chamber, involved sharp partisan differences over men and measures, whether it was the indemnity question in 1689, the Irish Forfeitures Bill of 1700, the impeachments of the three Junto lords in 1701, or the handling of the Scotch Plot and the Aylesbury election case in 1703–4. But perhaps the most notorious instances of parliamentary partisanship arose out of the Commons' treatment of controverted elections for, as one pamphleteer remarked, 'tis so natural for every party to strengthen their own, that all attempts against it will be insignificant'.[26] So partisan was the House's attitude towards election cases that sometimes, as in the early days of the first session of the 1690–5 Parliament, votes on petitions were used as a gauge 'to try the strength of the House' and 'to determine how the House stands affected'.[27] The usual procedure for hearing such petitions was to delegate this work to the Committee on Privileges and Elections, and the most common tactic consisted simply of the committee majority burying most petitions and allowing very few to be tried against members of their own party. However, in Anne's third Parliament, the Whig majority resorted to trying elections in a more summary manner at the bar of the House. And one of the first victims (despite the merits of his petition) was Sir Simon Harcourt, singled out for his treatment of Whig petitioners in former sessions. Nor did the Whigs trouble to conceal their motives: as one observer reported, 'more of the same corner [of the House] will follow the same fate till they have made up the number that the Tories in the days of peace turned out in one session, I think 13, in which Sir Simon was particularly eminent'.[28] This was party politics in its most flagrant guise, but it was of a piece with the markedly partisan orientation of both Houses. Indeed, in the light of the evidence now available, intra-party ties and inter-party conflict clearly stand out as prime factors both in the conduct of parliamentary business and in the voting behaviour of most M.P.s.

From the evidence for the importance of the two parties in the structure of parliamentary politics it is time now to turn to consider how and to what extent political conditions qualified the role and strength of the Whig and Tory parties. And here we may isolate two sets of limiting conditions, operating more or less constantly throughout the 1689–1714 period. In the first place, there were those conditions imposed on the party men by external pressures and circumstances. Thus not all parliamentarians consistently kept to the path of party orthodoxy, while by no means all parliamentary business was determined on a strictly partisan basis. One important factor militating against straight party voting was loyalty to the Court – whatever the party cast of the current ministry. This seems to have weighed heavily with a good many peers. During Anne's reign between 40 and 50 per cent of the peers active in the Lords were obliged to the Court for offices and/or pensions, and the voting records of many of these 'Queen's Servants' reflected these ties. Furthermore, though the majority of placemen in the Commons were less amenable to Court influence, there remained – even in Anne's reign – a small nucleus of non-party officials whose expert guidance on administrative issues and in the preparation of legislation was often sought by the House.[29]

Just as there was a substantial minority of the Lords and a smaller minority of the Commons who experienced a loyalty to the Court stronger than the pull of party, so too there were certain issues which were usually determined on a non-party basis. For one thing, much of the time of the Houses was taken up by private and local bills which were not often treated as party questions. For another, private and provincial interests frequently appear to have outweighed partisan considerations in such matters as the control and regulation of overseas trade or the allocation of the tax burden among the various industries and regions. For instance, when the Commons turned in the 1691–2 session to consider by what method the land tax should be raised, 'the members that served for the associated counties laboured hard to have it by a pound rate . . . which they urged to be the more equal tax . . . but the majority of the House especially the western and northern members being for a land tax by a monthly assessment, it was carried for the same'.[30]

But perhaps most important were those issues which tended to divide the Commons along Court–Country, rather than Whig–Tory, lines. Even when the party conflict was near fever pitch, the 'Country tradition' remained a lively one, capable of arousing country gentlemen (whatever their partisan leanings or loyalties) against Court corruption, administrative abuses, electoral irregularities and, above all, the profusion of officials and military men in the Commons. So it was that the Parliamentary Qualifications Act of 1711 was preceded by at least four other bills between 1695 and 1705 attempting to secure the 'freedom' of the Commons by establishing possession of substantial landed estates as a qualification of parliamentary candidates, while from 1692 onwards the introduction of Place bills or clauses seeking to exclude all or some categories of placemen from the House became a nearly annual event.[31] It is true that neither these devices nor other

Country panaceas such as the parliamentary commissions of accounts lived up to their backers' hopes, and also that such proposals were sometimes subverted to party purposes, especially by the Tories of Queen Anne's day. Nevertheless, the frequency with which such measures were brought forward and the enthusiasm with which they were supported by the country gentlemen stand as striking reminders of the continuing vitality of the Country tradition in these years.

If the first set of limiting conditions on the strength and role of the parties lay outside them, the second set lay within them. Above all, we must remember that the parties of this era were not the closely arrayed and well-disciplined phalanxes of contemporary Britain. On the one hand, close to half the members of the House were independent country gentlemen, unburdened by electoral obligations to the great party magnates and, whatever their partisan loyalties, reluctant to labour unremittingly in the stygian chambers of Westminster Palace. So it was that probably the greatest challenge to the party leaders was that of getting their supporters up to the capital and then ensuring their attendance at St Stephen's Chapel. Not only did many gentlemen prefer their rural pleasures to the expenses of London, but also there were many diversions to keep them from the House even when they did come up to Parliament, such as 'the baiting of a tiger near St James's Park' arranged, so one pamphleteer claimed, in order to draw off the opponents of the bill for establishing the new East India Company.[32] To be sure, the two largest divisions of the entire period, those of 26 February 1702 and 15 April 1714, produced the very respectable totals of 456 and 464 members.[33] But such large numbers were rare, and the average attendance on all Commons' divisions recorded in the *Journal* during William's reign was 238 – less than half the total membership.

On the other hand, each party was a composite of country gentlemen, courtiers and one or more 'power groups' consisting mainly of the professional politicians and bound together by electoral dependence, professional obligation, kinship, neighbourhood and/or personal friendship. Moreover, at times other intra-party groupings might emerge – 'pressure-groups' bent on the achievement of specific programmes or policies to which the party leaders were reluctant to commit themselves, such as the Hanoverian and Jacobite alignments which developed within the Tory party during the closing years of Anne's reign. Hence neither the regular attendance of most party members nor complete party solidarity among those who did meet at Westminster was by any means assured. And these problems, which plagued both parties, were especially acute on the Tory side, where the Country element grew stronger, where the chief leaders were often at odds with one another, and where the stable and effective core supplied on the Whig side by the Junto and their adherents from the early 1690s onwards was lacking.

If the parties' primacy within Parliament was qualified throughout this period by contemporary political conditions, on occasion their very predominance was called into doubt. Indeed, as we suggested earlier, the overall pattern of parliamentary politics was never fully stable during this period. Even in Anne's reign there were times, as in 1714, when intra-party divisions loomed larger than inter-party rivalry, or, as in 1707–8, when the Court–Country division seemed to overshadow that of Whig and Tory. As one knowledgeable observer remarked early in the 1707–8 session: 'there seems a disposition in both [Houses] to come to the old division of Court and Country, laying aside the distinctions of Whig and Tory, or at least burying them for a time'.[34] Even more important, what was the exception in Anne's reign was virtually the rule for much of William's – a period of transition in Parliament, as in the country at large, when a sizeable group of members gradually shifted their allegiance from one party to the other, while the Commons as a whole wavered and oscillated between orientation along a Whig–Tory or a Court–Country axis.

Here we cannot provide an account in full of the shifts in the pattern of parliamentary alignments between 1689 and 1702, but a bare outline of the main developments may be briefly sketched. To begin with, we should note that despite the general revulsion against James's rule which the Revolution revealed, the Convention Parliament was soon riven by the pre-Revolution division between Whig and Tory over such questions as Protestant dissenters' political privileges, the treatment of James's servants and collaborators, and the regulation of municipal corporations. Furthermore, the General Election of 1690 saw bitter partisan conflict as Whigs and Tories sought to besmirch each other's reputations with the publication of 'black lists' of M.P.s who had opposed the crowning of William and Mary or supported the purge of the corporations proposed under the 'Sacheverell clause'.[35]

But though the rancour of the election campaign was carried over into the first session of the 1690–5 Parliament, especially in the struggle over the terms of the Act of Recognition, by the autumn of 1691 William's preference for mixed administrations and the effects of the costly and largely unsuccessful war effort were combining to confound the partisan division and to accentuate Court–Country differences. As Robert Harley (destined with his kinsman Paul Foley to become the leader of the so-called 'New Country party') wrote to his father early in the 1691–2 session: 'the House seems in a very strange temper and which way the parties will determine is very difficult to say, but at present very much intermixed and jumbled together'.[36] Thus, during the remaining sessions of this Parliament party questions, such as abjuration bills and attacks first on Tory and then on Whig ministers, jostled uneasily with Court–Country questions, such as Place bills, treason trial bills and triennial measures.[37] Moreover, though William reluctantly but gradually reconstructed his administration between 1693 and 1695 by removing Tories from positions of influence and replacing them with members or adherents of the emerging Whig Junto, at the same time the New Country party – a fusion of 'old' or 'true' Whigs such as Foley and Harley with pre-Revolution courtiers such as Sir Christopher Musgrave – gained strength in the Commons.

Nor did the General Election of the autumn of 1695 reverse the trend in favour of anti-Court measures and men, and in the opening months of the 1695–6 session the New Country party, with Tory backing, appeared to be on the verge of toppling the Junto. Even the great ministerial undertaker, the earl of Sunderland, seemed to be ready to throw his support to Foley and Harley.[38] But the sudden disclosure of the assassination plot against William late in February 1696 gave the initiative back to the Junto, and they quickly capitalised on this windfall by reviving the issue of loyalty to the Revolution regime as a partisan question both with the Association and with the bill of attainder against Sir John Fenwick. The upshot was that the second half of the 1695–6 session and also the 1696–7 session saw a reversion to a partisan axis in alignments within the Commons, while the Junto's hold on office was consolidated.[39]

However, the conclusion of peace with France in the autumn of 1697 was the signal for the reopening of the Court–Country breach, and the General Election of the summer of 1698 was fought along those lines. As Lord Somers dolefully observed to the duke of Shrewsbury in the autumn of 1698, 'the elections were made on an ill foot; uneasiness at taxes, and the most dangerous division of a Court and Country party; so that there is reason to doubt of the behaviour of many of your best friends'.[40] And Somers's gloomy prognostications proved only too accurate, for the two sessions of the 1698–1700 Parliament saw the New Country party, in conjunction with the Tories, in command of the

Commons and the members of the Junto forced or edged out of office.[41]

In turn, the General Election of the winter of 1700–1 was followed by new successes for the increasingly close alliance between Harley and the old Tory leaders during the spring session of 1701 – especially the passage of the constitutional provisos of the Act of Settlement with their strictures against placemen, secret councils and foreigners. On the one hand, then, the 1701 Parliament saw the virtual completion of the transit from Whig to Tory ranks that Harley and other 'old' Whigs had begun in the early 1690s. And on the other, the old Tory or 'Church' party (with its bias in favour of royal prerogative) had by this time been no little transformed by the infusion of new blood and the adoption of a marked Country bias. As the author of an outspoken Whig pamphlet wrote after the close of the 1701 session:

> The Tory Party, as they affect to be called, is that part of the House of Commons which has governed this session . . . If we consider the men, and compare what they have done with the pretended principles of their party, 'twill hardly seem odder to see Sir Edward Seymour bring in a bill to prevent bribery, or Mr John How exclaim against exorbitant grants, or Sir Christopher Musgrave violent either against grants, or a standing army . . . than to see them assume the name of Tories. Is not Robert Harley a ringleader in this Tory party? . . . Does he not attend all Ordinances, and as constantly every weekday frequent the service of the Church (for his is a Church-party) in St Stephen's Chapel, as he does the Conventicle every Lord's day? Are not the Foleys, Winningtons, St John, Harvey of Weymouth, Barnardiston, Hammond, Randyl, and others of that leaven, members of this fraternity?[42]

Yet the reconstitution of the Tories, coupled with their vindictive attacks on the Junto lords, their slowness in taking strong measures against the revived French threat on the Continent and at sea, and their lukewarm adherence to the Protestant successor, also set the stage for the revival of Junto fortunes and the orientation, once more, of the Commons on a Whig–Tory axis. The General Election of December 1701 was chiefly fought as a party struggle, and the last Parliament of William's reign – with the conflict over Whig proposals for a voluntary abjuration of James III coupled with Tory attempts to resurrect the impeachments of the preceding Parliament – was dominated by party rivalry.[43] Thus, despite the shifting and often confused alignments of the 1690s, the chief parliamentary groupings in the final year of William's reign were – as they had been in its earliest years – Whig and Tory, though in the interval the Whigs had lost the Harleys and their associates to the Tories. By the spring of 1702, then, there had emerged a pattern of parliamentary politics which, despite occasional intra-party fissures and temporary relapses into a Court–Country division, was to continue to prevail throughout Anne's reign.

IV

As we look back from the vantage point of the late 1960s upon the recent debate over the structure of parliamentary politics between 1689 and 1714, two final notes might be briefly recorded. Firstly, it is evident that Walcott's revisionist interpretation has not succeeded in holding the field. Rather, the findings of more recent studies would seem to suggest that the differences between the politics of the post-Revolution years and those of the mid-eighteenth century are greater than their similarities. But secondly, it would be mistaken to assume that the scholarly activity of the last decade, sparked in no small part by Walcott's provocative conclusions and 'Namierite' methods, has resulted in a mere recasting of older accounts. For one thing, despite their disagreement with many of Walcott's conclusions, most political historians of the period have accepted the utility of Namier's techniques, when carefully applied and used in conjunction with traditional approaches. Current research, then, is based on the application of a variety of modes of analysis to a far wider range of sources than was used or available in the past. Furthermore, though by no means all the results are in as yet, already a good deal of illumination has been cast on hitherto dimly lit corners of post-Revolution politics. And, above all, it is now possible to conclude, with greater certainty yet with more subtle shadings than ever before, that the clash of the Whig and Tory parties was the prime, though not always the prevailing, element in the complicated and sometimes very fluid structure of parliamentary politics between 1689 and 1714. In sum, we may at last have reached the stage where knowledge of the structure of parliamentary politics has been sufficiently clarified for political historians to feel free to take up once again the work of narrating the course of politics in the days of King William and Queen Anne.

BIBLIOGRAPHICAL NOTE

The best narrative guide to the parliamentary history of our period, especially through the political thickets of William's reign, is still K. Feiling, *History of the Tory Party 1640–1714* (Oxford, 1924). J. H. Plumb's *The Growth of Political Stability in England 1675–1725* (1967) is a most suggestive survey of many aspects of post-Revolution politics, including the crucial changes of George I's reign, while G. Holmes's *British Politics in the Age of Anne* (1967) is a masterly dissection of the structure of politics at the centre between 1702 and 1714. One book published after the completion of this essay, D. Rubini, *Court and Country 1688–1702* (1968), differs from these authorities, and from the present writer, in attaching relatively little importance to the Whig–Tory dichotomy in Parliament during William III's reign: its handling of evidence does not always inspire confidence.

Two essays dealing with the character and impact of Namier's work in eighteenth-century political history are W. R. Fryer, 'The Study of British Politics between the Revolution and the Reform Act', in *Renaissance and Modern Studies*, i (1957), and J. M. Price, 'Party, Purpose, and Pattern: Sir Lewis Namier and his critics', in *JBS* i (1961): the former focuses on specific substantive problems and the latter on methodological ones. Biographies of three of the leading politicians of the day contain much useful general information about politics: A. Browning, *Thomas Osborne, Earl of Danby . . . 1632–1712* (Glasgow, 1944–51); J. P. Kenyon, *Robert Spencer, Earl of Sunderland 1641–1702* (1958); H. Horwitz, *Revolution Politicks: The Career of Daniel Finch, Second Earl of Nottingham 1647–1730* (Cambridge, 1968).

The best collection of political documents for these years is in *The Divided Society: Party Conflict in England 1694–1716*, ed. G. Holmes and W. A. Speck (1967), and its utility is enhanced by the informative introductions provided to the documents.

NOTES

1. For a brief resumé see R. Walcott, 'The Idea of Party in the Writing of Later Stuart History', in *JBS* i (1962).

2. R. Walcott, 'English Party Politics (1688–1714)', in *Essays in Modern English History in Honor of W. C. Abbott* (Harvard, 1941), p. 131.

3. W. R. Fryer, 'The Study of British Politics between the Revolution and the Reform Act', in *Renaissance and Modern Studies*, i (1957), 103.

4. L. Namier, *The Structure of Politics at the Accession of George III*, 2nd ed. (1957), p. xi.

5. R. Walcott, *English Politics in the Early Eighteenth Century* (Oxford, 1956), p. 34.

6. These figures are drawn from ibid. pp. 69, 115, 215. They do not quite total 513 (the full membership of the Commons before 1707) and are calculations made by the present writer from Walcott's data. In his 1941 essay Walcott suggested a rather higher figure for the country gentlemen – about 200 (see *Essays . . . in Honor of W. C. Abbott*, p. 130).

7. Ibid. p. 131.

8. D. J. MacDougall, 'Some Recent Books in British History', in *Canadian Hist. Rev.* xxxviii (1957), 140.

9. *William and Mary Q.* 3rd ser., xiv (1957), 118.

10. e.g. D. G. Barnes, *American Hist. Rev.*, lxii (1956–7), 192–3; A. S. Foord, *His Majesty's Opposition 1714–1830* (Oxford, 1964).

11. M. A. Thomson, in *History*, NS xlii (1957), p. 153. See also J. H. Plumb, in *EHR* lxxii (1957), 126–9.

12. W. A. Speck, 'The House of Commons 1702–1714: a study in political organisation' (Oxford D.Phil. thesis, 1966), folios 10–11, 151–248.

13. G. Holmes, *British Politics in the Age of Anne* (1967), p. 329.

14. H. Horwitz, 'Parties, Connections, and Parliamentary Politics, 1689–1714: review and revision', in *JBS* vi (1966–7), 49–52.

15. Plumb, in *EHR* lxxii (1957); Speck, 'House of Commons', folios 20–1.

16. Ibid. p. 21.

17. *JBS* i (1962), 61. See also *American Hist. Rev.*, lxxiv (1968), 600.

18. J. G. Sperling, 'The Division of 25 May 1711, on an Amendment to the South Sea Bill: a note on the reality of parties in the Age of Anne', in *HJ* iv (1961); W. A. Speck, 'The Choice of a Speaker in 1705', in *BIHR* xxxvii (1964). Quotations drawn from Sperling, p. 202.

19. Speck, in *BIHR* xxxvii (1964), 35, 34.

20. For the identity of these lists see Horwitz, in *JBS* vi (1966–7), p. 50 n 30, and pp. 58–9.

21. Unpublished calculations of this writer.

22. For Speck's calculations see Holmes, op, cit. pp. 34–5; cf. I. Burton *et al.*, 'Political Parties in the Reigns of William III and Anne...', in *BIHR* Suppl. 7 (1968)

23. Ibid. pp. 36–7 and app. A.

24. Of the seventeen, five involved the legality of William's title and/or the security of the succession, five foreign policy and related problems, while the remaining seven ranged from the regulation of municipal corporations to the duke of Hamilton's right to a seat in the Lords.

25. Holmes, op. cit. p. 45.

26. *An Answer to an Infamous Libel Entituled, A List of One Unanimous Club of Members of the Late Parliament* (1701), p. 21.

27. Add. MS 43586, fo. 86: W. Brockman to J. Deedes, 27 March 1690.

28. Add. MS 33225, fo. 17: F. Hare to H. Watkins, 28 Jan 1709. Hare's reference to the Tory 'corner' of the House reminds us that informal seating arrangements tended – at least in Anne's reign – to reflect partisan alignments, though not with complete uniformity. See Holmes, op. cit. p. 249 n 2.

29. Ibid. pp. 356, 387 and app. A and B.

30. All Souls College MS 158, i, 109. For examples of provincial clubs among parliamentarians see J. H. Plumb, *The Growth of Political Stability in England 1675–1725* (1967), p. 33.

31. H. E. Witmer, *The Property Qualifications of Members of Parliament* (1943), ch. 1; G. S. Holmes, 'The Attack on "The Influence of the Crown" 1702–1716', in *BIHR* xxxix (1966).

32. *England's Enemies Exposed, and its True Friends and Patriots Defended* (1701), p. 17.

33. These totals exclude tellers. By 1714 the House had been enlarged by the addition of forty-five Scottish members.

34. E. Gibson to H. Humphreys, 6 Dec 1707, printed by C. M. Griffiths, 'Letters from Edmund Gibson to Bishop Humphreys', in *National Library of Wales J.* x (1957–8), 372.

35. These lists are reprinted by A. Browning, *Thomas Osborne, Earl of Danby and Duke of Leeds 1632–1712* (Glasgow, 1944–51), iii, 164–72.

36. BM Loan 29/185, fo. 240: to Sir E. Harley, 7 Nov 1691.

37. It seems no accident that most of the surviving Commons' lists from these years, by contrast to the party compilations of 1690, are lists of placemen. See Browning, *Danby*, iii, 184–7; BM Loan 29/206, folios 170–1; Bodl. Rawlinson MS D846, folios 1–6.

38. J. P. Kenyon, *Robert Spencer, Earl of Sunderland 1641–1702* (1958), pp. 276–7.

39. Again, the extant Commons' lists from March 1696 through the 1696–7 session reflect this revival of a Whig–Tory alignment. Browning, *Danby*, iii, 194–213; Add. MS 47608 (Fenwick attainder bill list).

40. Printed in *The Divided Society: Party Conflict in England 1694–1716*, ed. G. Holmes and W. A. Speck (1967), p. 18.

41. All four surviving Commons' lists from this period reflect the Court–Country orientation, viz. those in *A Letter to a Country Gentleman . . . To Which is Annexed a List of the Names of some Gentlemen who were Members of the Last Parliament, and now are (or lately were) in Publick Employments* (1698), reprinted in *The Harleian Miscellany* (1810), x, 361–71; *A Compleat List of the Knights, Citizens and Burgesses Of the New Parliament* (1698), placemen on this list indicated by crosses beside their names (see Add. MS 40772, fo. 8); BM Loan 29/35/12, printed by Horwitz, in *JBS* vi (1966–7), 62–9; *A List of the Members of the last House of Commons . . . who Voted for a Standing Army* (1700).

42. *Jura Populi Anglicani: or the subject's right of petitioning set forth* (1701), p. vii.

43. The two surviving Commons' lists of this period again reflect the re-orientation of politics. See [J. Drake], *Some Necessary Considerations of Members to Serve in Parliament, Humbly offer'd to all Electors* (1702), reprinted in *A Fourth Collection of Scarce and Valuable Tracts* (1751–2), iii, 16–41.

5. William III and the Politicians

E. L. ELLIS

'ALL of them look upon your Highness as the great wheel which, under God, must give life and motion to any good project.'[1] Sir Patrick Hume, the future earl of Marchmont, who wrote thus to William of Orange on 22 April 1687, was retailing the hopes of deliverance from James II of the many English and Scots refugees then in exile in Holland. It is unlikely that William was over-impressed by this statement of total commitment to his cause by men who had forfeited their right to speak for Britain by fleeing from their homeland. But during the next twelve months the authentic spokesmen for the political nation in England were driven to the same conclusion: that in William alone was salvation to be found.

In the light of the bitter political hatreds that had riven England in the early 1680s, this unity of purpose among former enemies in circumstances of the utmost hazard, in which their lives were at risk for months on end, is an astonishing phenomenon. Only so consistent a blunderer as James II could have achieved such an effect in so short a time. Few of the Whigs had been under any illusions about the likely consequences of James's accession: since 1681 they had been pilloried and proscribed and many of their leaders executed or driven into exile.[2] But the Tories, too, were to have their shocks: the crudity of James's attacks on property and settled institutions, the ruthless fervour of his dismissals of non-cooperators, created a growing army of bewildered Tories and ex-Court politicians. Moreover, whatever the domestic differences of Whig and Tory, both were Protestant; and more, both were furiously anti-Catholic and anti-French. When James II turned on the Church of England he shattered the remaining illusions of the Tories and quickly drove them into alliance with the Whigs. 'Whig and Tory was forgotten for a year or two, and only the distinction of Protestant and Papist made use of.'[3] In this mounting emergency, rendered finally intolerable by the prospect of a Catholic heir to the throne, it was to William of Orange, the King's nephew and son-in-law, that the united political nation in England turned; and when William (who for years had hoped to enlist English support for his resistance to

the exorbitant power of France) finally responded to these appeals in
November 1688, the Glorious Revolution was in train.

As a result of the Revolution, Crown and political nation were brought
to new terms of accommodation and the English political system
achieved a new viability. But most of the Revolution Settlement was too
purely negative to provide a clear blue-print for effective government in
the future, and much of the interest of William III's reign[4] lies in the
attempt to give detailed practical effect to the broad settlement of 1689.
Initially, William, 'the Great Deliverer', was popular, but when the
consequence of his accession – England's involvement in large-scale,
costly, not strikingly successful war – became apparent, new political
difficulties ensued. Indeed, the whole reign was dominated by a search
for a degree of domestic stability that would enable England to maximise
her military effort abroad. This search, if we may anticipate, was
unsuccessful until 1693–4, when a new model of government was
established which made a considerable contribution to the war effort.
By 1698 this scheme had exhausted its utility and the remainder of
William's reign was a time of confusion in which the relations of King
and political nation again approached breakdown.

This essay, therefore, attempts to answer the question: what caused
the political instability of William's reign? In particular, how far was it
attributable to the difficulties of the King's new position after 1689,
and how far to the foreign, military and domestic policies he pursued,
and the responses to them of a political nation that could no longer be
ignored?

With his accession as King in 1689, William, who had been clear in his
own mind all along that he would not accept any subordinate status, had
inherited an amplitude of formal power scarcely less in essentials than
that of his two predecessors. The abolition of the suspending power, the
condemnation of the dispensing power as lately exercised, and the
elimination of the Ecclesiastical Commission were small losses easily
borne by a sensible monarch; the only important power immediately
surrendered, as time was to show, was that of raising and keeping a
standing army in time of peace. On the face of it, therefore, William was
well placed to achieve his main purpose in coming to England: first, to
commit his new realm to war against France, and thereafter to mobilise
her resources for full-scale operations on land and at sea. In other
circumstances William might well have encountered some difficulties

here. Of course there were plenty of men in England who believed that war against France was the logical, even wholly desirable, consequence of the Revolution. Bishop Burnet, for example, considered William 'a person raised up by God to resist the power of France';[5] in February 1689 the great John Locke was delighted with 'the designs which his Majesty has so gloriously begun for the redeeming England and with it all Europe'; and there were no doubt many, especially among the Whigs, at least initially, who would have endorsed Locke's opinion that every one of his countrymen was

> bound in conscience and gratitude not to content himself with a bare, slothful . . . loyalty, where his purse, his head or his hand may be of any use to this our great deliverer. He has ventured and done too much for us to leave room for indifferency or backwardness.[6]

But of course not all Englishmen shared these sentiments: indeed had the issue of peace or war, and especially the scale and method of England's participation, been coolly and fully considered at the outset, it is probable that William would have met strong opposition. For the fact was that for most Englishmen William had been called over, as he himself stated in his Proclamation on landing, to rescue the religion and domestic liberties of Englishmen, not to involve them willy-nilly in a great and inordinately expensive continental war. In the event, as on so many occasions previously, William's difficulties, actual and potential, were resolved for him by the actions of King James. In March 1689 James landed in Ireland at the head of a French army; on 7 May 1689 William III declared war on France and the decision was popularly, even rapturously, received in England. From William's point of view Ireland was an irritating and dangerous distraction from his main military business on the Continent.[7] Nonetheless it was not without its advantages: by the time the Irish war was over in 1691, England's full involvement in the European struggle was established, and there was no real question thereafter of limited liability.

It is doubtful if William ever fully brought his very considerable political talents and his vast experience of men and affairs to bear on English domestic politics. His aim was quite simple: he wanted the maximum amount of national unity as the best foundation for successful war abroad; he was not seriously interested in Englishmen's domestic concerns, nor their personal and party feuds, except in so far as these promoted or hampered the military effort. He saw himself as the agent of reconciliation, and nearly all his domestic policies were directed to this end: but these efforts were blessed with only limited success and certain weaknesses in William's position were soon apparent.

One difficulty was that the newly cauterised regime initially inspired too large expectations of its virtue, especially among those 'country' politicians who had been the most consistent opponents of the post-Restoration monarchy; disillusion was all the greater when, inevitably, it fell below the impossibly high grace expected of it. Lord Ashley, the future third earl of Shaftesbury, was driven into semi-retirement by disgust at what he regarded as the cynical compromises that had been made in a reign when, as he told Locke, 'we expected virtue and honesty should have succeeded better than ever'.[8] Not all men were as high-toned as Ashley, and some Englishmen of the highest rank with much to lose were more concerned at the seeming frailty of the new Settlement than appalled by the occasional subsequent compromises of political morality; several of them hedged their bets by making a peace of sorts with James II. Of course many Englishmen from the outset had only grudgingly accepted William as King. Nor had he the obvious winning charm and popular manners that could have won people over. William's warmth and affection had to be earned and were sparingly given; little that he saw of England and Englishmen inspired this sort of evident fondness (which might well have been reciprocated) in the King for his new subjects. On the contrary, his genuine affection was kept for his family circle, which, despite the presence there until 1694 of a native-born and popular Queen, had an unmistakably foreign flavour and included far too many Dutch favourites on whom William lavished wealth and honours, to the growing fury of his English subjects.

But the King's domestic difficulties went deeper than these general disgruntlements and personal inadequacies. The fact was that there was no simple formula for effective government in England after the Revolution; indeed, in some respects the King's position after 1689 was more difficult than ever. There was no shortage of guidance on paper, but it was much easier to describe the constitution in general terms than to work it in practice. All the commentators were agreed that the monarchy was limited, but none was very clear, much less precise, about the practical extent of the limitations: presumably experience and the merits of the case could be expected to provide the determining judgements for the future. Stripped of divinity, the King must take his chance along with other mortals, and he had been amply warned of the perils of ill-behaviour.

But many problems remained. It was agreed on all sides that the King must be, in the common phrase of the time, 'the Father of all his people': but this was not easily reconciled with the fact that the relatively sophisticated political nation in England, after its brief period of near-consensus in 1688, very quickly returned to its customary party discords. Party activity in the late seventeenth century was like sin, universally condemned and widely indulged; it remained almost as formally undefended as fornication and was usually denounced with the same vehemence. It amounted, declared a typical opinion, to 'a propensity to ruin more than natural'.[9] But despite this common-form disapproval (which, with the bitter memory of the Civil War close at hand, reflected a yearning for peace and amity), the party men quickly showed in the Convention that they had not changed their spots. 'Fear of Popery has united: when that is over, we shall divide again', warned a Whig member, Pollexfen, in the Commons on 29 January 1689.[10] There were too many bitter memories, too many unsatisfied hopes of revenge, too many genuine ideological differences unresolved, for amity to continue. Parties quickly reappeared to furrow the brows of ministers and wear the patience of angels.

Indeed, in some respects post-Revolution political circumstances heightened the party fight. The continuing need for unprecedented sums of money for the war ensured that there would be annual sessions of Parliament, and Westminster was the great focus of, and stimulus to, the struggle of Whig and Tory. Moreover, when in 1694 William, after a determined resistance, was forced to accept the Triennial bill, the consequent certainty of regular General Elections and the very short period of intermission between them kept the country at large at or near the boiling point politically for years on end. In 1708 when the seventh General Election since 1694 was in train, Daniel Defoe, an acute and sophisticated observer of English politics, while still ultimately convinced that the Triennial Act had 'a complication of advantages . . . lodged in the bowels of it', was nonetheless forced to admit that:

it has this fatal consequence in it, which all England feels . . . viz: that the certainty of a new election in three years is an unhappy occasion of keeping alive the divisions and party strife among the people which would otherwise have died of course. Had the election to come been remote and uncertain, the interest of this or that person had been equally uncertain, and men had not applied themselves so much to the cultivating their interest and riveting themselves in the opinion either of people or parties. . . . This beautiful rose has its prickle: this certainty of the return of an election occasions a constant keeping alive of innumerable factions. . . . Parties are ever struggling; they contend on every occasion, choosing their parish officers, their Recorders, their magistrates, and everything that has the least face of public concern; all runs by parties, all eye the grand election . . . and have that occasion in view.[11]

What, in fact, could the King do to minimise party hostilities? Experience suggested that he should at any rate not declare fully for one side or another; that he should not withhold at least the promise of his patronage from either or any side. With this thesis William fully agreed. The 'Trimmer' Halifax's notes of his conversations with the new King are strongly laced with William's repeated assertions that he, too, was and ever would be, by temperament and necessity, a 'Trimmer'.[12] This delicate balancing of parties had much to recommend it in parliamentary terms, for it was the best method short of heaven of obviating the growth in Parliament (which, despite its increased authority, was better equipped to wreck than to construct) of a formidable group of irresponsible irreconcilables. And it was also the best guarantee that the men of interest and influence in the localities would continue to give a precarious regime that minimum of support without which it could not hope to function effectively, perhaps even to survive.

At the executive and administrative levels, however, it was otherwise. Nothing demonstrates this fact more sharply than the administrative paralysis in the all-party Council of nine set up to assist Queen Mary to administer the country during William's absence in Ireland in 1690. Though inexperienced, the Queen was quick to see the weaknesses of this Council formed ostensibly to guide her, but in reality one more of the King's trimming devices for masking party rancour.[13] Even in the dire national emergency after the naval defeat off Beachy Head, when the French commanded the Channel and an invasion seemed likely, this cross-grained crew of Whigs and Tories in the Council blithely engaged in a bitter party fight for supremacy. It is evident, too, in these early years of the reign, when the King clung to his hope of cancelling the disruptive power of party by including the two sides in more or less equal strength in his government, that ministers did not hesitate to be 'insolent' at Council or Cabinet if their proposals did not find favour; nor did they shrink from fomenting, even openly leading, opposition in Parliament to a government of which they were members. As a consequence, as Lord Sunderland, a man brilliantly skilled in political management, pointed out, 'the whole government is loose, no respect paid to it'.[14]

It is possible that William could have significantly reduced this ministerial irresponsibility by his permanent presence in England. But he was abroad for several months each year commanding his armies in person; and in his absence it was clear by 1692 that, despite Queen Mary's brave attempt to fill the void, 'nobody else has authority enough to keep things from the uttermost disorder and confusion'.[15] In 1701 it was perfectly plain to John Toland the pamphleteer, as he said in a sober review of William's reign, that 'Whigs and Tories are incompatible in the ministry . . . drawing two ways is making no way at all. [It was, he said,] a sort of neutral government'.[16]

In fairness to William, he had reluctantly come to concede at least partially the truth of Toland's maxim some years before the end of his reign, and by doing so the King achieved for a time that political stability at home that he so desperately needed. The history of William's search after stable government between 1689 and 1702 falls into four unequal periods, with a hint at the end of at least the beginnings of a fifth period dramatically cut off by his death.

The first period was of short duration: it began with the opening of the Convention and ended late in 1690. William initially seemed to take the Whigs at their own valuation; in December 1688 he told Halifax that the Commonwealth party (that is, the Whigs in pejorative terms) was the strongest in England. 'He had then that impression given', said Halifax. 'They made haste to give him that opinion.'[17] Accordingly he conceded rather more places to the Whigs than their real strength and experience warranted, though not perhaps more than the unequivocal nature of their service to his cause hitherto made reasonable. Everywhere, in all his appointments, there was an attempt to mobilise the maximum amount of general support that was consistent with even a show of co-operation and a bare minimum of competence. One Secretaryship went to Nottingham, a strong Tory, the other to Shrewsbury, the rising hope of the Whigs; the Great Seal, the Treasury and the Admiralty were put into commission – a means of increasing the loaves and fishes of office – and shared largely by the two sides.

The King's hopes of general unity and an effective administration were soon dashed. In the vital consideration of money bills, ministers of both parties gave no clear lead and allowed the House to fall into profitless debates and reflections on recent history. Impatient for the sinews of war, William was soon complaining to Halifax that Parliament 'used him like a dog' and that his ministers were culpably remiss.[18] But worse was to follow: the Whigs, almost to a man, were determined on wholesale revenge for the injuries they had suffered, in particular atonement for the blood of the martyrs of 1683, and the total vindication of their activity before 1688, including the formal reaffirmation of the reality of the Popish Plot. All of this was completely at variance with the King's desire for oblivion and indemnity for the past; moreover he began to suspect that most of the Whigs were Republicans or republican fellow-travellers who would reduce him to the level of a figure-head Doge. On closer acquaintance he discovered his growing distaste for many of them – Delamere, Monmouth, Harbord, Capel, Sacheverell and Wharton, especially – on personal grounds.

This disillusionment was mutual; many of the Whigs had naïvely believed that, with William at their head, they, the chosen people, would move into the Promised Land. They were infuriated at the King's willingness to employ Sir Edward Seymour and the like, malevolent survivors from the worst period of Whig persecution. In December 1689 Thomas Wharton, the newly appointed Comptroller of the Household and future stalwart of the Whig Junto, wrote to the King quite the most downright, most hectoring letter William ever received. Wharton violently denounced the King's 'trimming between parties', bitterly assailed his employment of the Tories who were 'knaves' and 'villains' with whom the Whigs, 'the honester part of the nation', who had confidently expected to have 'all power put into [their] hands', would no longer serve. At the same time Shrewsbury also wrote to the King to much the same purpose, though in characteristically milder terms, except that he, too, asserted that many of the Tories were disloyal and, 'questionless, would bring in King James'.[19]

But William remained unmoved; he discounted Whig claims to principled virtue and believed that a proper share of offices was an infallible means of cooling party zeal. He was almost daily appreciating the merits of Nottingham and the ever-useful Godolphin and was seriously contemplating counter-measures against the Whigs in a Parliament which was rapidly reaching the ultimate in recalcitrance and party violence.[20] When early in 1690 the Whigs added a Draconian clause, designed to emasculate Tory electoral strength, to the Corporation bill, William threw his influence against them and the bill was ultimately lost. Nor did he stop there; by this time most of the outstanding money bills had been grudgingly passed and on 5 February

Parliament was dissolved. It was a shock to the Whigs and William, not without relish, 'saw their faces, long as an ell, change colour twenty times' during his dissolution speech.[21]

According to Burnet, the 1690 Election 'went generally for men who would probably have declared for King James, if they could have known how to manage matters for him'.[22] Refined of its party malice, this suggests a moderate but not overwhelming Tory preponderance. It should be remembered that every Parliament at this time included numbers of men who were either independent of party or only nominally Whig or Tory; these were often members with noses of wax capable of being turned either way, and it was a normal party gambit in the early days of a session to try to sweep up these troublesome doubt-fuls in a distinguishing vote. The Whigs did not abandon their party offensive in the new Parliament but they won scant success: they had an apparent success when Halifax, who was never to be forgiven for his part in defeating the Exclusion Bill, resigned in disgust, but they failed to dislodge Nottingham or Carmarthen (Danby of old), against whom they were especially virulent. In fact, during 1690 the Whig leaven in the ministry was much reduced: some had resigned, some were dis-missed, Wharton, in pique, neglected all business, and, most important of all, Shrewsbury, the essential Whig in William's scheme, insisted on retiring. The King's first experiment, an almost equal balance of parties, had ended abruptly in failure; and thus far Whig intransigence, the determined combativeness of the Tories, and some miscalculation by William himself had all contributed to the prevailing instability.

The second period, from the close of 1690 to March 1693, was marked by a refinement to the trimming policy. William, who fully appreciated the threat to monarchy and even to civil peace implicit in the claim to single-party dominance, would have nothing to do with a party mono-poly of his government. However, he was now prepared to give his ministry a stronger party tilt and, heartily sick of most of the Whigs, it was to Carmarthen, Nottingham and the administratively experienced Tories that he turned. The remaining Whig ministers, a disgruntled minority, consisted in the main of Wharton, John Somers, Charles Montague, Edward Russell and their friends, younger men of ability, the future Whig Junto, who, whatever their discontents, were avid for the war and would rally in the final reckoning to William's side. This experiment, too, was soon an evident failure.

Nor was political weakness at home counter-balanced by decisive success in the military campaigns abroad. Time after time William was outmanœuvred by his French opponent, Luxembourg, who fully exploited the natural advantages that the terrain of the Low Countries (brilliantly improved by the great French engineer Vauban) gave to the side content with a predominantly defensive campaign relieved by occasional opportunist sallies. These are the years of defeat at Steinkirk and Landen. Increasingly William, who longed for a war of movement and an assault on France itself, was driven by mounting frustration to pin his hopes on allied naval power; ultimately, if and when command of the Channel had been achieved, the King planned an amphibious 'Descent' on the French coast. There were great expectations that in 1691 the fleet, now led by Edward Russell, would achieve mastery of the seas. But the French would not play, despite risky efforts to draw them out; and meantime French privateers caused havoc by their depredations on allied shipping and something near to panic by appearances off the English coast. In 1692 Russell did at last defeat the French at La Hogue: but he failed to capitalise on the victory, and the 'Descent' was again postponed.

These almost unrelieved failures and discouragements had their repercussions on English opinion and politics: people were furiously 'angry with the fleet for doing nothing', there were public allegations of ministerial betrayal of war plans, and in mid-1691 there was even a project on foot for a parliamentary committee to take over direction of the war.[23] Before long the King's whole conception of strategy was being questioned; in Parliament and in the Press he was bluntly told that his hope of conquering France was 'the passion of fools, the hope of women'; as for the English army on the Continent, 'what have we to do there?' England's native element was the sea, as La Hogue fitfully showed.[24]

In the parliamentary inquests on all these disappointments the government was hard put to hold its own, not least because of the growing vendetta between Russell and Secretary Nottingham. The ministry was clearly living from hand to mouth; there were frequent tinkering changes usually bringing in Tories in place of Whigs: 'Our revolving government', Monmouth wrote sardonically to Locke, 'always affords us something new every three or four months, but what would be most new and strange, were to see it do anything that were really for its interest.'[25] Early in 1693 the government's weakness was even more evident: a bill for frequent Parliaments, reduced en route by a desperate defence from an annual to a triennial proposal, passed both Houses, and William, left unscreened, had to apply his royal veto. The King's second experiment, a Tory preponderance, was rapidly exhausting its limited utility. Carmarthen and Nottingham had failed: Tory administrative experience, unsupported by any great enthusiasm for the new regime and its war policies, was not enough to guarantee stable government.

Meantime the King, forced at last to face the facts, was beginning to respond to the adroit persuasions of Lord Sunderland (James II's old minister, discreetly retired since 1688), who had been advising him unofficially since 1692, hitherto unavailingly. Sunderland now began to argue strongly that, all along, the King had backed the wrong horse; William had mistakenly assumed that Whigs and Tories were equally committed to his cause whereas, in Sunderland's opinion, while 'the whole' of the Whigs were loyal, 'not one quarter' of the Tories could ever be relied upon. Sunderland began to urge the case for switching the government's dependence from Carmarthen and Nottingham to Somers, Montague, Wharton and the Junto Whigs; he pointed to their proven abilities, their body of loyal supporters in the Commons and their unqualified commitment to the Revolution and the war.[26] Sunderland was insistent that there must be a thorough change, patching would not do: but the King, with his inveterate preference for little by little, proceeded at snail's pace. In March 1693 Somers was made Lord Keeper and Sir John Trenchard became Secretary of State; but it was not until nearly a year later that a Whig preponderance in the government was effectively established, when Shrewsbury replaced Nottingham and the Treasury and Admiralty boards were stocked with Whigs. At long last William was in sight of an effective ministry.

The third period of William's reign, the middle years from 1694 to 1698, is in some ways the most interesting politically of all, for it demonstrates the possibilities and limitations of party government in the late seventeenth century. Sunderland was never at any time the advocate of a Whig monopoly. On the contrary, he insisted that the King should employ all who would serve him and 'make the foundation of his government as broad and as firm as he can'.[27] The mechanics of this successful ministry are instructive. By 1694 one thing was crystal clear: with the King abroad for months on end, and even the Queen's weak substitution no longer possible because of her death, the vital need was for a general supervisor or, in the language of the time, a chief 'manager' of the government. No one hitherto had enjoyed the King's confidence sufficiently to wield this authority: Sunderland did; moreover he had the skill, energy and experience to do so effectively. He now began directing the ministry, but thought it wiser not to expose himself to attack by accepting an official position. Sunderland proposed to buy some support in Parliament by the straight bartering of pensions and greasing the palms of some of the troublesome and the necessitous; to keep all placemen up to the mark by effective discipline; to rely on the skill of the Junto Whigs for parliamentary management and hope that Shrewsbury would soften their party asperities sufficiently to make them acceptable to the King. For two years or so the scheme worked superbly.

It was well that it did, for these were the slogging, apparently unrewarding years of the war. William's brilliantly imaginative idea of asserting English naval power in the Mediterranean promised much, but ultimately disappointed; on land the campaigns were bogged down in dispiriting stalemate. Furthermore England's capacity to finance the war seemed in doubt; the land tax brought home annually the cost of England's new European role to the country gentlemen, the vital political class, who were beginning to demand tangible results for their money. From first to last this was a ministry whose stability was under pressure; but its organised strength enabled it to meet most of the demands made on it. Charles Montague, who headed the Treasury, did not have a particularly original mind, but he had a keen eye for the political possibilities in other men's notions. It was Montague who piloted through Parliament legislation establishing the Bank of England and the New East India Company, who floated the useful expedient of Exchequer bills, and it was this ministry which, perhaps more by luck than good management, surmounted the great crisis of the recoinage in 1696. Somehow or other, by good discipline, parliamentary skill (in which again Montague shone) and fertile invention the money for the war was forthcoming until William was able to make at least an honourable peace.

In the General Election of 1695 the government had improved its parliamentary position, and the Junto especially pulled every available string with considerable success. As a result they were less willing than formerly to be content with a mere preponderance of offices and began to aim at monopoly. From the outset they had regarded their sponsor, Sunderland, with suspicion, and there was an endless tug-of-war with him over appointments and much furious in-fighting with his creatures, Henry Guy and the like. In February 1696 a plot to assassinate William was discovered. The government acted with decision and the danger was soon over: but the Junto now had a party opportunity that they could not resist. They proposed an 'Association', to which all office-holders must subscribe, for the defence of King and country; it included an affirmation that William was 'rightful and lawful King', an obvious arrow aimed against those Tories who had resisted that notion in 1689.[28] 'This is a conjuncture such as cannot be hoped for again', wrote one Junto adherent, and the Association was pushed for all it was worth.[29] Although the King would not give his Whig ministers the blank cheque for the proscription of Tories that they asked for, nevertheless the magistracy and the militia throughout the country were substantially purged of non-subscribers.

But there was an embarrassing aftermath. Sir John Fenwick, one of the plotters, alleged that Shrewsbury, Russell and others had been disloyally in touch with James II, and later in the year Shrewsbury, the vital honest broker between Sunderland and the Junto, insisted on retiring, despite the King's pleadings. With Shrewsbury lying doggo, Sunderland's relations with the Junto deteriorated sharply: the ministry was beginning to disintegrate.

At first sight this mattered less than formerly, for in September 1697 both sides in the war accepted the verdict of a draw and peace was signed at Ryswick. William and Sunderland mistakenly believed that this gave them more room for manœuvre and they could now mercifully reduce their reliance on the Junto Whigs. They were sadly wrong. William saw the peace as no more than a truce, and in these continuing conditions of cold war it was vital for England to keep up her military strength. But the country would have none of it. All the pent-up resentments of the country gentry at long years of high taxation to pay for new-fangled, not strikingly successful policies, burst out irresistibly. In Parliament the ministry was on the run, Sunderland hastily retired, and the country was in a ferment over William's attempt to keep a standing army in time of peace. Unluckily, at this juncture, under the terms of the Triennial Act, an Election in 1698 could not long be avoided. The last four years had shown how much in difficult circumstances a well-organised government, substantially based on party, could achieve. But now a price had to be paid for this success: the power of a disgruntled Parliament and political nation and the constraints on the post-Revolution monarchy were soon made plain.

The 1698 General Election was something of an oddity: this time the possession of office did not confer its usual decided advantage. The King was obviously temporising to see which way the wind would go, and the lack of royal support dispirited the ministers.[30] Moreover, by now politics had reverted from the recent classic conflict of Whig and Tory to the older, and potentially more dangerous, struggle of Court *versus* Country. For the fact was that since 1689 increasing numbers of men had been soured by the high cost of the war, its seemingly unrewarding outcome, and the wholly unacceptable prospect of a standing army in peacetime. By now a formidable Country opposition, based on a chronic distrust of King and Court and all their expensive works, had come into existence. It consisted of some old Tories seeking a new dynamic, renegade Whigs bitterly disappointed that their constitutional and other expectations in 1688 had gone astray, resentful ex-placemen, independent gentlemen who simply wanted lower taxes, and the habitual opposers who eyed all governments askance.[31] A hodge-podge marshalled with increasing dexterity by Robert Harley, himself a former Whig, into a furious Commons' majority determined on a 'Little Englander' programme of reduced taxation, no further continental commitments, and the humiliation of an alien monarch who did not hide his contempt for Englishmen and had outlived his usefulness.

The Junto ministers, publicly lashed as 'beardless politicians . . . upstart apprentices in business . . . who began like patriots, to conclude like parasites',[32] had fought the election doggedly and at least prevented a rout of their supporters. But they were under no illusions about future difficulties. Quite apart from domestic problems there was an extremely dangerous international situation. William did not intend to be thwarted in his life-time's purpose; he was already negotiating with France a partition of the Spanish empire to preserve the balance of Europe when the ailing Spanish King, who had no direct heir, should die. Undeterred by the collapse of his first arrangement, William later negotiated a second partition agreement with France: in both instances English ministers were consulted only to a limited extent.

It was soon clear that the King was badly out of touch with the parliamentary situation – the price of long absences abroad and his lack of real interest in English politics. William believed that it would be possible to persuade the Commons to agree to an army of 20,000 men: in fact the House was adamant for 7000 only. The King was furiously angry, spoke wildly of coming to 'resolutions of extremity'[33] (presumably a dramatic but scarcely seriously intended threat to abdicate), and insisted on his ministers returning to the charge again and again – a policy of attrition that failed dismally. The fact was that Harley and his supporters had wrested control of the Commons from the government. So gloomy were the Court's prospects that even Sunderland, usually endlessly fertile in expedients, was reduced to a pathetic Micawberism:

'as long as there is life there is hope, and whilst there is hope, accidents may happen and expedients may be found to prevent ruin'.[34]

As for the Junto ministers, they now had their backs to the wall and had to face the unremitting attacks of an opposition determined to punish them for engrossing too much favour to themselves for too long. Although they had to be dug out, one by one over the next two years they were prised out of office and ultimately impeached for the partition agreements for which they were only minimally responsible. Meantime, William tried to disarm criticism by moving the ministry into neutral and by recruiting innocuous mediocrities such as Bridgwater and Jersey: he was not, of course, deflected in the slightest from his main aims in international matters. These weak gestures at home had no effect; the continuing instability resulting from the absence for the moment of an effective party stiffening to the ministry was well described by Sir William Trumbull: 'We are like a rope of sand', he told young Henry St John, 'easily untwisted and no cement looked for to join us together.' The King's manœuvres, said Trumbull, illustrated the truth of 'a late maxim: that changing hands without changing measures is as if a drunkard in a dropsy should change his doctors and not his diet'.[35]

The Country opposition in Parliament continued to drive on furiously with a bill to resume William's notoriously lavish grants to his favourites of lands forfeited in Ireland. When for a time the bill hung in doubt, the opposition, mindful that a king's last argument is often the sword, moved that the army should be entirely disbanded. Finally, to William's disgust, the bill passed. The King was not far short of the last extremity. Through his agent Sunderland (who had soon returned unofficially to play) William tried to reach an accommodation with the opposition whose critical power was currently so evident; Godolphin and Rochester took office, but Harley, easily the most adroit of those who had so recently harassed the King, was content to take the Speakership after an Election early in 1701 had, if anything, reduced Whig strength in the Commons.

From the King's point of view, this makeshift administration was hardly a success. Certainly the Act of Settlement, vesting the throne in the Protestant Hanoverians in the event of the death of the successor, Anne, without further issue, was passed; but it included a great Country catalogue of protest against William's governmental practices since 1689 and humiliating prohibitions on their continuance. Moreover, as part of the bargain with his new ministers, William had agreed to summon

Convocation, the deliberative body of the Church of England. After the various efforts in 1689 to comprehend most Protestants in a broader national Church had failed, the less ambitious compromise of the Toleration Act had been agreed. For some time the King acted cautiously on the advice of the most moderate spokesmen of the Church and subsequently virulent clerical Toryism had been anaesthetised by allowing Convocation to lapse. Now in 1701 the Lower House immediately assailed the bishops, and a furious controversy, the preface to the even more bitterly disruptive one of Anne's reign, began.

Worse was to follow: the ministry's support in the Commons was a curious army of negatives united largely by grievances, a brittle party of fault-finders who were still hot in pursuit of the Junto and manifestly unwilling to face up to a thoroughly menacing international situation. At last Charles of Spain had died bequeathing his entire empire in the first instance to the French claimant, and Louis had accepted the offer on behalf of his grandson.

For William it was time to consider desperate remedies. Mercifully, Louis' arrogance was jolting even a purblind Commons to a sense of responsibility, and there were signs (admittedly partly stage-managed) in the Kentish petition, the 'Legion' letter and a hail of Addresses calling for war that the political nation was ahead of the Commons. By midsummer war was not seriously in doubt, but, horses for courses, it was perhaps time to call in the Junto again. Sunderland, inventive to the last, endorsed the proposal and quickly produced a scheme for a more efficient war administration. Somers, now clearly at least *primus inter pares* among the Whig leaders, pressed for a snap dissolution to make the projected ministry a tenable proposition.[36] The Election was inconclusive and, in consequence, the return to Whig party government was postponed, but the King was sufficiently encouraged to insist in his Speech to the new House that it was to be war in the old terms, on land as well as at sea. At the last, before he died, William had triumphed and Marlborough, his brilliantly successful heir as leader of the Grand Alliance, was already astir.

If the Civil War and the succeeding years of government by the sword represented the ultimate failure of the English political system, the Restoration was no more than an uneasy partial recovery, and it was not until after the Revolution, mercifully largely bloodless, that England had the chance to return to more civilised ways. It was not to be expected that so vague and so limited a compromise settlement would have produced political stability immediately, and of course it did not. Many difficulties in detail remained and only time and experience could suggest their solution, or partial solution. A monarch who could devote all his attention to England's insular concerns would have been at his wits' end to contain the remaining sources of discord in a political nation determined on further contention. It was not surprising, therefore, that William, who annexed England to the wider politics of Europe, had to cope with additional exceptional strains.

Considering the novelty of his policies abroad, their mounting cost, and the continuing absence of really heartening military success, William held England to his version of her proper place in the world surprisingly successfully, although it is fair to say that it was Louis rather than William who guaranteed England's resumption of the leadership of Europe in 1701. Despite a crude rule-of-thumb approach to English domestic politics, here, too, William had his successes: if trimming between parties produced a ramshackle divided administration, it at least kept the Tories, potentially the larger part of the nation, from extremity and a dangerous new truck with Jacobitism. Moreover, by dividing and confusing the Whigs, it helped to hold off a further remodelling of the constitution to the detriment of royal power; and when he could afford to be, William was every inch a king, even in some respects an authentic Stuart king.

But every obverse gain contained a reverse disadvantage, and the intra-ministerial strife of 1690 followed by the administrative near-collapse of 1693 made necessary at least an experiment with a qualified form of party government. This had the virtue of providing stable government in the most testing time of the war and it was not until after the peace that the price for this, as well as for William's other heavy demands on England, had to be paid in the dangerous confusions of the last years of the reign.

In some respects the King was unlucky: his Queen, who softened the xenophobia of the English, died off. There was no obvious or generally acceptable candidate for the vitally important office of chief manager, the King's effective proxy in the ruck of politics, particularly essential in view of William's absences abroad: Carmarthen was in the fag-end of his career, Halifax too detached to try; Sunderland succeeded substantially so far as his vulnerability would allow; Harley was still serving his apprenticeship. Furthermore, even when the King had accepted the necessity of employing a middleman to mediate between himself and the party leaders, he found that the latter soon chafed (as in 1696 and 1701) against the restraints such a system imposed on them. And the fact that the parties themselves remained for much of his reign in a state of flux, their ideological position partially confused in the aftermath of the Revolution, their lines of division criss-crossed by those of Court and Country, inevitably made stable government a more elusive goal for William III than for his successor.

Despite his genuinely noble purposes, William had his frailties. He indulged his private friendships too heavily at the public expense; he allowed personal antipathies to obtrude too much in his political dealings; occasionally he procrastinated when swift decision was called for; he was indifferent to the ceremonial of a monarchy which perhaps needed a touch of visible majesty. His foreign policy, though far-sighted in conception and not in conflict with Britain's long-term interests, was tactlessly executed. Clearly he made mistakes, and these mistakes made political stability more difficult to achieve. But they are scarcely surprising, least of all when it is remembered that, puny and ailing, he nevertheless fulfilled, for more than a dozen years, responsibilities shared subsequently by Marlborough, Godolphin and Queen Anne. Much of their brilliant success had its roots in William's time.

BIBLIOGRAPHICAL NOTE

The best starting-point is the superb introduction (the distillation of years of work in the field) to *English Historical Documents, 1660–1714*, ed. A. Browning (1953). Miss L. Pinkham's interpretation of the events of 1688 as a mere palace revolution – *The Respectable Revolution* (1954) – should be compared with the broader view of M. Ashley, *The Glorious Revolution of 1688* (1966). R. Walcott, *English Politics in the Early Eighteenth Century* (Oxford, 1956), has merit, but should be taken with reserve and consulted only after reading the heavy strictures on it in J. H. Plumb's fine monograph, *The Growth of Political Stability in England 1675–1725* (1967). S. B. Baxter, *William III* (1966), is an excellent man, scholarly and wide-ranging, whereas Nesca Robb, *William of Orange* (1966), vol. ii, is more restricted and personal. The best studies of individual politicians, the biographies of Sunderland, Danby and Nottingham, have been referred to in an earlier note (p. 112 above).

The recent publication of many of these books reflects the great renewed interest in the period, from which many important revisions have followed. On the other hand, T. B. Macaulay, *The History of England*, ed. C. H. Firth (1915), despite many attempted demolitions, remains easily the best narrative, and the scholarship of K. Feiling, *History of the Tory Party 1660–1714* (Oxford, 1924), has withstood magnificently the passage of time.

On more limited topics, G. V. Bennett, 'King William III and the Episcopate', in *Essays in Modern English Church History*, ed. G. V. Bennett and J. D. Walsh (1966), is a very good revisionist introduction to the religious history of the reign, and J. P. Kenyon, 'Lord Sunderland and the King's Administration, 1693–5', in *EHR* lxxi (1956), is of special importance for this essay. Also of value is A. McInnes, 'The Political Ideas of Robert Harley', in *History*, NS l (1965).

NOTES

1. *Correspondentie van Willem III en van Hans Willem Bentinck*, ed. N. Japikse (1928), ii, 13.

2. 'Read the annals of England . . . from 1681 to 1686 if there is any need to justify Whiggism', says *Party No Dependence* (1713), Bodl. Misc. Pamph. Mar. 842.

3. Ibid.

4. Technically William and his wife, Mary, were declared joint sovereigns in Feb 1689: but as the regal power was vested in William, the short-hand version is not incorrect.

5. G. Burnet, *A History of My Own Time* (1833), iv, 567.

6. Bodl. MS Locke C24, fo. 198: to Mordaunt, 21 Feb 1689.

7. *Wilhelm III von Oranien und Georg Friedrich von Waldeck*, ed. P. Muller (The Hague, 1880), ii, 210: William to Waldeck, 4 Feb 1690.

8. Bodl. MS Locke C7, fo. 210: 9 April 1698.

9. 'The State of the Parties' (*c.* 1692, anon.), in *State Tracts*, ii, 208.

10. *Miscellaneous State Papers 1501–1726*, ed. earl of Hardwicke (1778), ii, 401ff.

11. D. Defoe, *The Review*, ed. A. W. Secord (New York, 1938), v, 142.

12. H. C. Foxcroft, *The Life and Letters of Sir George Savile . . . Marquis of Halifax* (1898), ii, 'The Spencer House Journals', *passim*.

13. Sir J. Dalrymple, *The Memoirs of Great Britain* (1771–3), ii, app. pt ii, 120–3: the Queen to the King, 20 June 1690.

14. Nottingham Univ. Lib. Portland MSS: Sunderland to Portland, June [1693].

15. Ibid. 5 May 1692.

16. *The Anatomy of Parties* (1701), p. 102.

17. Foxcroft, op. cit. ii, 203.

18. Ibid. ii, 107, 221.

19. Dalrymple, *Memoirs*, ii, app. pt ii, pp. 84–95: Wharton to the King, 25 Dec 1689; W. Coxe, *Correspondence of Charles Talbot, Duke of Shrewsbury* (1821), pp. 14–16: 22 Dec 1689.

20. Foxcroft, ii, 202–3, 242, 244–6.

21. Japikse, op. cit. i, 95: William to Portland, 7 Feb 1690.

22. Burnet, iv, 73.

23. HMC *Downshire MSS* I, i, 380–1; *A Memento to Englishmen . . . a Call to their Duty*, Bodl. Pamph. 233; Dalrymple, *Memoirs*, ii, 188.

24. 'A Honest Commoner's Speech' (1692), in *Somers Tracts*, x, 324–31; Bonet's report in L. von Ranke, *A History of England* (1875), vi, 184.

25. Bodl. MS Locke C16, folios 113–14: 19 Nov 1692.

26. Nottingham Univ. Lib. Portland MSS: Sunderland's letters to Portland, 1693/4. The words quoted are in Sunderland's letter of 5 Aug 1694.

27. Ibid: to Portland, 13 July 1694.

28. *Parl. Hist.* v, 987.

29. HMC *Fitzherbert MSS*, p. 39: Sir Francis Drake to Lord Chief Justice Treby, 6 April 1696.

30. *Hardwicke State Papers*, ii, 433–6: Somers to Shrewsbury [Oct 1698].

31. A. Grey, *Debates in the House of Commons, 1667–94* (1769), x, 141, for the apt comment: 'If an angel came from Heaven that was a Privy Counsellor, I would not trust my liberty with him for one moment'.

32. 'A Letter to a Country Gentleman' (16 July 1698), in *Parl. Hist.* v, app. xv.

33. *Hardwicke State Papers*, ii, 362.

34. Portland MSS: to Portland, 9 Jan 1699.

35. Berks RO, Trumbull MSS Misc. Corr. (1685–1705), fo. 92: 9 Nov 1699.

36. *Hardwicke State Papers*, ii, 449–62: letters to and from Sunderland, Somers, the King and others for these negotiations.

6. Conflict in Society

W. A. SPECK

HISTORIANS frequently describe political struggles of the past in social and economic terms, even when those actively involved in them gave less material explanations of their own motives. Paradoxically, in the period 1689–1714, contemporaries often attributed the violence of their politics to economic rivalries which scholars have tended to discount. Above all, post-Revolution politicians claimed that the contest between Tory and Whig was exacerbated by a serious conflict in society between the landed and the monied interests. Yet Sir George Clark, an eminent authority on the period, has insisted that 'this conflict of interests . . . was almost fictitious'.[1] More recently Professor Lawrence Stone, while prepared to admit 'that there was severe friction between the landed and the monied interests during the wars with Louis XIV', nevertheless asserts that 'the conflict between the two interests . . . never remotely threatened to destroy the stability of the political system'.[2] This paper seeks to test these historical verdicts against contemporary evidence, and to answer the question: was the conflict between the landed and the monied interests in post-Revolution England a myth or a reality?

Before we can answer this question it is vital to define its terms. It has often been assumed that the two interests comprised all landowners on the one side, and all businessmen on the other. In fact by the 'landed interest' contemporaries did not mean landowners at large, but only those who lived exclusively on their incomes from rents, deriving no supplementary revenues from other sources such as office-holding, commerce or even the mineral resources of their estates. The 'monied interest' was an even more precise term. It referred not to traders and merchants in general, but to those elements in society who were involved in the new machinery of public credit which was created after the Revolution along with the setting up of the Bank of England in 1694. The Bank and the East India Company were the principal elements in this new system, and those who lent money to the government, especially through the holding of stock issued by the two corporations, together with those who handled their affairs on the Exchange – factors, jobbers and brokers – were all comprehended in the expression 'the monied interest'.

There can be no doubt that contemporary landowners thought that economic and political trends were benefiting the monied men at their expense. Country gentlemen looked askance at this powerful new interest based on money rather than on land. Its very novelty, coupled with its rapid progress, frightened them. In 1709 Henry St John referred to it as 'a new interest . . . a sort of property . . . not known twenty years ago, [which] is now increased to be almost equal to the terra firma of our island'.[3] Landed men found it difficult to comprehend the methods by which this had been achieved. To many of them the terminology of public credit – Bank stock, Exchequer bills, National Debt and so forth – sounded like baffling incantations chanted by a strange new sect practising its mysterious rites, while the mechanism of the system appeared to be a diabolical machine for creating wealth out of thin air. They were the more perplexed because their own alternative schemes to raise money from apparently more substantial terra firma – the Land Bank projects of the 1690s – foundered. Many suspected that fundamentally the monied interest was dishonest. Swift played skilfully on this ignorance and suspicion when he wrote: 'through the contrivance and cunning of stock-jobbers there hath been brought in such a complication of knavery and cozenage, such a mystery of iniquity, and such an unintelligible jargon of terms to involve it in, as were never known in any other age or country of the world'.[4]

The monied interest acquired a political influence commensurate with its new economic role. Government required the confidence of monied men to keep going the system of public credit, without which the national finances would collapse. Consequently financiers, though a tiny minority of the Commons, exerted an influence in Parliament quite disproportionate to their numbers. Despite being much the strongest element in the House, country gentlemen became apprehensive of the influence of the monied interest, and campaigned to preserve the power of the landed interest for all time by demanding property qualifications for M.P.s. In 1711 they succeeded in passing an Act which stipulated that knights of the shire were to have estates worth £600 per annum, while borough members had to own real estate valued at £300 per annum. St John, moving the commitment of the bill, stated that 'he had heard of societies . . . that jointed stocks to bring in members', and suggested that without it the time would come 'when the monied men might bid fair to keep out of that house all the landed men'.[5]

The men who supported the Property Qualifications bill did so because they believed, or were led to believe, that not merely were their interests threatened but that their very survival was at stake. At their most exaggerated these fears found expression in accusations that there was a deliberate design to ruin the landed interest by members of the government who were in league with the monied interest. Thus in 1702 Robert Harley was told: 'you certainly ruin those that have only land to depend on, to enrich Dutch, Jews, French and other foreigners, scoundrel stock-jobbers and tally-jobbers, who have been sucking our vitals for many years'.[6] In William's reign the King himself was accused of seeking to create a vested interest in his regime by diverting capital from land into government loans. Under Anne the main charges came to be directed against the duke of Marlborough, Lord Treasurer Godolphin and the Whigs, who were said to be deliberately prolonging the war of the Spanish Succession in order to enrich themselves and their monied friends. The argument ran that direct taxation of estates in order to pay for the war was bleeding the landed interest white, while those who lent money to the government were making handsome profits. Sir John Pakington vented his spleen on this subject in 1709 in an angry speech to the Commons which was subsequently printed and widely dispersed: 'if [a gentleman] speaks against the continuance of the war', he declaimed, 'to prevent the beggary of the nation, to prevent the monied and military men becoming lords of us who have the lands, then he is to be no object of Her Majesty's favour and encouragement'. Swift summed up the alleged conspiracy in *The Conduct of the Allies* when he wrote: 'We have been fighting to raise the wealth and grandeur of a particular family, to enrich usurers and stock-jobbers, and to cultivate the pernicious designs of a faction by destroying the landed interest.'[7]

Behind the arguments and the propaganda of politician and pamphleteer there lay genuine anxiety. To what extent the fears of the landed interest were justified can best be gauged by examining some of the economic facts of life between the Revolution and the Hanoverian succession.

To a generation that expressed profound belief in Providence, economic trends in the late seventeenth century might well have seemed to be fulfilling the Scriptural prophecy 'unto every one which hath shall be given; and from him that hath not, even that he hath shall be taken away from him'. The widening gap between those who had little and those who had much was particularly noticeable among the landowning classes. During the second half of the seventeenth century and the first half of the eighteenth the aristocracy and substantial squires tended to extend and consolidate their estates, while the bulk of the landed gentry found it hard to hold their own, and a significant minority were squeezed out of landed society altogether.[8]

This shift in the pattern of landownership is attributable to a variety of long-term economic tendencies. The larger landowners prospered to a slight extent through employing more professional methods of estate management, and because they had the capital to improve their estates; and to a large extent because they were in a position to raise money from sources other than land. Thus they cornered the more attractive bargains in the marriage market, engrossed the more lucrative posts in the administration, and invested surplus capital in the profitable public funds and private companies. The smaller landowners were finding the going tough, perhaps because the produce of their estates was not flexible enough to withstand violent price fluctuations and poor seasons, while a few fell by the wayside after a surfeit of conspicuous consumption provoked by a vain attempt to keep up with the more extravagant social standards set by the wealthier squires. The plight of the smaller landowners was worsened by their difficulties in tapping alternative sources of wealth and their increasing inability to maintain, let alone augment, their revenues from land alone. They lacked surplus capital to invest in profitable stock, and there were neither sufficient official posts nor enough well-endowed brides to rescue them from complete reliance on the resources of their own estates.

These resources were, unfortunately for them, shrinking. Three possibilities presented themselves to a landowner anxious to raise money from his lands: to increase rents, to mortgage or to sell. Between 1689 and 1714 all three were becoming less and less profitable.

During these years rents at best remained static, at worst declined. An investigation by G. C. A. Clay into lands owned by the Grimston family in East Anglia discovered that 'the course of rents on both Essex and Suffolk lands in the second half of the seventeenth century was uniformly downwards. The rent of every single farm . . . had to be reduced sooner or later.' Between the early 1660s and the late 1690s rents on the Grimston estate in Essex dropped by over a fifth. One holding – Rishangles – realised £481 15s. in 1662 and only £365 in 1698.[9] This fall in the level of rents was occasioned partly by the failure of tenants to make farming profitable and partly by a shortage of capital for investment in farms. The inability of tenants to pay their rents was a constant complaint of the gentry in this period. Many were unable to do so because poor harvests recurred with disastrous regularity in the 1690s, while a slight improvement early in Anne's reign was succeeded in 1709 by the biggest crop failure of the period. Tenants piled up arrears of rent which had all too often to be written off as they went bankrupt. The turnover of tenants in the late seventeenth century could be prodigious. A farm owned by the Grimstons had no fewer than ten between 1662 and 1700.[10] Other farms could not always be let immediately they fell vacant and were untenanted for months or even years.

Although legal devices adopted during the century had made it less hazardous to mortgage such lands than it had been earlier, during the period 1689–1714 there was a tendency to restrict mortgage loans because alternative investments were more attractive. And in any case the fall in rents depressed the amount which could be raised by mortgaging land no less than it reduced the price.

By Anne's reign contemporaries were convinced that the bottom was falling out of the land market. They calculated the price of land in terms of the number of years' purchase: that is, the purchase price divided by the annual value. In 1707 Lord Hervey wrote to a relative: 'I can have no thoughts of making any further purchases outright . . . the value of lands being so considerably fallen that those estates in this county [Suffolk] which I would formerly have given 20 years' purchase for, now go a-begging at 18, and I have actually refused to buy them so.'[11] Four years later the duke of Newcastle's agent observed that 'land about London and all other parts of England is fallen at least 4 or 5 years' purchase'.[12]

The fall in the price of land was not always reflected by a reduction in the number of years' purchase. Where it accompanied a drastic drop in rents it could even be concealed by an actual increase in the number. Thus the normal price of lands investigated by Dr Clay was about twenty years' purchase in the third quarter of the seventeenth century, and between twenty-three and twenty-five years' in the late seventeenth and early eighteenth centuries.[13] But when over the same period the actual annual value of land had been sharply reduced this still represented a real fall in price. Take Rishangles for example. If sold in 1662 at twenty years' purchase it would have realised £9620. Put on the market in 1698 at twenty-five years' it would have fetched only £9125.

Prospective buyers, therefore, paid particular attention to the level of rents before fixing on the number of years' purchase. If they felt that it had reached rock bottom they were prepared to go over the norm of twenty years' on the prospect of raising it. Certainly the biggest and perhaps the shrewdest speculator on the land market at this time was the duke of Newcastle. Between 1701 and 1711 he spent in the region of £250,000 on land. In an account of these transactions O. R. F. Davies observed:[14]

> In November 1709 he declined to buy an estate at 23½ years' purchase, which he wrote 'is far above the country rate and most especially for lands so lately improved to their utmost rent . . .' Earlier the same year he had agreed to pay 24 years' purchase for a manor worth £752 per annum on an agent's report that 'this estate is very improveable as it is. But if the rest of the freeholders . . . can be bought out this estate may be improved to above £1200 per annum at very little charge.' Twenty-four years' purchase was an exceptionally high price for Newcastle to pay. Twenty was more normal and sixteen not unknown . . .

The best prospects of improving rents at very little charge were afforded by estates which had been kept in first-class condition. As James Brydges informed a landowner anxious to sell in 1713:[15]

> Tis very true, Sir, I have given 22 years in some cases. But then it was where the houses & barns etc. were in good repair, & where there was some timber upon the ground, to make amend for the hardness of the bargain. Now in this case, as there is no help of the latter so the first is so far from being the condition of these farms that I understand I must expect to be at considerable expense in repairs, more than will balance the advantage I shall receive by the improvement of the rents when the leases come to be expired. All these considered make me judge 20 years' purchase a very reasonable offer, & I believe is rather more than land generally sells for in Herefordshire.

Well-maintained estates, however, were not common in this period because landowners were having difficulties in finding enough money to keep farm buildings in good repair.

A major reason why many landowners lacked capital to improve their estates in this period was that their incomes were being very heavily taxed. 'I believe all country gentlemen are under the like pressures and uneasiness', William Bromley wrote to James Grahme in 1707, 'and all cannot so well bear them. Tenants are breaking every day, and the quarterly payments of the taxes takes away the little money we receive.'[16] After the Revolution the land tax became the most important individual source of revenue to be annually voted in Parliament, calculated to bring in between £2,000,000 and £2,250,000. Originally designed as a tax on all property this was for all practical purposes a rate on land, fixed in 1693 by an assessment of rental value. In peacetime the rate was two shillings in the pound, though the assessment was more favourable to some areas, especially the north-western and south-western extremities of England. In wartime the rate was doubled to four shillings, and since rents did not rise until after the war of the Spanish Succession, then in those areas where the assessment had been reasonably accurate it really was a 20 per cent income tax on rents. The rate was kept at this high level from 1693 to 1713, apart from a brief interlude at the end of William's reign. This meant, to cite an example from Norfolk, that 'a higher rate of direct taxation on income was levied on the Coke estates under Queen Anne than ever again until the twentieth century'.[17] The landed interest, therefore, was not only feeling the squeeze of adverse economic trends but the bear hug of the land tax. As an Act of 1714 put it: 'The heavy burden of the late long and expensive war hath been chiefly borne by the owners of the land of this kingdom, by reason whereof they have been necessitated to contract very large debts, and thereby and by the abatement in the value of their lands are become greatly impoverished.'[18]

The preamble to the same Act continued with a pointed reference to another development which had a significant bearing on increasing social tensions in this period: 'by reason of the great interest and profit which hath been made of money at home, the foreign trade of this nation hath of late years been much neglected'. War and war finance were also responsible for this situation whereby many overseas ventures had become less attractive than domestic investments. Warfare adversely affected one branch of overseas trade directly through the rigid prohibitions on both sides of Anglo-French commerce, and some other branches through the activities of French privateers, which considerably increased the normal hazards of oceanic enterprise.[19] War finance was indirectly responsible since it tied up money in London which would normally have been channelled into other outlets. As a Member of Parliament complained in 1702, a 'merchant finds a better return between the Exchequer and the Exchange than he makes by running a hazard to the Indies'.[20]

In order to sustain the wars against Louis XIV the government had to raise vast sums on the money market – vaster sums, indeed, than ever before in English history. Loans were raised in immediate anticipation of revenues voted in Parliament, £1,850,000 being borrowed by the Treasury as soon as the land tax bill received the royal assent in years when the rate was four shillings in the pound. Money was also obtained on the security of remote revenues, and ultimately on confidence – public credit – alone. Of course governments had borrowed for centuries from private individuals and companies, and they continued to do so after 1689. Where pre-Revolution governments had tapped private wealth through intermediate channels, such as goldsmiths, after the Revolution they appealed directly to individuals, for example by offering annuities on loans. Thus a Tontine subscription was first organised in 1693. Lotteries were also held to divert private capital into public funds. Corporate wealth, too, was channelled directly into the Treasury. The East India Company was frequently tapped for loans in return for the confirmation of its privileges. During the 1690s, when there were two companies vying for the government's favours, the State received substantial sums from this source. Thus in 1698, when the 'New' company was incorporated, it lent £2,000,000 to the government, while in 1708, just before the rival concerns joined to form the United East India Company, a further sum of £1,200,000 was advanced.

Ad hoc negotiations between the Treasury and City financiers, however, proved inadequate to raise the unprecedented amounts required to combat France, and nothing less than a financial revolution was necessary to establish a permanent machinery of public credit. At the centre of this new system was the Bank of England. By the terms of its charter in 1694 the Bank advanced £1,200,000 to the government at 8 per cent interest. In 1709 an Act of Parliament increased its capital to £4,402,343 and authorised it to lend another £2,900,000.[21] In 1711 the financial mechanism was completed with the launching of the South Sea Company, which incorporated the government's short-term creditors and transformed some £9,000,000 of debt into the new corporation's stock.

The government's growing dependence on the City's three great monied concerns made their stocks the most coveted in the market. The fluctuations of the price of £100 Bank stock is perhaps the best indicator of confidence, since the competition of its rivals tended to depress 'Old' East India Company stock between 1693 and 1702, when the first step towards amalgamation with the 'New' company was taken, while the

South Sea Company was founded too late to influence the wartime money market. During its first two years of operations Bank stock never fell below par, while in January 1696 it stood at 148. Between 1696 and 1698 the country passed through a severe financial crisis, aggravated by the recoinage of the currency as well as by the pressures of war finance. Where many other ventures sank the Bank weathered the storm, though the price of its stock subsided and at the depth of the depression in February 1697 reached 62½. Towards the end of 1698 there was a recovery, and apart from a brief setback in 1701 Bank stock remained buoyant until 1704, when there was another recession for two years. Thereafter its price reflected a confident market, and it fell below par only once between 1707 and 1714, during the credit crisis of 1710-11, dubbed by contemporaries 'the famine of funds'.

During the period between the foundation of the Bank and the death of Queen Anne, therefore, there were fifteen years when prices for its stock were on the whole up, as against only five when they were down. The dividends from profits declared justified the confidence of proprietors of Bank stock, who regularly received a return on their investments, the lowest dividend in any one year, apart from the grim year 1696 when none was declared, being 7 per cent, and the highest 16 per cent. Returns on East India stock were more haphazard. After initial post-Revolution payments of 50 per cent in 1689 and 1691 there was no further dividend to stockholders by the 'Old' company until 1700, when a 10 per cent dividend was declared. In the last years of the company's life it paid out 8 per cent per annum. The complicated finances of the 'New' company make comparisons between it and other Corporations unsatisfactory, but after 1709 the United East India Company could offer enticing returns to proprietors of its stock. The first full year's dividend was 9 per cent, a figure repeated in the following year. After 1712 the company made dividends of 10 per cent per annum until 1720.[22]

The profits to be made from the institutions of public credit, therefore, made investments in them increasingly attractive in the period 1689-1714, especially as they came to be regarded as not only lucrative but secure. Many who might well have hesitated to advance money to earlier regimes, and with good reason considering the shaky credit of the Stuarts before the Revolution, could entrust their fortunes to the public with almost complete confidence under Queen Anne. By her reign this new phenomenon – what would now be considered gilt-edged securities – tempted anyone who had surplus capital to invest it in the public funds rather than in land. Lord Cowper was one of the many who yielded to the temptation. He kept the Great Seal from 1705 to 1710 and again from 1714 to 1718, and his income from office was considerable enough to provide him with ample opportunities for investment – in Anne's reign alone receipts from the Seal amounted to over £41,000. Yet he spent only £8084 on land between 1705 and 1718, keeping the bulk of his capital in paper securities.[23] Such affluence was relatively rare. Only the more successful members of the business or professional communities benefited from investments in the public funds; men such as the eminent lawyer Nicholas Lechmere and the enterprising coalowner James Lowther, who gambled shrewdly on the stock market in July 1711, when Lechmere wrote to his accomplice: 'South Sea stock gets ground . . . The ministry seem determined to exert all the powers of the Crown to give it credit. When they have made their best effort . . . 'twill be time for you and I to clear of them, & sell out.'[24] Similarly only the wealthiest landowners could afford to speculate with the funds. Thus among the Warwickshire gentry Andrew Archer, a country gentleman with an income of over £2000 a year, was almost unique in holding Bank and East India stock during this period.[25]

The wealthy few whose money was tied up in the new machinery of public credit numbered about 10,000, of whom roughly a third were proprietors of Bank and East India stock. An analysis of those who held stock in the two corporations in 1709 has shown how far they formed a monied interest distinct from the landowning section of society. Of the seventy-four men who held £5000 or more Bank stock, only three lived outside London and the Home Counties. The remaining seventy-one have been described as:

> a group of capitalists of international outlook and connections, and of mixed origins. A substantial minority were Huguenots and Jews, who were excluded from formal participation in local or central government. Nearly all were self-made men, whose vast wealth had been built up during the long wars since 1689. Even if it was not due to these wars, it must have been tempting to hostile critics to say it was.

Below these plutocrats was a solid body of a thousand or so men who held between £500 and £5000 in Bank stock. Even at this level there were very few landowners, the bulk being made up of merchants, financiers, office-holders and professional men, nearly all of whom lived in London and the Home Counties.[26] The monied interest was therefore overwhelmingly London-based, a phenomenon which did not go unnoticed at the time, when the term 'the City' began to be used to describe the business section of the capital.

The fiscal needs of government, then, produced a genuine rift between the two interests, which was not merely the product of contemporary imaginations. Indeed during the wars against Louis XIV these needs created a powerful force which counteracted the social forces binding those interests together. Even if these bonds had been strong they might well have snapped under such great strain; but there is reason to believe that in fact they were weak, and getting weaker. It is often alleged, for instance, that the distinction between the landed and the monied interests was socially and economically unfounded because the two were cross-fertilised by intermarriages and investments. Thus Professor Stone has asserted that 'the monied classes often used their wealth to buy land, the landed classes often used their children to marry money'.[27] Marriage and capital, however, did not mix into a social cement quite so easily.

Intermarriage between landed and monied families was almost certainly on the increase in the late seventeenth century. Superficially this suggests a breaking down of barriers, but it is vitally important to take into account the pattern of such marriages. Though it still aroused comment and provoked satire, it was by then socially quite acceptable for a landowner or his son to marry a City heiress. The availability as well as the desirability of wealthy brides to rescue impoverished gentry families from ruin is delightfully illustrated in the following letter which Sir William Massingberd, second baronet of Gunby, wrote on 3 May 1703 to his cousin Burrell, a fellow-commoner of Emmanuel College, Cambridge:[28]

> There goes a report about the country that you are courting a young lady. What truth may be in it, I know not. But before you engage in such a concern I hope you will seriously consider how far your own happiness, as well as that of your family, depends upon your discreet management of so important an affair . . .
> You are too well acquainted with the unfortunate circumstances of your family to stand in need of any information, and unless you marry a prudent person with a considerable fortune I fear you will let slip the most likely opportunity of retrieving it . . . A discreet wife with five or six thousand pound (and if she have more 'tis the better

still) would put you in a condition to pay your brother and sisters'
portions, clear the estate, furnish you wherewithal to build or repair,
and give you a comfortable prospect of living easy in the world. Such
matches there are to be had, and though you should stay a while
ere you meet with one, yet the future success would compensate for
the delay, and I believe you will grant that 'tis more eligible to be
happy at last than to repent at leisure. Tis your advantage I aim at in
what I write, though I must confess there is something of self-
interest too in the case, but no more than this (viz) that your welfare
will always contribute to my satisfaction . . .

Although clearly not averse to monied brides, Sir William had no time
for monied men. He rejoiced when the Property Qualifications bill
became law, and hoped another would be passed to qualify justices of
the peace 'for when landed gent[lemen] represent us in Parliament, and
do our business at home in the country, we may justly look for better
times, and that our tottering constitution may be once more fixed to the
confusion and amazement of all its adversaries'.[29]
Though it was permissible for landed men to marry money, landowners were not prepared similarly to barter their daughters. On the
contrary, for landed brides to marry monied men was socially out of the
question. Thus, though he had an unusually large family to provide for,
the earl of Nottingham made sure that all his daughters who married
contracted alliances with peers except one, and she became a baronet's
lady. These conventions go far to explain the inflation of marriage
portions which occurred during the seventeenth century, though
casualties inflicted by the wars and a tendency for more men to remain
bachelors might also account for the enhanced price of husbands in the
period 1689–1714. Their market value was rising so rapidly that
Governor Thomas Pitt, grandfather of the Great Commoner, was
advised in 1707 to dispose of his daughter as soon as possible since 'men
of estates are scarce, and women plenty, so that they do not easily go
off without a great deal of money, though they be never so virtuous and
pretty'.[30] In order to maintain their standing in society landowners were
obliged to marry their daughters into landowning families, but when
they put them on the marriage market they could find themselves in
fierce competition with monied men like Pitt, who had made a fortune
in the East India trade. Substantial landowners could match City
dowries pound for pound – it cost Lord Nottingham £52,000 to endow
his daughters[31] – but to save face many landed gentlemen had to cripple

themselves financially to provide competitive portions. To many a small landowner numerous female progeny spelt disaster. So far from being a cause of social harmony, therefore, marriages could provoke strident discord between the landed and the monied interests.

The land and money markets did not produce a harmony of interests any more than the marriage market. Capital was not flowing from land into the City, nor from the City into land, as readily as it had done earlier in the seventeenth century. Very few landowners, as we have seen, were investing in Bank or East India stock. At the same time, when such stock realised handsome dividends, land became an uninviting proposition for other investors. The duke of Newcastle's agent attributed the fall in the price of land to 'the great difference of advantage between money and land'.[32] Lord Hervey observed in 1707 'how much better money yields than land, which after taxes and repairs allowed never answers above 3 per cent'.[33] His observation was borne out by the experience of Lord Cowper, whose estates in Hertfordshire and Kent realised 'just under $3\frac{1}{2}$ per cent and just over 3 per cent according to the current rate of the land tax. By contrast Cowper's paper investments yielded between 4 per cent and 6 per cent, with the average about 5 per cent, and no deductions to be made for land tax and repairs.'[34]

The flow of money from the City into land seems to have been most restricted during the wars against Louis XIV. Where earlier in the seventeenth century monied men had featured very prominently in the land market, after the Revolution relatively few of them were concerned in the purchase of estates at a time when the funds offered more attractive returns on their investments. Consequently 'there was less interlocking of the two classes than there had been under Elizabeth and the early Stuarts'.[35] After the end of the Spanish Succession war the gap began to be bridged again as reductions in both the land tax and the rate of interest eased the burden on landowners, so that land became an attractive investment just at the time when the Property Qualifications Act obliged monied men to purchase estates if they wished to enter Parliament. The peaceful accession of the house of Hanover and the defeat of the '15 Rebellion doubtless helped to convert the trickle of money being invested in estates into a stream, by removing political uncertainties affecting the land market; but it became a flood in 1720 when the bursting of the South Sea Bubble shattered the early confidence in paper securities and led to a panic rush for less profitable but more secure investments in land.[36] Thereafter comparatively little is heard of an incompatibility of interests between monied and landed men except in the propaganda effusions of Country politicians.

The conflict between the landed and monied interests, therefore, reached its peak in the period which separated the Revolution from the Bubble. It was no mere coincidence that the same years witnessed the rise and fall of what came near to being a two-party political system. The Tories were linked by contemporaries with the landed interest, while the Whigs were associated with the monied interest.

Not that mere landowners were to be found exclusively in the ranks of the Tories, or that the monied interest was Whig to a man in the period 1689–1714. Since the landed interest formed the bulk of the political nation, no party could have existed without significant support from its members, let alone win elections as the Whigs did in 1695, 1698, 1708 and 1715. On the other side there were influential Tory financiers. The 'Old' East India Company was largely Tory, while Robert Harley drew on monied men with Tory leanings to launch the South Sea Company in 1711. Nevertheless the preponderance of the landed interest was Tory, while the monied interest was predominantly Whig. As one contemporary put it 'the majority of the gentry upon a poll will be found Tories'.[37] This conclusion can be tested from an analysis of election results in the counties, where the gentry held sway. Thirty-five of the county seats in England and Wales were held by the same party through seven General Elections between 1701 and 1715. Of these 'safe' seats thirty-one returned Tories and only four returned Whigs.[38] Though the Whigs were weak in the counties, they were strong in the City. The Bank was a Whig institution from its foundation, and while the 'Old' East India Company was linked with the Tories, the United Company fell into Whig hands at the start. Not only were the financial corporations directed by Whigs, but the principal subscribers and stockholders also seem to have been that way inclined. It is not too difficult to ascertain the politics of forty-two men who subscribed to the doubling of the Bank's capital in 1709, or who were leading holders of both Bank and East India stock at that date,[39] since they all sat in Parliament during Anne's reign. Of these monied men only seven were Tories.[40] Information about the political attitudes of others who invested in the public funds is not as readily forthcoming, but there seems no reason to doubt that there would be at least the same proportion of Whig investors outside as there was inside Parliament.

It was about 1709 that the conflict in society reached critical proportions. During the years 1708–10, when the Whigs were in power, the country gentlemen nearly reached their last gasp as the severest winter of the period was succeeded by the worst harvest. Meanwhile the Bank, following the doubling of its stock, made three dividends amounting over the whole year to 16 per cent, which easily beat all records in the century following its foundation. Tory gentry could scarcely blame the government for the crop failure – though Addison once caricatured a squire who remarked pointedly on the good weather they had enjoyed in Charles II's reign – but they did suspect the Whigs of cashing in on their distress. There was some foundation for these suspicions in 1709, when a House of Commons with the biggest business representation in the post-Revolution period, in which no fewer than eleven Bank Directors sat,[41] increased the rate of interest on loans advanced in anticipation of the land tax from 5 to 6 per cent. Thus the point at which the burden of the tax became most intolerable for those who paid it coincided with the point at which the return was made more attractive for those who lent on its security. It was no further coincidence that in the same year the cries that the government was deliberately prolonging the war for private gain and to the ruin of the landed interest began to be taken seriously.

The idea that where the landed interest was being crippled by the war other interests were gaining by it became a stock-in-trade of Tory complaints. Lord Nottingham grumbled about it to William Bromley in December 1708:[42]

I agree that we are not likely to have a peace, for the circumstances of our enemies are not yet such as that we may from thence hope for a good one and (bad as our condition is) this is a good reason for continuing the war. I wish there were no other reasons for it, but while it lasts 'tis plain some persons get immensely, and all inquiry into miscarriages is stopped by loud clamours that such proceedings would disturb the Queen's affairs and discourage our allies . . .

When Nottingham wrote those words he cannot have foreseen that France was so desperate for peace that by the following May she would agree to all but one of the peace preliminaries proposed by the allies at the Hague. The failure of the allies to make peace in 1709 was held by many to be due to their insisting upon terms in regard to Spain that France was manifestly unable to accept, which fostered the rumours that monied and military men were conspiring to perpetuate the war.

Though the conspiracy thesis was absurd, there was just enough connexion between the Whigs, the City and the 'hard' line on the war to

give it a specious plausibility. Certainly the monied men were not prepared to sacrifice the Spanish throne to the Bourbon candidate, while
the Tory gentry were so desperate for peace that they were ready to
recognise him as Philip V. Sir Gilbert Heathcote, Governor of the Bank
in 1709, was one of the leading Whigs in the House of Commons. After
the battle of Malplaquet Lord Treasurer Godolphin discussed with
him the circulation of more Exchequer bills on the strength of the
victory, and passed on to Marlborough remarks exchanged in their
conversation.[43] Heathcote said:

> 'Pray, my Lord, don't let's have a rotten peace.' 'Pray tell me,'
> I answered, 'what you call a rotten peace?' 'I call anything a rotten
> peace,' he said, 'unless we have Spain.' 'But, Sir Gilbert,' I said 'I
> want you a little to consider the circumstances of the duke of Marl-
> borough and me. We are railed at every day for having a mind, as
> they call it, to perpetuate the war, and we are told we shall be
> worried next winter for refusing a good peace, and insisting upon
> terms which it was impossible for France to perform.' He replied very
> quick, 'They are a company of rotten rogues that tell you so. I'll
> warrant you, we'll stand by you.'

Heathcote stood by Godolphin the following year to the extent of
waiting on the Queen, along with three of his colleagues, the day after
the Whig earl of Sunderland's dismissal to seek her assurance that there
would be no more ministerial changes. Their presumption scandalised
the Tories, who regarded it as proof, if proof were needed, that the
power of the monied interest had increased, was increasing, and ought
to be diminished. The four Bank Directors were unable, however, to
prevent the collapse of the Godolphin ministry and its replacement by
one determined to bring the war to a conclusion.

Thus the Peace of Utrecht owed something to the conflict in society.
The landed interest sought through the Tories to put an end to the
crushing burden of war taxation, and to the country gentlemen one of
peace's greatest blessings was a reduction in the land tax from four to
two shillings in the pound. The monied interest combined with the
Whigs to resist what they regarded as reckless moves towards peace at
any price.

The accession to office of a largely Tory ministry in 1710 precipitated
a crisis of confidence, and Harley had his work cut out until the spring
of 1711 to restore financial stability. This was the most significant
indication of how far the stock market had come to act as a sensitive

barometer of political confidence. Market reaction was particularly observable whenever confidence in the Hanoverian succession was shaken, it being generally agreed that the Pretender would repudiate the National Debt. During the Pretender's abortive invasion in 1708 panic hit London, there was a run on the Bank, all funds and stocks fell, and people were so anxious to realise their assets that the price of guineas rose by threepence. This occurrence gave substance to the nightmare which Addison depicted for the benefit of the *Spectator*'s readers in March 1711, wherein Public Credit shrank to nothing at the approach of the Pretender and gained health with the arrival of the Hanoverian successor.

Addison wrote his essay just before a bid by the Tories to wrest control of the Bank and East India Company from the Whigs. Mighty interest was made on both sides to procure a majority of directors. In the elections for the Bank 'Dr Sacheverell . . . not only qualified himself for voting by purchasing £500 [stock], but was very busy and industrious in soliciting for the cause'. On the Whig side Lord Hervey 'travelled all the night between the 11th and 12th of April from Newmarket to London to choose Governors and Directors of the Bank'.[44] His journey was not in vain, for he helped the Whigs to elect the Governor, Deputy-Governor and all twenty-four Directors. The Tories, thus routed, were not much more successful a few days later in the elections of directors for the East India Company, carrying only four to the Whigs' twenty. Thus the two great monied corporations of the City remained entirely under Whig control. It was partly to offset them with a Tory rival that Harley launched the South Sea Company on 1 May.

St John would have gone much further than this. He was prepared to smash the Whigs' hold on the City completely, as he later revealed:[45]

> We supposed the Tory party to be the bulk of the landed interest, and to have no contrary influence blended into its composition. We supposed the Whigs . . . to lean for support on the Presbyterians and other sectaries, *on the Bank and the other corporations*, on the Dutch and other allies. From thence we judged it to follow, that they had been forced, and must continue so, to render the national interest subservient to those who lent them an additional strength, without which they would never be the prevalent party. The view, therefore, of those amongst us who thought in this manner was to improve the Queen's favour to break the body of the Whigs, *to render their*

supports useless to them, and to fill the employments of the kingdom, down to the meanest, with Tories.

St John never got the chance to put this programme completely into action. Had he done so he might well have turned the conflict in society into civil war. The political sparks produced by the friction between the landed and the monied interests, therefore, were no mere flashes in the pan. On the contrary, their rivalry generated heat so fierce that it threatened to melt the foundations of the political nation.

BIBLIOGRAPHICAL NOTE

GENERAL
In general there has been more assertion than analysis. Geoffrey Holmes, *British Politics in the Age of Anne* (1967), ch. 5, 'The Clash of Interests', though it extends beyond the conflict between the landed and the monied interests, provides one of the few overt discussions of the problem. It amply demonstrates that 'politics after 1701 was materially affected by a clash of interests in society for which there were genuine and rational causes'.

THE LANDED INTEREST
H. J. Habakkuk, 'English Landownership 1680–1740', in *EcHR* x (1939–40), 2–17, was a pioneering article, the main conclusion of which, that the land market was dominated by big landowners who were consolidating their estates, was confirmed by the more detailed study of G. E. Mingay, *English Landed Society in the Eighteenth Century* (1963). W. R. Ward, *The English Land Tax in the Eighteenth Century* (Oxford, 1953), discusses the effects of taxation on the landed interest, though its usefulness is marred by vagueness on crucial points.

THE MONIED INTEREST
W. R. Scott, *The Constitution and Finance of English, Scottish and Irish Joint-Stock Companies to 1720*, 3 vols (1912), was an astonishing achievement of scholarship, invaluable as a quarry of information. Sir John Clapham, *The Bank of England*, 2 vols (1944), is the standard work on the main institution of public credit, while P. G. M. Dickson, *The Financial Revolution in England: A Study in the Development of Public Credit 1688–1756* (1967), admirably elucidates the complicated technical problems of finance.

NOTES

1. G. N. Clark, *The Later Stuarts*, 2nd ed. (Oxford, 1955), p. 36.
2. L. Stone, 'Social Mobility', in *Past and Present*, xxxv (1966), 157.
3. Bodl. MS Eng. Misc. e.180, fo. 4: to Lord Orrery, 9 July 1709.
4. *Prose Works of Jonathan Swift*, ed. H. Davis, iii (1940), 6–7.
5. *The Wentworth Papers*, ed. J. J. Cartwright (1883), p. 167: Peter Wentworth to Lord Raby, 21 Dec 1710.
6. HMC *Portland MSS* viii, 96: Anon to Harley, 10 March 1702.

7. *Prose Works*, vi (1951), 58–9.

8. See bibliographical note on 'the landed interest', p. 152 above.

9. G. C. A. Clay, 'Two Families and their Estates: the Grimstons and the Cowpers from *c.* 1660 to *c.* 1815' (Cambridge Ph.D. thesis, 1966), folios 60–1. I wish to thank Professor J. H. Plumb for drawing my attention to this extremely useful thesis, and Dr Clay for permitting me to draw on his conclusions.

10. Ibid. p. 63.

11. *The Letter Books of John Hervey, first Earl of Bristol* (Wells, 1894), i, letter 270: to John Hervey, 18 Nov 1707.

12. T. Lawson Tancred, *Records of a Yorkshire Manor* (1937), p. 231: W. Wenman to G. Wilkinson, 8 July 1711.

13. Clay, op. cit. p. 458.

14. 'The Wealth and Influence of John Holles, Duke of Newcastle, 1694–1711', in *Renaissance and Modern Studies*, ix (1965), 43–4.

15. Huntington Library, Stowe MSS 57, ix, 254: to Sir John Williams, 17 Nov 1713. Brydges was not merely driving a hard bargain, for a week later he told Captain Herring, 'by all I can understand land does not sell anywhere in Gloucestershire for above 20 years' purchase'. Ibid. 273.

16. Levens Hall, Bagot MSS: 11 Oct 1707.

17. R. A. C. Parker, 'Direct Taxation on the Coke Estates in the Eighteenth Century', in *EHR* lxxi (1956), 247.

18. 13 Anne c.15.

19. For a discussion of the effects of the wars on English trade see pp. 27–30, 32–4 above.

20. Bodl. MS Carte 117, fo. 177: 'The Speech of an M.P. on the malt tax, 19 Feb 1702'.

21. P. G. M. Dickson, *The Financial Revolution in England* (1967), p. 374.

22. For stock prices and dividends see W. R. Scott, *The Constitution and Finance of . . . Joint Stock Companies to 1720* (1912), ii, 179, 189, 206; iii, 244.

23. Clay, op. cit. pp. 181, 215.

24. Carlisle RO, MSS D/Lons.

25. A. M. Mimardiere, 'The Finances of a Warwickshire Gentry Family', *Birmingham H. J.* ix (1964), 134.

26. Dickson, op. cit. pp. 262, 265 (quotation), 267.

27. Stone, in *Past and Present*, xxxv (1966), 157.

28. Lincs RO, Massingberd MSS 20/43.

29. Ibid. 20/93: to Burrell Massingberd, 1 April 1711.

30. HMC *Fortescue MSS* i, 28: R. Raworth to Thomas Pitt, 7 Feb 1707.

31. H. J. Habakkuk, 'Daniel Finch, 2nd Earl of Nottingham: his house and estate', in *Studies in Social History*, ed. J. H. Plumb (1955), p. 159.

32. Lawson Tancred, op. cit. p. 231: W. Wenman to G. Wilkinson, 8 July 1711.

33. *Hervey Letter Books*, i, letter 270: to John Hervey, 18 Nov 1707.

34. Clay, op. cit. p. 188.

35. H. J. Habakkuk, 'English Landownership, 1680–1740', in *EcHR* x (1939–40), 17.

36. 'In the 18 months after the Bubble burst [Lord] Cowper spent £12,998 on lands, almost as much as in the previous thirteen years since he first took up office.' Clay, op. cit. p. 215.

37. Christ Church, Oxford, Wake MSS 17, i, fo. 243: W. Wootton to Wake, 21 March 1710.

38. The evidence on which these figures are based will be discussed in my forthcoming book *Tory and Whig: the struggle in the constituencies 1701–1715.*

39. See Dickson, op. cit. pp. 262–7.

40. Lords Ashburnham, Brooke, Delawarr and Leominster; Sir James Bateman, Benjamin England and Sir Thomas Powys. The William Bromley whom Dr Dickson identifies (p. 267) as 'the prominent High Tory . . . M.P. for Worcestershire' was in fact a Whig. His Tory namesake represented Oxford University.

41. G. Holmes, *British Politics in the Age of Anne* (1967), pp. 164, 172.

42. Leics. and Rutland RO, Finch Papers, vi, 23, fo. 77: 20 Dec.

43. Add. MS 9107, folios 60–1.

44. A. Boyer, *The Political State of Great Britain for 1711* (1718), p. 261; *The Diary of John Hervey first Earl of Bristol* (Wells, 1894).

45. Viscount Bolingbroke, *A Letter to Sir William Windham* (1753), pp. 19–22. My italics.

7. Conflict in the Church

G. V. BENNETT

IN the generation after the Revolution the Church of England was torn apart by a great conflict of parties. It was clear even to the most detached observer that her clergy and laity were involved in a radical reappraisal of the whole role of the national Church in English society. Their discontent, anxieties and confusion of purposes went far to provide the very stuff of political conflict. During Queen Anne's reign many of the great issues which agitated the statesmen and members of Parliament, and sharpened the pens of the newsmen and pamphleteers were, or purported to be, religious in character.

This essay attempts to penetrate beneath the slogans of 'High' and 'Low' churchmen to discover what was the nature of the great Anglican crisis after 1688. How did the Establishment weather the sea-change from the Stuart regime of personal kingship to the new age of party management? What effect did the Toleration Act have on the Church's authority and influence? How can we account for the seething discontent of the ordinary parish priests? How was it that an Anglican divine could by a single sermon in 1709 throw the whole world of politics into violent motion? It is these questions which we must now attempt briefly to answer.

Preaching in 1661 at the consecration of a new bishop, Dr Robert South expressed succinctly the political faith of the Restoration Church:

> The Church of England glories in nothing more than that she is the truest friend to kings and kingly government, of any other church in the world; that they were the same hands that took the crown from the King's head and the mitre from the bishops.[1]

After all the disasters of the Civil War and the Commonwealth, as by a miracle, the hereditary monarchy and the Anglican order of the Church had been re-established. Few doubted that in the future they would stand or fall together. The divines accepted without hesitation their role as servants of a regime of personal monarchy and as advocates of an authoritarian view of society. The national Church was cherished as a bulwark against civil strife and religious anarchy. As a class the clergy became deeply committed to a high religious theory of kingship. Each 30 January, the anniversary of the execution of Charles I, and each 29 May, the day of his son's return, the pulpits thundered forth the doctrines of the divine hereditary right of kings and the utter sinfulness of resistance to their commands. The most single-minded of the servants of the House of Stuart was undoubtedly William Sancroft, archbishop of Canterbury from 1677 to 1691, a man who combined an almost mystical reverence for monarchy with a passion that the influence of his Church should be extended. In the great struggle between King Charles II and those who sought to exclude from the succession his Roman Catholic brother, James, duke of York, Sancroft was immovable in the duke's cause. After 1681 he united with Court politicians, and especially with the Hyde brothers, the earls of Clarendon and Rochester, to build up a strong Yorkist party. When the King created an Ecclesiastical Commission to advise him on all senior appointments in the Church, the archbishop used it as an instrument to promote only those of proved loyalist opinions.[2]

In return for so energetic a contribution to the Stuart cause, Sancroft hoped that a revived and strengthened prerogative might be put to work to serve the Church. Closely associated with a religious theory of kingship was a religious interpretation of human society and social obligation. With obedience to kings went reverence and submission to parsons and squires, to fathers and employers. Indeed loyalist doctrines tended to the position that all rightful authority was a reflection of God's providential rule of the world, and that disobedience was sinful in character. Sancroft's voluminous papers reveal how thoroughgoing were his efforts to refurbish Anglican discipline over the nation. Many of his projects were reminiscent of those of Laud; and he was anxious to increase the reputation, learning and income of the parish priests who were to be the agents of this policy. His greatest concern was with the Church courts. It is commonly stated by historians that after 1660 the ecclesiastical courts were never able to recover the vigour of their jurisdiction, but the evidence is quite otherwise. Perhaps a few technical questions they did yield to Chancery, but Restoration common-law judges showed a far greater readiness to lend their assistance to the ecclesiastical system than had their early-seventeenth-century predecessors. The consistory court of a bishop or the court of an archdeacon dealt with a wide range of matters which would now be considered wholly civil: matrimonial causes, probate, tithe and even cases of brawling or unseemly conduct. They also exercised a comprehensive control over the morals and religious duties of the laity. Once a year the churchwardens of every parish had to 'present' to the archdeacon all moral offences and all cases of ecclesiastical neglect. It was open to any private person to 'promote the office of the judge' and accuse his neighbours of similar defects. In fact the records of the Church courts after 1661 abound in the moral offences of the laity: adultery, fornication, begetting bastard children, blasphemy and acting as physician, midwife or schoolmaster without proper episcopal licence. Ecclesiastical offences were even more frequent: not coming to church on Sundays, working on holy days, not receiving the sacrament at Easter and not sending children or servants to be catechised.

It is important not to underestimate the effectiveness of this Anglican discipline. Doubtless there were abuses, but the profession of ecclesiastical lawyers flourished, and careful manuals were written of their practice. The courts were certainly not without sharp teeth; and their chief sanction, the excommunication of an offender, had serious consequences for any man of position. An excommunicate could neither make a will nor bring an action in a civil court, and he could not qualify himself for public office under the Test and Corporation Acts by receiving the sacrament of Holy Communion. If the ecclesiastical judge 'signified' him to the secular authority he could be imprisoned until submission. What Sancroft's policy achieved, when the government lent its aid, was impressive. In 1676 two country parsons recorded their figures of Easter communicants. William Sampson, rector of Clayworth, Nottinghamshire, was a grasping, ungenerous man for whom his parishioners can have felt little affection, yet he noted the names of no less than 200 communicants where only 236 persons were of an age and qualified to receive the sacrament. Between 1676 and 1686 his numbers remained constant at this high level. In the Kentish village of Goodnestone the curate, Francis Nicholson, recorded 128 persons who communicated out of a possible 144.[3] The year 1676 was, of course, a time when the government of Danby was lending its full support to Anglican efforts, but the fact remains that when virtually the whole population of a village from the squire down to the labourers and their wives knelt at the altar rails, the power of the Church, at least in the countryside, was still strong.

The Anglican scheme possessed one fatal flaw. Both Charles II and his brother were earnest in their endeavours for a toleration. Perhaps the

King may have had some sympathy with Roman Catholicism, but it is extremely unlikely that he would have risked bitter resentment and divided politics on this count alone. The explanation of his strangely ambivalent attitude towards his Anglican subjects must surely lie in his fear of becoming utterly dependent on the body of churchmen who monopolised office, lay and clerical, throughout the country. A tempting alternative policy was to endeavour to raise up a new 'King's party' out of the minority groups of Restoration England – Roman Catholics, dissenters and former Cromwellians – and to unite them under the banner of a toleration granted by an exercise of the royal prerogative. It was a dangerous course, and in 1672 Charles's Declaration of Indulgence precipitated a grave political crisis from which he emerged defeated and humiliated. Under Danby the alliance with the Church had been patched up again, but influential Anglicans always recognised that the royal desire for a general toleration posed a serious threat to their ecclesiastical polity. Their position was especially difficult at a time when educated opinion was hardening against the coercion of respected and peaceable dissenters. It thus became their tactic to counter every suggestion of a 'toleration' with an offer to consider a 'comprehension'. A toleration would obviously shatter the whole disciplinary machinery of the national Church, but a comprehension would at least preserve the theory that all citizens came under the aegis of ecclesiastical authority. Thus at all moments of political crisis discussions were held with leading dissenters with a view to relaxing the stricter terms of membership of the Anglican Church: ceremonies were to be optional, oaths and subscriptions attenuated, and easy conditions laid down by which nonconformist ministers might receive preferment and benefices. Comprehension was always the policy of avowed High churchmen such as Daniel Finch, earl of Nottingham; and Sancroft lent the notion his support. Its underlying aim was to comprehend all moderate dissenters in the Church of England, but then to continue the persecution of obdurate sectaries or admit them to only the barest form of a toleration.

The blow which ruined everything was struck by King James II. When the duke succeeded to the throne in 1685 Sancroft and his friends staked everything on his willingness to work with and through Anglicans, and they were not without reason for their hopes. Although an emphatic and devout Roman Catholic, James had repeatedly promised his many Anglican allies that he would 'support and defend' their Church. During the time of his 'personal rule' in Scotland he had associated himself firmly with the episcopalian party. But from 1686 the King reversed his whole policy and attacked the Anglican regime in both Church and State. In April 1687 his Declaration of Indulgence decreed that 'all and all manner of penal laws in matters ecclesiastical for not coming to Church or not receiving the sacrament, or for any other nonconformity . . . be immediately suspended'. Whatever the legality of such a declaration, its effect on the Church of England was immediate and catastrophic. From the summer of 1687 the whole class of business in the Church courts concerning attendance at church drops away, and the number of moral cases against the laity perceptibly diminish. Amid the collapse of their whole scheme of things, Sancroft and his brethren hoped desperately that the King might come to his senses and return to his Anglican alliance. As reports came up to them from the dioceses of the full extent of the ecclesiastical revolution, they found themselves moved, however unwillingly, to protest. The famous petition of the Seven Bishops was an uneasy bid by a group of Court loyalists to save the authority of their Church by warning the King and calling him back to the path of moderate authoritarianism. Yet, even when their master had them publicly prosecuted and tried for sedition, they prayed and looked for a reconciliation with him. The invasion of William of Orange and James's flight to France brought them no joy; it was the final stroke which laid in ruins their whole concept of the alliance of Church and State.

The events of the Revolution put the clergy under the severest strain. Although the Tory lay politicians did their best to secure some formula which would satisfy the old beliefs about kingship, the outcome was stark. In March 1689 the throne was declared to be vacant, and a resolution of both Houses of the Convention Parliament offered the crown jointly to William and Mary. New oaths were prescribed by statute to be sworn by all office-holders and by all beneficed clergy. Private diaries and surviving correspondence attest the agony of spirit endured by those faced with the oaths to the new rulers. Could Anglican divines disavow their preaching for a generation? Was not James II rightful king still, and was not the Revolution a prime example of rebellion and resistance? If they thus shifted their allegiance, where stood now the religious view of society and social obligation? For some their course was clear. Archbishop Sancroft refused by word or action to acknowledge the new regime; five of his episcopal brethren followed him out into the wilderness of deprivation and poverty, and just over 400 of the clergy. The Nonjurors were few in number, but their effect on the great body of conforming Anglicans was profound: they were like a ghost of the past, confessors who stood in the ancient ways, devout, logical and insistent. For the Nonjurors the conforming Church of England was no true Church at all; it had apostatised from its distinctive doctrines by adhesion to a usurper. Men such as George Hickes or Henry Dodwell, who had given up everything in the cause of loyalty, treated conformists with an angry contempt. The majority of the clergy took the oaths, usually on the casuistical argument that they would obey William as *de facto* king, but continue to honour James as their *de jure* prince. Most went into the new era with deeply uneasy consciences. They sought around nervously for some theory or formula by which they could preserve as much as possible of the old ways of thought in the conditions of a changed age.

During the course of the year 1689 it became possible that there might be a total rupture between King William and the clergy. The new monarch was a convinced Dutch Calvinist; on previous state visits to England he had joined in the worship of the established Church, but in Holland he had clearly resented the services in Mary's Anglican chapel and he had bullied and harassed her chaplains. Once in England he acted with great unwisdom; he received prominent dissenters with cordiality and dropped them hints of a comprehension on the terms 'wherein all the Reformed Churches do agree'. By the summer, churchmen were deeply suspicious, and were already planning defensive action in Parliament. But suspicion turned to grievance and anger when in July it became known that William had consented to an Act of the Scottish Parliament which abolished prelacy and established a Presbyterian church-order. In fact the King had little choice in the matter: episcopal authority in Scotland had always been weaker than in England, and almost to a man the Scottish bishops had refused the new oaths. Now the episcopalians went out, a tiny, persecuted, Jacobite remnant. It was perhaps inevitable that the King should receive the blame for their sufferings. Before 1688 there had at least been the appearance of ecclesiastical unity in all the three kingdoms. Now Anglicans saw their church-order diminished to England and Wales, with the precarious outpost of the Church of Ireland.

That the situation did not deteriorate into an open clash was due primarily to the timely intervention of the earl of Nottingham, who in the autumn of 1689 persuaded William to reconsider his policy and accept an alliance with moderate Tory churchmen. Nottingham was a politician of an impeccable Anglican and royalist background. He had never been close to the Yorkist party of Sancroft and the Hydes, and his particular brand of churchmanship laid more store by theology and the laws of England than high-flying political theory. But a feature of the Finch family was the way in which they had built up an important and distinguished connexion of London clergy who looked to the earl as their patron and mentor. As William's Secretary of State Nottingham was able to offer the King a useful alliance with moderate-minded but indubitably Tory politicians and divines; and it was this which William eventually had the wisdom to accept. Bishop Burnet put the point clearly: 'I reckon that I do not exceed the severe rules of history when I say that Nottingham's being in the ministry, together with the effects which it had, first preserved the Church and then the Crown.'[4] In the two years following the Revolution an unprecedented series of vacancies occurred in bishoprics and deaneries, by death and by the refusal of Nonjurors to take the oaths. With the notable example of Nottingham's close friend and ally, John Tillotson, who became archbishop of Canterbury in 1691, the places were filled by moderate Tories, men of real distinction and learning. It is often said that King William packed the episcopal bench with 'Whig Latitudinarians', but the evidence is quite otherwise.

The most delicate question of the year 1689 was that of the degree of toleration to be allowed to the dissenters. Its solution was strangely unsatisfactory. On 27 February Nottingham introduced two bills into the House of Lords: one for a comprehension, the other for a toleration. The two were designed to go together. The first laid down generous terms by which dissenters might be admitted to the Church of England, while the second provided carefully limited terms for the toleration of the relatively small number who would not allow themselves to be so comprehended. On 14 March both bills received a second reading. But two days later King William made a grievous error. Without testing the opinion of his Tory ministers, he appeared in the House of Lords and proposed the abolition of the Test and Corporation Acts. Anglican anger and alarm were difficult to keep within bounds. Not only was the King's proposal overwhelmingly defeated, but the Comprehension bill itself was lost, and the Toleration bill alone went on to become law. The result was that the new Act, which had been designed to deal with a small number of intransigent nonconformists, now had to apply to nearly half a million sober and respectable citizens. It was a modest document. Dissenters who took the oaths of supremacy and allegiance and made the declaration against transubstantiation were allowed to worship separately in their own meeting-houses. Ministers had to subscribe to such of the Thirty-nine Articles as did not directly concern church-government, and all places of worship had to be registered with a bishop or at the Quarter Sessions. Services had to be conducted with the doors unlocked. No mention was made of permission for dissenting education; and nonconformists still laboured under the disabilities of the Test and Corporation Acts. The Toleration Act specifically laid it down that the old laws about attendance at church on a Sunday still applied to those who did not resort to a licensed meeting-house. But it was clear that such stringent provisions could not stand, and in the autumn of 1689 Nottingham attempted to revive his comprehension project. A royal commission was set up to prepare a scheme which should be laid before the Convocation of Canterbury. The commissioners laboured hard and produced a carefully devised but generous set of proposals which owed their inspiration above all to the Secretary of State's friends. But when the Convocation met all his plans came to nothing. The ordinary parish clergy had elected some of the most intransigent of their brethren to represent them in the Lower House, and the word went forth that there was to be no change in the formularies of the Church of England at the will of a Calvinist foreigner. In opposition to Nottingham's candidate for the chair the lower clergy proceeded to elect Dr William Jane, canon of Christ Church, Oxford. His forthright speech and his rousing cry of *Nolumus leges Angliae mutari* spelt the doom of comprehension. Without delay, and with his ministers' ready consent, the King brought the sessions to an end. So truculent an assembly was clearly too dangerous in an ecclesiastical situation of such delicate balance.

The result was that the meaning of the Toleration Act was always in doubt. Although the clergy professed to stand by its strict provisions, it was interpreted quite differently by the government and by the great majority of ordinary lay-people. Churchwardens and others insisted on regarding the Act as a statutory continuation of the state of affairs which had existed since James II's Declaration of Indulgence. The wardens of Ditton in Surrey may be taken as typical. When chided by the archdeacon in 1690 as to why they had not presented absentees from church, they replied defiantly: 'liberty of conscience being allowed by the supreme authority, we have nothing of neglect or defect to present'.[5] Another archdeacon, that of Norwich, complained bitterly that the Toleration Act had not so much given a liberty to dissenters as destroyed any control he could exercise over churchgoing:

The mischief is, a liberty being granted, more lay hold of it to separate from all manner of worship to perfect irreligion than go to the [meeting-houses]; and although the Act allows no such liberty, the people will understand it so, and, say what the judges can at the assizes, or the justices of the peace at their sessions, or we at our visitations, no churchwarden or constable will present any for not going to church, though they go nowhere else but to the alehouse, for this liberty they will have.[6]

Obviously where squire and parson united to bring social pressure to bear on a rural community, something of the old order endured, but in the absence of a Sir Roger de Coverley congregations decreased year by year. After 1689 Parson Sampson's Easter communicants at Clayworth diminished remorselessly; and in 1701, the last year of his records, they had fallen to 126 souls. A generation later an energetic vicar, such as Thomas Leigh of Lower Heyford, Oxfordshire, had to rest content with an average of only twenty of his parishioners at the Easter sacrament, out of a qualified population of 220.[7]

The evidence is clear that the middle years of King William's reign provided bitter conditions for the parochial clergy. The number of licences taken out under the Toleration Act was a great surprise. In the first year of its operation 796 temporary and 143 permanent meeting-houses were licensed, and the Quakers set up an additional 239. In the years from 1691 to 1710 no less than 2536 places were licensed.[8] Many of these would have been private houses or temporary structures, but up and down the land parsons were facing a new and disturbing phenomenon: a local dissenting congregation meeting openly and competing with them for the minds and hearts of their parishioners. A different but equally heavy cause of grievance was the flood of heterodox and anti-clerical literature which now poured onto the popular bookmarket. In 1695 the Licensing Act expired. Pamphleteers still had to walk circumspectly when writing on political questions, and until well into the eighteenth century it was a hazardous business to defame ministers of the Crown, but heresy and attacks on the clergy became virtually unpunishable. Deists such as John Toland, whose *Christianity Not Mysterious* caused such a scandal in 1696, could publish without fear; and Socinians such as the indefatigable Thomas Firmin or plain anti-clericals such as Anthony Collins, Matthew Tindal or Charles Blount had been given their freedom. The Blasphemy Act of 1697 was passed as some defence against the new writings, but proved a dead letter from the start. Bishop Burnet described how 'it became a common topic of discourse to treat all mysteries in religion as the contrivances of priests to bring the world into a blind submission to them; *priestcraft* grew to be another word in fashion, and the enemies of religion vented all their impieties under the cover of these words'.[9] Even this might have been supportable had there not been a serious decline in the economic position of the clergy. Clerical poverty was no new theme, and it was a recognised fact that a poor parson who could not buy books, distribute charity or keep his family above servile labour could not command the respect of rustics nor do effective work among them. Throughout the Restoration era great endeavours had been made to raise and augment the incomes of benefices by a host of sympathetic patrons and benefactors, but this work was now undone. During the period from 1689 to 1702 no less than £58 million was raised in taxation, mostly through the land tax. The parson who lived mostly off the profits from land, by his tithes and glebe, had to pay on a major part of his income. In addition tithes were assessed to the poor-rate, and the various attempts during the 1690s at a poll tax gave clergymen a high rate of payment. By 1697 beneficed clergy were paying between a quarter and a third of their income in some kind of tax or levy. Writing in 1704 of the bitterness of party conflict, Charles Davenant remarked shrewdly that 'the scandalous poverty of the clergy has very ill effects'.[10]

That this bitterness and sense of betrayal among the ordinary parsons could easily become the matter of political agitation was readily apparent, and the Williamite bishops made great efforts to turn their clergy's attention to pastoral concerns. A new vigour came into the episcopal office. Archbishop Sharp of York and bishops Burnet, Stillingfleet, Patrick and Kidder travelled to remote corners of their dioceses which had scarcely ever before seen a confirmation service; episcopal visitations enquired into negligent incumbents, and unauthorised pluralists and absentees were called to account. The rise in standards was perceptible, but the process was scarcely a popular one. Burnet in particular handled his diocesan clergy with less than tact and earned a deep and lasting dislike. But the 1690s did see the beginnings of a spiritual revival. In 1695 Thomas Tenison succeeded Tillotson in the primacy, and under his direction a new policy began to emerge. Tenison was a dull and prosaic man, and yet by any account he was a great archbishop. He realised plainly that the Church of England could now expect little from the government, and that any increase in spiritual effectiveness would have to come from voluntary action. As vicar of St Martin-in-the-Fields he had shown an immense compassion for the poor and unchurched of his vast parish, and he had been a pioneer in voluntary relief work. Now in the middle years of William's reign a host of 'societies' sprang into existence, of which the Society for Promoting Christian Knowledge and the Society for the Propagation of the Gospel were to be the most notable. Missionaries were dispatched to the American colonies and a network of Anglican 'charity schools' covered the country. Cheap religious tracts were printed and circulated, and 'societies for the reformation of manners' attempted to supply the place of the ecclesiastical courts by initiating prosecutions for immorality under existing statutes. It was clear that a great and critical choice lay before Anglicans. Were they ready to accept the place in English society of a basically voluntary body working within the legal conditions of the establishment or were they going to agitate for a return to the past when Church and State had conjoined in a single authoritarian regime?

The dilemma was not, however, one for the clergy alone; nor could it be resolved on grounds of pastoral expediency. Inexorably the Church was drawn into the political conflict, and into an increasingly fierce differentiation of parties. After the Election of 1695 the King reversed his former Tory policies and put himself into the hands of the earl of Sunderland and the Junto group of Court Whigs; and there came into existence a powerful Country party, consisting of a union of 'Country Whigs' and Tories. It was an opposition coalition which thrived on discontent, and the grievances of the clergy were grist to the political mill. Thus from about 1697 there may be seen the formation of a 'new High Church party' as an aspect of that 'new Tory party' which attacked King William's ministers so remorselessly. The recruitment of clerical propagandists for the cause was no haphazard affair, and all was done under the supervision of the earl of Rochester, now a leading Opposition figure. Bishops Compton of London, Trelawny of Exeter and Sprat of Rochester, three survivors of the pre-Revolution regime, lent him their counsel and aid. Dean Henry Aldrich of Christ Church supplied to the fight a number of energetic and eminently literate young divines, and from Oxford came Francis Atterbury, a brilliant student of the House and soon to be the stormy petrel of the High Church movement.

In 1697, with the verve of the born journalist that he was, Atterbury launched on its way the pamphlet which began the famous Convocation controversy, and from which so much political division was to flow. The argument of *A Letter to a Convocation-Man* was ingenious and cleverly designed to fit in with the mood of the ordinary clergy. It rehearsed all the grievances of the Church, and not least the growth of heresy and blasphemy; and it demanded as the only remedy a sitting and acting Convocation. This was called for not as an act of grace, but as a legal right of the clergy of England. What Atterbury challenged was the King's right to silence and ignore the Church's own deliberative and legislative assembly. He did not rely on any theoretical notion of ecclesiastical independence of the civil power, but based his case on an elaborate review of English constitutional history and legal precedent. He was attempting to invoke the Church's 'rights, powers and privileges' under the legal terms of her establishment. No-one doubted the political object in view, and Archbishop Tenison knew that he had every reason to be deeply apprehensive of an assembly which would have a majority of clergy in the Lower House who would be hostile to the government and imbued with a swelling sense of their own grievances. At once the primate summoned to his aid some of the most notable medieval historians of the day, William Wake, Edmund Gibson and White Kennett; and it is certain that their historical case – that the summoning and licensing of a Convocation was entirely in the King's prerogative – was by far the better one in point of scholarship. But Atterbury's case was by far the more welcome to the country parsons; his books and pamphlets were distributed through the dioceses by willing helpers, and he became a popular hero and a champion. When in 1700 the Junto ministry finally collapsed and William had to admit Rochester and his allies to office, one of their prime conditions was that a Convocation should be allowed to sit and debate. It was at this point that the contest between High and Low Church really began. The meetings in the early months of 1701 saw some scenes of unbelievable disorder: the primate was personally insulted and his authority defied. The Lower House launched itself on an angry enquiry into heretics and their books, and efforts were made to begin a process against Bishop Burnet for some passages in his commentary on the Thirty-nine Articles. As the presbyters turned to an attack on the former administration, the session had to be prorogued in a state of total breach between the bishops and the lower clergy. Tenison and his colleagues found themselves looking to Lord Somers and the Whigs for support, while the majority of the Anglican priesthood looked eagerly to the Tory politicians to vindicate their cause, relieve their sufferings and lead them back to that fair country where they had dwelt before 1685.

The accession of Queen Anne in March 1702 raised Tory hopes immensely. Here was a devout and earnest Anglican churchwoman; her heart was, as she assured her first Parliament, 'entirely English'; and she was the daughter of an hereditary king. In her honour the old loyalist doctrines were quickly revived and the whole Church looked, as Archbishop Sharp expressed it, for a new 'nursing mother'. But in spite of her new Tory ministers and her gracious expressions of favour for the clergy, it was unreal and fanciful to imagine that Anne was about to inaugurate a period of Anglican reaction. One facet of her character was an acid dislike of factious clergymen or of any discord in religion. Her chief minister, the earl of Godolphin, was devoted to the great task of providing for Marlborough's campaigns in Flanders; and he had no intention at all of encouraging party strife at home. It thus turned out that the High Church agitation had to develop as an opposition to the moderate and conciliatory policies of the Queen and her ministers, Godolphin and Robert Harley. Rochester and Nottingham were soon forced out of the ministry and into an attack on their erstwhile colleagues, at first covertly but increasingly openly. While Marlborough was consistently successful in his campaigns, opposition was not easy, and only the emotional issue of the Church had the power to engage the support of the great mass of country M.P.s.

The vexed question of occasional conformity lay most easily to hand. Under the Test and Corporation Acts any person appointed to a place of trust under the Crown or to any municipal office had to receive the Holy Communion according to the Anglican rite and obtain from the officiating minister a qualifying certificate. On re-election or reappointment another certificate had to be acquired. The device was plainly intended to exclude all non-Anglicans from public office, and it did effectively exclude Roman Catholics; but it became a widespread practice that dissenters should pay a single visit to the parish church, receive the sacrament and their certificate, and thereafter go regularly and cheerfully to a meeting-house. Some borough corporations, and notably the great cities of London and Bristol, were heavily stocked with such 'occasional conformists'. As the Anglican squirearchy saw their monopoly invaded, their anger knew no bounds. To William Bromley, one of the most able and respected Tory politicians, it was 'that abominable hypocrisy, that inexcusable immorality of occasional conformity'.[11] A few clergy went so far as to refuse the sacrament to dissenters, though this could legally be done only on the grounds that the intending communicant was 'an open and notorious evil-liver'.

In each of the years 1702 to 1704 an Occasional Conformity bill was introduced under the auspices of Rochester and Nottingham. Each would have made it a penal offence to attend a dissenting chapel after receiving the sacrament in an Anglican church for the purpose of qualifying for office. It was a deeply divisive issue. Against the bills were not only the Whigs and the dissenters, but a substantial body of 'moderate' opinion which had come to accept that a wide interpretation of the Toleration Act was inevitable, unless the country was prepared for continuing religious strife. Bishop Burnet, speaking in the House of Lords in 1703, put in an eloquent plea for the many dissenters who went to the Anglican sacrament not out of selfish interest, but as an occasional act of religious charity. But this above all was a 'party' issue which divided the nation into two camps. In two successive years it filled the prints and impeded the voting of supplies; in 1704 it provoked one of the major political crises of the reign when the High Church zealots tried to 'tack' the Occasional Conformity bill to the Land Tax bill for that year. It took all the determination of Godolphin and the subtle political management of Secretary Harley to defeat a move which came very near to breaking the ministry. But the high-flying agitation was a failure. Rochester had deeply alienated the Queen, and when in 1705 he raised the cry of 'the Church in Danger' he was defeated in the Lords in the most humiliating manner. By 1707 the ecclesiastical issue had become associated with sterile factious politics, and the clergy's case seemed to be going down into the limbo of lost causes.

The second stage of the High Church movement began with the General Election of 1708, which proved so disastrous for the Tories. Godolphin and Marlborough were forced to rely more and more heavily on the Junto, and gradually a Whig party regime was inaugurated. During the years 1708 and 1709 thousands of foreigners, persecuted Calvinist refugees from Germany, were brought into the country and granted a general naturalisation. Using these 'poor Palatines' as a convenient excuse, the Whigs began an agitation to allow a man to qualify for public office by receiving the sacrament in *any* Protestant congregation. Rumours were heard that a radical reform of the religious tests at the universities was planned, and pressure was put on the Irish bishops to agree to a repeal of the Irish Test Act. Anglican anger was rising fast, and it was a propitious time for Tory unity. Robert Harley was now out of the ministry, and he, Rochester and Bromley joined forces for a new and more responsible campaign. Harley had little use for factious opposition; his aim was office, and in season and out of season he preached to his friends the doctrine of gaining the Queen's confidence, forming an administration, and then putting into effect that renewal of the Church for which they so earnestly looked.

To keep the growing movement under control was the difficult task. News came in of inflammatory sermons at Oxford, at distant country assizes and at episcopal visitations in defiance of the presence of the bishop. It was at this time that the Nonjurors, a small but vociferous group of propagandists, made their great literary endeavour. The danger was clear. Amid all this emotional preaching and writing, would the Tory churchmen, as a whole, find themselves irrevocably associated with, and led on to, Jacobitism? The doctrine of non-resistance was to most Tories simply an assertion of the religious view of the state and society, but its implications for the succession question were obvious. And the Whigs had no intention of missing their chance. What indeed *had* happened at the Revolution? Was it a sinful resistance to a rightful king or a proper defence of the liberties of the people? How did the high-flying divines reconcile their theory and their practice, or were they just waiting their time to restore the legitimist Pretender? Among the Whig controversialists the most sour and tenacious was Benjamin Hoadly, the crippled little rector of St Peter-le-Poer in the City of London. When Bishop Blackall of Exeter preached before the Queen a somewhat injudiciously phrased exposition of the text 'Let every soul be subject to the higher powers', Hoadly attacked him with cutting sarcasm and the repeated accusation that he was recommending tyranny and popery.

As Harley's principal ecclesiastical lieutenant, Francis Atterbury attempted to offer a moderate solution to the resistance problem and ward off the dangerous possibilities of the debate on the Revolution. Preaching as early as 1704 he had offered a formula – that of 'the providential revolution'. Men (so he argued) could not resist even evil kings, but God retained the sovereign power to overthrow them. At the Revolution James had been set aside by divine intervention; even the winds and waves had conspired against him, and the extraordinary unity of the nation at that time had shown that no mere human power was at work. Even so, the doctrine of passive obedience was not equivalent to submission to unreasoning tyranny. This was a Whig lie. The obedience due was that to 'the legislature' not to a monarchical tyrant. Phrased thus, the theory became the unexceptional one of peaceable citizenship under constitutional government.

But not all the High divines saw it in this way, and one of their number caused Atterbury and his friends great apprehension. Dr Henry Sacheverell, Fellow of Magdalen College, Oxford, was a handsome young man of modest intellectual equipment. His speciality lay in emotional discourses in which he lashed around him in exaggerated language at a whole range of Tory bugbears. On 5 November 1709 he was given his great chance for fame when an ultra-Tory Lord Mayor of London asked him to preach on Gunpowder Day. The doctor's explosive sermon, *In Perils among False Brethren*, was worthy of the commemoration; and he launched himself into a furious rant against dissenters, occasional conformists, unlicensed schools, 'moderate' bishops, Burnet, Hoadly and all who gainsaid the primitive doctrines of loyalty and obedience. The whole affair might have passed off as a seven days' wonder, if the ministry had not decided to prosecute the preacher. It was true that Sacheverell had referred to the Lord Treasurer as a 'Volpone', but the government's action was not based merely on personal pique. Clearly the Whigs hoped to seize this opportunity to initiate a grand national debate on the nature of the Revolution and of political authority; they wanted to set the stigma of Jacobitism on the Tory theories once and for all. It was an astute move. They knew that at bottom the great majority of squires and parsons were not Jacobites; the ordinary Tories were fighting for a way of life, not for a Stuart succession. As one country divine put it: 'Whig and Tory, High and Low Church, are names – Hanover and St Germains are Things!'[12] But Sacheverell was inept and foolish enough to give the Whigs all they desired; and when the House of Commons voted formally that he should be impeached for 'high crimes and misdemeanours', the Tories were in deadly danger. At once, rather than leave the doctor to extreme advisers, Atterbury and Sir Simon Harcourt took over his entire cause and its advocacy.

The trial took place amid a rising popular clamour. Pamphlets, broadsheets and cartoons flooded onto the market, and the cry went up that the Church was attacked and a priest under persecution. The memory of these Sacheverell riots remained with eighteenth-century politicians as a bitter recollection of religious faction. Lords and M.P.s found that their passage to and from the trial lay through ugly crowds shouting for 'High Church and Dr Sacheverell!' As the proceedings went on, even the 'moderate' bishops became alarmed at the terrible passions which had been aroused among their clergy. Tutored by Atterbury and Harcourt, Sacheverell's defence was brilliant. He was (he claimed) an ordinary priest grievously misrepresented by spiteful opponents; he had done nothing more than proclaim that teaching on loyalty and obedience which had ever distinguished Anglican beliefs; he did accept the Revolution as a providential work of Almighty God; he prayed for the Queen with his whole heart; and he looked to the House of Hanover as the only safeguard for the Protestant religion. It was a triumph. At the end of his speech Tory peers were weeping openly. When the vote came, the doctor was found guilty by the narrow margin of seventeen voices, and he escaped with the derisory sentence of three years' suspension from preaching. Soon the excitement spread to the provinces and market towns. Church bells were rung and toasts drunk: Low churchmen and prominent Whigs found it expedient to keep indoors. During the summer the hero of the hour went on a kind of triumphal tour through the Midlands to a new living in Shropshire and was received rapturously by the Tory mob. It was clear that the whole Whig plan had rebounded on its authors' heads. As the ministry staggered before popular feeling, the churchmen began to feel that their day had at last come.

The new administration which Robert Harley formed in the summer and autumn of 1710 was destined deeply to disappoint. Neither he nor his royal mistress really intended to deliver themselves into the hands of the extreme Tories; both wanted a moderate regime above party faction. In his first months of office the chief minister had to struggle with serious financial problems, and the return of an overwhelmingly 'Country Tory' House of Commons in the General Election of November 1710 was a grave embarrassment. There was little in the moderation of his policies and the dexterity of his political manœuvres which could satisfy the party zeal of the backbenchers or the hopes of the high-flying divines. Now Harley's many promises to his allies came home to roost, and it could not be disguised that a great gulf was fixed between the needs of responsible government and the implementation of the High Church programme. Almost immediately his relations with some of his erstwhile followers were under strain, and not least with Francis Atterbury, who had been until now his willing agent and counsellor in Church affairs.

It was clear that the churchmen had a coherent set of measures in mind and were eager to be at work. Atterbury, as Prolocutor, or chairman, of the Lower House of the new Convocation, was in close touch with William Bromley, Speaker of the Commons. Their method of proceeding was in close accord with past precedents for promoting ecclesiastical legislation. First Convocation should discuss the various

measures and work out their provisions in detail; then the matter should
be embodied in a petition to the Queen, who in her turn would refer the
matter to Parliament where a bill would be introduced on the lines set
out by the clergy. Atterbury had in mind a radical scheme: new
coercive procedures to re-establish the jurisdiction of the ecclesiastical
courts over the laity; new powers to allow the bishops to license all
schools; legal protection for the revenues of benefices; easier means to
set up new parishes; and provision of money to build new churches. But
at an early stage the programme began to run into difficulty, not just
from the delaying activity of 'moderate' bishops and Whig clergy, but
from the underhand opposition of the ministry. Only the famous
'Fifty New Churches' Act, to provide additional buildings in London
and the suburbs, got through to the statute-book. By the summer of 1711
disillusion with Harley, now Lord Treasurer and earl of Oxford, was
almost complete.

The last phase of the High Church movement in Anne's reign was
thus peculiarly unhappy and frustrated. The Queen appointed to the
bench of bishops men of mild Tory inclinations, and denied promotion
to Atterbury, Jonathan Swift or others of a more vigorous temperament.
Any proposals for an out-and-out regime of Tory appointments were
blocked by the Treasurer's devious skill. The only measure to become
law was Lord Nottingham's Occasional Conformity Act of 1711,
obtained by a 'devil's compact' between the Junto and an angry group
of dissatisfied Tories. In fact the Act never seems to have bitten
deeply into the practice of occasional attendance at the sacrament, and
prosecutions were rare. The country clergy, however, remained eager
for counter-revolution. In 1710 in one county after another they had
exhorted their flocks to vote for 'Church' candidates, and often they
had marched to the poll in a black-coated phalanx. The surviving poll-
books stand as evidence how few clergymen ever voted Whig. In 1713
clerical ardour was still undiminished, and again the Tories were
returned to the Commons as a substantial majority.

High Church numbers remained strong, but, as the Queen's health
declined perceptibly, confusion and division fell upon the cause. The
critical question was, without doubt, that of the succession. It is
virtually certain that Atterbury was not a Jacobite before 1714; like so
many he hoped for a Hanoverian succession with a new king who would
have to come to terms with a strong and united Tory party. But the
enemies of this political realism lay on the left hand and on the right. On
the left the Whig writers were unwearied in their theme that the Tory

leaders were in league with St Germains and preparing the way for
Popery and a French invasion. On the right the professed Jacobites
wrote as if this were in fact true. It was the great moment for the
Nonjurors. In pamphlet and treatise they threw into the political arena
a whole series of intriguing questions, all subtly devised to insinuate
Jacobite sympathy into the minds of the clergy. Roger Lawrence, the
author of *Lay Baptism Invalid*, put forward the ingenious theory that
only those who had been baptised by an episcopally ordained minister
had received valid Christian initiation. At one stroke he had delivered an
attack on the dissenters *and* on the baptism of the Lutheran House of
Hanover. Other theories from the pens of Jacobites and quasi-Jacobites
were equally embarrassing to Atterbury and his friends. Thomas Brett
proclaimed the necessity of absolution from a priest before a person
could be admitted to the Holy Communion, and it was clear that he was
claiming for the clergy the right to grant or withhold admission to the
sacrament and to public office. So dangerous were these issues, and so
likely to create division even among Tories, that the High Church
efforts in Convocation could not be pursued.

By the spring of 1714 the succession issue overshadowed every other
topic of public interest. Atterbury, now at last bishop of Rochester,
had thrown in his lot with Henry St John, Viscount Bolingbroke, in
disgust at Oxford's continual moderation and procrastination; and the
two worked for a single-party regime in Church and State. If Oxford
had to be forced out before they could achieve their aim, then go he
must. But everything depended on Tory unity, and it was not only the
politicians but the churchmen who were divided. On one hand Atterbury
represented all those who desired urgent measures to effect an Anglican
reaction before it was too late; on the other hand Archbishop Dawes of
York led a substantial body of senior Tory divines who were deeply
afraid of what this might involve. Dawes's 'Hanoverian' party was
earnestly in favour of a Church programme, but their growing suspicion
of the ministry forced them into an uneasy opposition. It was thus as a
last bid to reunite the High Church party that in May 1714 Atterbury
advised the introduction of the Schism bill. It laid down stringent
penalties for anyone who taught in a school or academy without
subscription to the articles and licence from the bishop. It was a
shrewd move. Oxford would be forced to choose whether to support
Anglican measures or not, and the churchmen would unite to resist
dissenting 'encroachments'. In a last effort of zeal the bill was passed
through the Commons and on to the Lords, where the archbishop of

York supported it warmly. In the weeks after the passing of the Act the Treasurer was struggling for his political existence, and on 27 July he was dismissed by the Queen.

But time had run out for the High Church movement. On 1 August, the very day on which the Schism Act became effective, Anne died. And with her went any hope that the Stuart past might be restored. In the new Hanoverian age the Whig politicians took their revenge, and the Church of England went under the iron hand of patronage. The churchmen had sown discord, and now they reaped pastoral ineffectiveness.

BIBLIOGRAPHICAL NOTE

There is no satisfactory history of the Church for this period, and the pioneer works of the late Norman Sykes remain indispensable. His *Church and State in England in the Eighteenth Century* (Cambridge, 1934; reprinted 1962) has some valuable early chapters on the post-Revolution situation; and his Ford Lectures, *From Sheldon to Secker* (Cambridge, 1959), illuminate important problems of administration and theology. George Every describes the theological viewpoint of *The High Church Party, 1688–1718* (1956), but is deficient in a knowledge of political history. Henry Horwitz, *Revolution Politicks* (Cambridge, 1968), is an important study of the second earl of Nottingham, the leading lay Anglican of his day.

There are numerous biographies of prominent bishops. Sykes's *William Wake* (Cambridge, 1957) is a compendious study of a leading moderate. E. F. Carpenter's *Thomas Tenison* (1948) is an ill-digested account of an important figure. G. V. Bennett has written a life of *White Kennett* (1957) and hopes soon to publish a new biography of Francis Atterbury.

Much recent work is to be found in articles or essays. R. Thomas has a useful essay on 'Comprehension and Indulgence', in *From Uniformity to Unity, 1662–1962*, ed. G. F. Nuttall and O. Chadwick (1962), while G. M. Straka has written on 'The Final Phase of Divine Right Theory in England, 1688–1702', in *EHR* lxxvii (1962). G. V. Bennett has attempted a revised view of 'King William III and the Episcopate', in *Essays in Modern English Church History*, ed. G. V. Bennett and J. D. Walsh (1966); and has tried to show the interaction of politics and an ecclesiastical issue in 'Robert Harley, the Godolphin Ministry and the Bishoprics Crisis of 1707', in *EHR* lxxxii (1967).

NOTES

1. R. South, *A Sermon preached at Lambeth Chapel upon the Consecration of the Lord Bishop of Rochester, Nov. 25, 1661*. Quoted in G. R. Cragg, *From Puritanism to the Age of Reason* (Cambridge, 1950), p. 162.

2. See the excellent article by R. A. Beddard, 'The Commission for Ecclesiastical Promotions, 1681–84: an instrument of Tory reaction', in *HJ* x (1967).

3. *The Rector's Book, Clayworth, Notts.*, ed. H. Gill and E. L. Guilford (1910); P. Laslett, *The World we have lost* (1965), p. 71.

4. *A Supplement to Burnet's History of My Own Time*, ed. H. C. Foxcroft (Oxford, 1902), p. 314.

5. Greater London Council Archives Office, AB 1–3: churchwardens' presentments, 1664–1927.

6. *Letters of Humphrey Prideaux to John Ellis 1674–1722*, ed. E. M. Thompson (1875), p. 154.

7. Bodl. MS Top. Oxon. fo. 50: incumbent's book of Lower Heyford.

8. E. D. Bebb, *Nonconformity and Social and Economic Life 1660–1800* (1935), pp. 45, 174.

9. G. Burnet, *History of My Own Time* (Oxford, 1823), iv, 378.

10. Add. MS 773, fo. 17.

11. Bodl. MS Ballard 38, fo. 137: to Charlett, 22 Oct 1702.

12. Christ Church, Oxford, Wake MS 17, i, fo. 243: W. Wootton to Wake, 21 March 1710.

8. The Road to Union

T. C. SMOUT

THE Act of Union of 1707 is at once a major event in the development of the British constitution and the great hinge on which the domestic history of Scotland turns. The road towards the treaty, however, was long and tortuous. There was a clear century between the first feelers following the Union of Crowns in 1603 and the final Union of Parliaments in 1707. What were the driving forces that brought the two countries towards one another in the seventeenth century, and what finally clinched the partnership in Queen Anne's reign?

One of the most notable features of the bargain struck in 1707 was the creation of a British common market embracing almost 7 million people, much the largest free-trade area in contemporary Europe; and in consequence it is pertinent to enquire how far the forces behind the making of the Union were pre-eminently economic in character. Recently, however, a more cynical interpretation has been put on the actions and motives of those involved in the final bargain: one that would relegate to comparative insignificance not merely the economic arguments deployed at the time, but for that matter all arguments of statecraft that might conceivably have been weighed, by Scotsmen at least, in an atmosphere of free choice. Instead it has given prominence to the effects of 'political jobbery' and crude bribery. It is with these sharply contrasting emphases that this essay is mainly concerned. But it also poses a final problem. How far, in the last analysis, can the historian ever hope to discover what motivates a political decision of this kind?

The idea of Incorporating Union was first seriously mooted by James I and VI when he became the first monarch to occupy the throne of England as well as that of Scotland. He made the proposal as soon as the Court moved from Edinburgh to London: to him it was the logical solution to the executive problems of trying to rule two kingdoms at once. James envisaged a threefold marriage: the law of the two kingdoms was to be joined by assimilating the Scottish legal system to that of England; the Church was to be joined by a common hierarchy of episcopacy; the economies were to be joined by a common coinage, customs system and body of commercial regulation. Initially he also wished for the Parliaments to be joined, but a taste of the independency of the English Parliament convinced him that this would be a mistake, and so parliamentary Union was actually omitted from the programme. He probably felt he could ultimately use Union to undermine the powers of the English Parliament by relegating it to the status of an advisory regional assembly.

The King's plan was discussed over the years 1604 to 1607, but for many reasons went no further. The English Parliament smelt the rat lurking in a Union of law without a Union of Parliaments, and debates at Westminster revealed an almost pathological dislike of the Scots. 'Zoological metaphor', remarks S. G. E. Lythe, 'was strained to the limit to describe the ravening hordes of Scotsmen waiting the chance to flood southwards.'[1] The Scots took umbrage at this: besides, they just could not discover sufficient benefit in the proposed arrangements to persuade them to abandon their independence. Even their Privy Council, normally an obsequious royal tool, suggested to the King in 1607 that he should drop the matter, and dismantled what had already been done to establish free trade. James wisely withdrew in the face of unanimous protest, and sought other ways to solve the problems of government in two realms.

The Jacobean proposals therefore served only to emphasise how far Britain was from any form of Union. Three parties would have to be converted. The Crown would have to realise that nothing short of Incorporating Union would satisfactorily solve the problems of the executive. The English Parliament would have to be convinced that the gains from Union would offset the disagreeable prospect of opening their arms to the Scots. The Scots would also have to feel that there were advantages for them great enough to justify merging with that larger and richer state with whom they had so often and so bitterly fought in the past.

The story of the next century was the story of this conversion, but when Incorporating Union came in 1707 it was not much like that planned by James. It involved Union of Parliaments, and it repudiated Union of church and legal systems: of the original scheme only economic Union survived. On balance the Union of 1707 was rather less 'incorporating' than James's proposals, and it gave enough elbow room to certain Scottish institutions to ensure that national identity was not everywhere obliterated. Perhaps one consequence was to make the revival of nationalism much easier in the twentieth century than it would otherwise have been.

Of the three parties, the Crown was the first to be converted: for a long time after 1607, however, its attitude towards Union varied with its success in directing the government of the two realms without collision. King James never again pushed Union, yet he gained much of his purpose by guiding the Scottish Parliament through a steering committee, the Lords of the Articles, who were royal nominees, and by keeping religious and economic friction between England and Scotland to a minimum. His son apparently never gave Union a thought: indeed, Charles I was so overconfident about Scotland that he tried to use the Scots to demonstrate to his other subjects how a king should be obeyed. The only result was to provoke the violent explosion of the first Covenanting movement, which set off a chain of events that ended in the loss of both his thrones and of his head, and in the collapse of established government in both countries.

After a decade of civil uproar Oliver Cromwell seized power in England, and invaded and conquered Scotland only in order to protect his regime from enemies who had several times used the unbridled north as a base for operations against the south. Cromwell thus enforced Incorporating Union on Scotland in 1654 as the surest way of asserting English control over potentially unfriendly Scottish actions. The settlement had, admittedly, some indigenous support,[2] but it was ultimately dependent on an English army of occupation, and the actions of the Union government in Scotland were little more than extensions of military rule. Its abrupt collapse in 1660 showed how far both nations still were from the genuine sentiments of integration.

After the Restoration the constitutional position in Scotland reverted to what it had been under Charles I. Charles II, being able to control the restored Scottish Parliament by the reconstituted Lords of the Articles, was not greatly worried about carrying political integration further. On the other hand he would have preferred some kind of economic Union, because he could no longer restrain the English Parliament from passing laws harmful to Scotland: the Navigation Act of 1660, for instance, excluded Scots from the English empire and the English carrying trade; nor could he restrain the Scots from retaliatory action meant to hit English pockets, such as the imposition of an 80 per cent *ad valorem* duty on goods imported from the south.

This economic friction was the cause of negotiations for a form of Union being opened, by royal initiative, in 1667 and 1670. When they failed, however, Charles did not think the matter important enough to press further. As for James II and VII, in his short reign he showed no more interest in Union than Charles I had done, and, like him, lost his throne partly because he assumed too far on Scottish submissiveness.

At the Glorious Revolution, therefore, William III found that he had inherited in Scotland a peculiarly difficult problem. Firstly, he had before him plenty of evidence from the immediate past that failure to secure real control over Scotland could lead to endless friction and perhaps endanger his Crown. Secondly, he was obliged to relinquish the traditional ways of ruling the Scots, since the settlement of 1690 itself reflected Scottish determination not to allow their new king the same control over institutions as his predecessors had had. He was compelled to abolish the Lords of the Articles, to trim the powers of Privy Council and to accept a Presbyterian General Assembly to govern the Church. Thirdly, the alternative means of ruling Scotland by absorbing the Scottish Parliament into Westminster was temporarily blocked again: yet another tentative attempt to start Union negotiations in 1689 had fallen on barren ground in London. He was therefore left with the problem of ruling Scotland with such tools of patronage and persuasion as he and his English ministers could fashion in order to keep the Edinburgh Parliament reasonably co-operative.

Ten years were enough to convince William that this task was quite impossible. The odium that fell upon the Crown as a result of the Massacre of Glencoe in 1692 was bad enough. It paled into insignificance, however, before the complete failure of the Crown to keep Scotland under control in the affair of the Company of Scotland trading to Africa and the Indies. It was galling that the Scots should in 1695 set up this company, and thus collide with the jealous monopolists of the East India Company of London. It was also irritating for the King and his English ministers that the Scots went ahead with the company even after the Crown had discouraged or prevented investment in it in London, Amsterdam and Hamburg. But it was far worse when the Scots madly chose to use the company's funds to found a colony at Darien in Central America, since Darien was the property of the King of Spain and all William's foreign policy hinged on keeping Scotland out of the French alliance. William's ambassador was reduced to the absurd position of trying to explain to the Spanish Court that one of the nations over whom William ruled had invaded Spanish territory, but Spain should bear William no grudge since these particular subjects were acting against their monarch's expressed will. Only the feeble nature of the colony, snuffed out by disease, Spanish attack and Scottish mismanagement saved William's foreign policy from catastrophe on the spot. It was little wonder that one of the King's last acts was to urge upon his successor the necessity for bringing about an Incorporating Union as the only final and foolproof solution to the problem of governing the Scots. The main importance of the Darien episode in the history of the Union is that it finally converted the Crown to an enthusiastic pro-Union position.

Negotiations between English and Scottish representatives to discuss an Incorporating Union began in 1702. These were not, however, solely or even mainly inspired by the events at Darien. There was a still more urgent occasion: in 1700 the duke of Gloucester, the last surviving child in direct line to the throne, had died, and it became a matter of urgency to settle the question of succession. The English Parliament was content to choose the Hanoverian Elector; Anne's advisers thought it unlikely that the Scots would tamely follow suit without making some bid to loosen English control over Scottish affairs, least of all any new Scottish Parliament (and one was supposed to be called within twenty days of King William's death) which would be elected in the wake of bitter feeling about the failure at Darien. The negotiations were therefore an attempt to see whether a basis existed for Union which might even now be rushed through without calling a new Scottish Parliament. The talks collapsed after several weeks: the most obvious reason was that the English representatives were lukewarm. The only convert to Union so far was still the Crown.

In their attitude, the English in 1702 were behaving in a traditional way. England had never been able to see any good reason why it should share the many good things in her state with the undeserving and ravenous Scots. Why should they be admitted to the empire, acquired solely by English blood and treasure? The Navigation Acts kept them out. Again, why should Scotch linen and cattle be freely admitted to the English market if north-country clothiers and graziers could not sell their own cloth and stock? Westminster imposed tariff barriers and marketing restrictions on these goods in 1660 and 1663. The sale in England of Scotch salt (which competed with that of Tyneside) and of Scotch grain (which competed mainly with that of East Anglia) was stopped in the same period. Furthermore, overtures for a Union had come out of Scotland in 1667, 1670 and 1689, and had been as blankly received as their Jacobean predecessors. The new overtures in 1702 came after the events at Darien had shown up the Scots as, in English eyes, both fools and rogues. They could still see nothing to be gained by Union, and on this occasion contemptuously broke off negotiations when the Scottish representatives tried to insist on the Company of Scotland receiving compensation from England for its losses.

The sudden conversion of the English to a pro-Union position was a direct result of dramatic developments in Edinburgh in 1703 and 1704. After the failure of the Union talks the Crown called a new Scottish Parliament in accordance with the constitution. This assembly, despite efforts to influence the elections, turned out to be still more independent of the Crown and of the Court party (led by the duke of Queensberry as Queen's Commissioner) than anyone had anticipated.[3]

Its most famous member in 1703 was Andrew Fletcher of Saltoun, an East Lothian laird whose allegiances lay with the Country party, but a man of considerable intellect, courage and independence of mind, whose qualities were widely respected across party divisions. It was partly under his inspiration that the two main Acts of the session took their final form – the Act of Security and Succession, which in effect debarred a Hanoverian from the throne unless Scottish government was severed from 'English or any foreign influence', and the Act anent Peace and War, which demanded the consent of the Scottish Parliament in waging war and drawing up peace treaties. These served notice on the existing constitution and gave Scotland the option of contracting out of a 'British' foreign policy (in reality an English one) that had done her nothing but harm since 1689. In addition Parliament passed two lesser Acts that emanated from the ministry, vainly trying to increase customs revenue, and which were opposed by Fletcher, but did not appear in the south to be any less anti-English in tenor: the Wine Act, effectually legalising trade with France in wartime, and the Wool Act, legalising export of wool from Scotland even though it was known that a large proportion of this wool had been previously smuggled over the Border from England and was destined to feed the looms of England's principal industrial competitors.

To Englishmen, the Wine Act and the Wool Act were irritating, provoking and characteristically Scotch, but no worse. The Act of Security and Succession and the Act anent Peace and War, on the other hand, combined as they were with preparations to arm the Scottish militia (ostensibly against Jacobite dangers), pointed a dagger at a vital and vulnerable spot in England's military security. Suppose, through such legislation, the Crown and the English ministers lost all say in

Scottish affairs: suppose the independent Scottish government then made peace with France. How far would they stand from the next logical step of an offensive and defensive pact between Scotland and France, and revival of the Auld Alliance which so often in the past had threatened the encirclement of England? The English ministers decided after the session of 1703–4 that there was no solution possible to the dangers from Scotland except an Incorporating Union through which the Westminster Parliament could absorb the Scottish malcontents and render them tame. The English Parliament subsequently passed the Alien Act in March 1705, saying that unless the Scots appointed commissioners to negotiate for Incorporating Union within nine months all Scottish estates in England would be forfeited and all the main exports from Scotland to England banned. This threat marks the formal conversion of the English to the idea of Union.

We are now faced with the most difficult question of explaining what converted the Scots. Their initial reaction to the Alien Act (which was later repealed) was to intensify distaste for the English. The judicial murder of the crew of an English ship, the *Worcester*, on a fanciful charge of piracy took place in April 1705. Shortly after, Adam Cockburn of Ormiston was commenting in Edinburgh that he did not think 'ten men of the Parliament will go into an entire and complete Union'.[4] Eighteen months later the Scottish Parliament did vote by an overall majority of each estate for the first article of just such an Incorporating Union. Why?

This problem, like the last, must first be approached from the perspective of the attitude towards Union before 1700, which does not in Scotland appear to have been by any means as uniformly hostile as it was in England. In the early seventeenth century the Scots had admittedly been cold or indifferent, and the continuing separatist tradition came to light on such occasions as when, in 1649, Sir James Hope advised Charles II to be content with the throne of his ancestors and not to go adventuring again in England.[5] The Cromwellian Union had also been broken off joyfully, but whether from revulsion against Cromwell and his church policy or from revulsion against other aspects of the experience of Union is not clear.

A pro-Union Scottish lobby appears to develop first in the period after 1660, and then to have an economic basis. In the first half of the seventeenth century the Scottish economy had on the whole benefited from having a Scottish king in London: Scotland was internally more stable, peace was the ally of economic growth, and the situation at first allowed the Scots to expand very considerably their commercial contacts with England without encountering serious tariff barriers. But after the Restoration, as we have seen, the English took the opportunity to impose quite severe controls on Anglo-Scottish trade. Furthermore Scottish trade to Europe was in decline for various reasons from about 1680 onwards: exports of coal, salt, cloth, fish and corn, all of which had been important in earlier decades, began to sag sharply, and the search for substitute exports to Europe had little success. In these circumstances it is not surprising that some Scots began to agitate for a Union of Trade, with parliamentary amalgamation if necessary. From within she might hope both to gain access to the English market and to the markets in the English empire: left outside, she had now neither the benefits of unhampered trade with the rest of Britain nor the joys of prosperous trade with the rest of Europe. It is not easy to know how deep Scottish support for Incorporating Union was at this stage, since the negotiations of 1667 and 1670 were undertaken at royal instigation. Scottish mercantile spokesmen at least came forward readily at this juncture with arguments for Union, and on at least one further occasion before 1689, in 1681, a leading merchant pressed the Privy Council unavailingly for a Union of Trade. On the other hand, Sir George Mackenzie in 1669 reported considerable popular opposition when royal proposals began to go further than a simple customs union.[6]

The best evidence, however, of a strong pro-Union movement in Scotland comes at the moment of the Glorious Revolution itself, when the Scottish Convention, having disowned James VII and accepted William III, made overtures on its own account to the English Parliament for an Incorporating Union. These were ignored at Westminster: they had been passed in Edinburgh, according to one source by the 'unanimous consent of all our representatives'.[7] There exists a little-known letter from Fletcher of Saltoun dated 8 January 1689, written from London on his arrival with King William to a friend in Rotterdam, giving news of preparations for the Convention and mentioning with approval exactly the kind of Incorporating Union against which he was to set his face so resolutely fourteen years later:

The Prince he called together all of the [Scottish] noblemen and gentlemen here present, which are very numerous, though there be a great many more upon the road. The first have met these three days bygone and proceeded to things upon the matter much like what the

English have done, only we find great difficulty as to the regulation of
the elections for burghs in the desired Convention. For my own
part I think we can never come to any true settlement but by uniting
with England in Parliaments and Trade, for as for our worship and
particular laws we certainly can never be united in these.[8]

If Fletcher was satisfied with the prospect of Incorporating Union at
that point it is impossible not to believe that most Scots of political
significance would then have been happy to surrender their sovereignty
to secure their commerce and the liberties grasped at the Revolution. If
there had been this strong sentiment in 1689 it is perhaps not so
remarkable that it could be revived again after an interval in 1705 and
1706.

In William's reign, however, the tide turned to bitterness and at
times to Anglophobia. The failure at Darien was exclusively put down
to English malevolence. The war against France, so damaging to
Scottish shipping and markets, was seen, much more correctly, as
being undertaken purely in the interests of the King and of his southern
kingdom. Lastly, rank-and-file members of the Scottish Parliament
became aware of how far Scottish ministries were manipulated by the
strings of favour and patronage held by the Cabinet in London. Many
Scots by 1703 had therefore little affection for the existing constitution,
regarding it as a mockery of independence and a root cause of economic
depression. And none of the Acts that they passed that year gave any
hint that three years later they would be returning to the sentiments of
1689.

In explaining the *volte-face* of 1705 and 1706 the first thing to be
borne in mind is that the Scottish members, though able to muster a
parliamentary majority for the Acts expressing dissatisfaction with the
existing constitution, were deeply disunited on what should replace it.
Many, as Dr Riley has pointed out, voted against the government in
1703 merely to embarrass Queensberry in the party game, and had no
conviction behind their attitude. Others, the Jacobites or Cavaliers,
were committed to a Catholic Pretender whose regime could never be
acceptable to Revolution Whigs, or to the common people of the
Presbyterian parts of Scotland south of the Tay. Fletcher of Saltoun
ideally wished for a republic, but this was an intellectual's viewpoint
with no popular following, and he himself was fertile with other solutions. Yet others proposed Union with Holland, but this, too, was a
minority view. There were certainly very many in 1703 and 1704

thinking in terms of some kind of Federal Union with England. Fletcher himself travelled along this road far enough to contemplate Scotland and England sharing the same monarch, and then in Scotland so hedging him about with limitations that he would become a mere figurehead subjected to the will of the Scottish Parliament and unable to act as a front for English ministerial interference. His 'limitations', however, failed by a margin of twenty-four votes to get into the Act of Security. The final draft of the Act left the door ajar for a Federal Union that would combine two national Parliaments with one monarch and one free-trade area:

> Nor shall the same person be capable in any event to be King or Queen of both realms unless a free communication of trade, the freedom of navigation and the liberty of the plantations be fully agreed to and established by the Parliament and Kingdom of England to the Kingdom and subjects of Scotland.[9]

As long as the Scots were undecided among themselves about how to replace the *status quo* they were fatally weakened in resisting the increasingly well-organised and persuasive pressures brought by English and Scottish advocates of Incorporating Union after 1704.

A further critical factor was that Scotland could not afford any solution to her constitutional problems that was indecisive or resulted in weak government. What would happen if the Cavaliers' candidate was chosen? Everyone knew a Jacobite king would trigger off again the catastrophic religious war between Presbyterians and their enemies and another fratricidal war between Lowlanders and Highlanders. And if the Pretender won, would he be more satisfied with the throne than Charles II had been in similar circumstances? Would he not simply use Scotland as a base from which to recover the richer kingdom? Then, if he failed in that enterprise, the English would conquer Scotland and enforce a Cromwellian-type Union: if he succeeded, Scotland would be stuck again with a London king. Fletcher of Saltoun put it well enough: 'This country must be made a field of blood in order to advance a Papist to the throne of Great Britain. If we fail we shall be slaves by right of conquest; if we prevail have the happiness to continue our former dependence.'[10]

Furthermore it was plain by the end of 1704 that even a Federal Union which maintained Scottish control over foreign policy might form the pretext for an English invasion, since the English proved to be more apprehensive of having a military vacuum on their northern border than most people had anticipated. In December 1704 the House of Lords represented to the Queen 'the urgent necessity of taking immediate measures to put the Border in a state of defence', and Godolphin warned the Scottish Chancellor that if his fellow-countrymen would consider the history of previous wars 'they will not find the advantage of those breaches has often been on the side of Scotland'.[11] After Blenheim and Ramillies he was said to have remarked that if a Scottish war was inevitable, the sooner it came the better. Scotland might not in the last instance be dissuaded from independence by threats of force; yet it would be a rash statesman who staked everything on the belief that England was bluffing, and a blind one who could not see that while Incorporating Union with England would ensure the protection of English arms, anything less would only ensure that Scotland became a pawn, and possibly a bloody battlefield, in European power politics. This was the comment of the earl of Roxburgh in December 1704: it was he who had in 1703 phrased that clause in the Act of Security calling for Scotland to be freed from 'English or any foreign influence':

> I am thoroughly convinced that if we do not go into the succession or a Union very soon, conquest will certainly be upon the first peace: for supposing the Lord Treasurer [Godolphin] durst go into such limitations as were yielded last, England will never suffer Scotland's enjoying the Act of Peace and War, the Act for arming all the fencible men, the Wool Act, and what is necessary for maintaining of those. It's true, had Scotland virtue and power enough to maintain such a condition, I'm sure it's preferable to all; but that's the question in debate which, after all, depends upon occurring circumstances.[12]

There was also the matter of Scotland's economy. Most of those who had argued for closer association with England in any form since 1660 had done so on economic grounds. Even John Spreul, who wrote an important tract after the Alien Act with the object of showing that Scotland could survive the threatened economic sanctions if she had to, prefaced this by saying that no-one could be keener on a Union of Trade than he: it was only because, in his view, the price to be paid for a package-deal of Incorporating Union was so high that Scotsmen must look at the alternatives.[13]

This widespread desire for economic Union was mainly the consequence of a reorientation of the Scottish export trade during the seventeenth century. In 1603 Scotland had looked for trade mainly to France, Holland, Scandinavia and the Baltic; England's importance, though growing, was not yet obvious or overriding. By 1700 the continental trade was declining or stagnant; war had undermined relations with France and wiped out the special privileges Scotland had enjoyed a hundred years before under the Auld Alliance; Scottish exports had failed to stay competitive on the Dutch market; trade with Scandinavia and the Baltic also suffered, and had in any case never been able to match that of the other two regions. Trade with England, on the other hand, began to rise after 1603 as peace was established across the borders. Though it had not been uniformly prosperous throughout the century, by 1700 the three most important items on the Scottish export list were linen, black cattle and raw wool, and each of them was closely connected with England. Linen and cattle could be sold only in England. Wool was the standby of Scotland's remaining trade to France, as well as to Holland and Sweden: a large proportion of it was obtained by smuggling out of England, and sending it through Scottish ports as a re-export. Most people believed that if the Alien Act was ever to come into operation, and if the Border was to be effectively patrolled to prevent wool-running, Scottish external trade could be decapitated. Most people also saw that exports to England seemed to have a rosy future if free trade could be established by Union. Linen and cattle sales, important though they were, were obviously hampered by English tariffs and marketing restrictions imposed since 1660, while salt and corn, before Restoration England prevented their import, had once been important commodities in Anglo-Scottish trade and might become so again. It must be stressed that free trade between England and Scotland was the economic issue most anxiously pressed at the time. No-one was very anxious after the Darien fiasco to press the advantages that Scotland would gain by being admitted to England's American trade: that seemed too remote, too expensive and too speculative to occupy the forefront of men's minds in 1705 and 1706.

Were people persuaded into Incorporating Union by the economic advantages to be gained from it, or dissuaded from pressing their plans for separation or Federal Union by the economic penalties of the Alien Act? The matter was certainly explicitly debated at some length. In the very sharp pamphlet debate (mainly in 1706) the pro-Unionists, led by the English propagandist Daniel Defoe but supported by many Scottish writers, made out a convincing (though polemical and overdrawn) case for Incorporating Union on economic grounds, and the anti-Unionists totally failed to explain how Scotland could, at this late stage, hope to expand her European trade to compensate for a breach with England. Point was given to their contentions by the bad commercial crisis of 1704, 'one of the least years of trade that has been known in this age';[14] its main features had been a sharp drop in Border traffic and the temporary suspension of payments by the Bank of Scotland. Might not this be a foretaste of worse to come?

These economic arguments may seem to us convincing. How far did they convince those whose business was primarily in the commerce of their country? The answer must be that for many Scots, as for Spreul, the economic advantages or dangers were apparently not large enough or self-evident enough to weigh in the balance against the loss of national independence. The Convention of Royal Burghs, for example, petitioned against Union in 1706 by 24 votes to 20, with 22 abstentions. Edinburgh, Glasgow and Perth were among the more important towns that sent in separate protests against Union in the same year. These petitions must be taken as representing the viewpoints of many merchants and tradesmen at a relatively late stage in the negotiations, although when it came to a final vote on the Treaty of Union in January 1707 the burgess estate supported Incorporating Union by 30 votes to 20 (as they had also supported the first article of the Union two months earlier by 33 votes to 29). The merchants of the Royal Burghs, however, were not the sole or necessarily the most important of those whose interests were affected by the plight of the export trade: indeed with their interest in the exchange of wool for French wine (which would be illegal after Union), and their fear of competition from England in the manufacture of consumer goods otherwise produced by tradesmen in Scottish towns, they might have felt that their own economic interests were best served by keeping Scotland independent. The lairds, and more especially the nobles, on the other hand, with corn, cattle, coal and salt for sale off their estates, and with country tenants dependent on making linen in the villages, had at least as large a stake in external trade as the merchants, and would be more sensitive to changes either way in the accessibility of the English market. Their votes on the Union were appreciably more favourable towards it than those of the burgesses: the nobility approved the first article by 46 votes to 21, and the final version by 42 votes to 19: the barons did so by 37 votes to 33, and by 38 to 30. It is difficult to believe that this pattern of voting is not influenced by the economic interests of those concerned. It is probably unreasonable to attempt to be more specific since the criteria by which one can weigh economic considerations against other factors just do not exist.

In another letter, written on 28 November 1705, before the outcome was obvious, Roxburgh summarised the intellectual reasons why men of his class in Scotland would ultimately vote for Incorporating Union: 'Trade with most, Hanover with some, ease and security with others, together with a general aversion to civil discords, intolerable poverty and . . . constant oppressions.'[15] This passage has been frequently quoted by historians who believe that the Scottish assembly was primarily swayed by statesmanlike contemplation of the national plight. G. S. Pryde, for instance, speaks of the nobles' 'altruism' (on the grounds that the political influence of the nobles stood to be heavily reduced by sending a mere sixteen of their total to the Westminster House of Lords), and he concludes the Union 'was carried because a majority of Scotland's spokesmen honestly believed that it was the course that promised best for the nation'.[16]

There is another view, diametrically opposed to this, which has been most forcefully and clearly put by W. Ferguson. He sees eighteenth-century Scottish politicians as neither intellectual nor selfless, and indeed, as so much prisoners and manipulators of the British political game as to be virtually incapable of any statesmanlike decisions. He says of the passing of Union:

> Clearly it was not, like the Cromwellian Union, a *diktat* pure and simple; but equally clearly it cannot be regarded as a natural con-summation or even a triumph for honesty and right reason. It was, rather, a 'political job'. Indeed it was probably the greatest 'political job' of the eighteenth century.[17]

This introduces the most vexed question of all: what precisely is the role of parliamentary corruption or management (call the spade by whatever name you will) in accounting for the Scottish *volte-face* after 1704? Is it possible that this, after all, may have been the crucial factor clinching the treaty after a century of desultory discussion?

No historian could imagine that the blandishments of political management would not be tried. Pryde himself speaks, a shade evasively, of the 'routine political methods of the day'. It was Dr Ferguson's special contribution to the debate to be more explicit about them, and to show that they included such things as granting an outright demand from the duke of Argyll for military promotion before he would agree to 'serve the Queen in the affair of the Union', the use of threats that arrears of salaries would not be paid unless the recipients toed the line of the English ministers, and the activities of the earl of Glasgow, Treasurer-Depute in the ministry, who appears to have disbursed improperly some £20,000 made available from English funds for smoothing the way of the Queen's friends.

Dr Ferguson's difficulty lies in proving that bribery was carried on widely and systematically: since bribes are in the nature of things secret, it is not easy to secure unequivocal evidence of this. It also lies in establishing that, even if bribes were widely given, bribery was the factor that clinched the matter when it came to a vote: it is also almost impossible to establish for any individual that he changed his mind as a result of receiving a bribe. Ferguson's case therefore appears to rest, partly at least, on his demonstration of two pieces of circumstantial evidence.

Firstly, he is able to demonstrate a quite startling lack of consistency and principle among the Scottish nobility whom Pryde had considered so 'altruistic'. The most telling examples come from those who led the Scottish ministries for the Crown. The duke of Queensberry, Queen's Commissioner in 1703, allied himself with the anti-Union Jacobites in 1704 in order to sap the strength of his successor in office, the marquess of Tweeddale: he returned to the Unionist side in 1705 and once more became Queen's Commissioner in October 1706. Tweeddale, who had been a pillar of the Country party before the opportunity to form a ministry materialised in 1704, remained opposed to Incorporating Union while he was Queen's Commissioner. After the Alien Act, which put him and his friends in 'the Squadrone' in an intolerable position, he tried to reach agreement with Queensberry; but his ministry fell. In 1706 they became outright advocates of Incorporating Union, 'duped', says Ferguson, 'by a promise of handling that part of the Equivalent which related to the losses of the Company of Scotland and also undue representation in the sixteen peers'. The duke of Argyll became Queen's Commissioner in Tweeddale's stead in April 1705, ready to jump either way. To secure his co-operation for Incorporating Union it was necessary to bribe him with military promotion, to make him an English peer, and then to make his brother a Scottish peer as earl of Islay. Before each step he threatened to sabotage the proceedings unless his requests were granted: 'it is the most complete exposé of the hucksters' mood in which the Treaty passed the Scots Parliament'.

Secondly, Dr Ferguson is able to contrast this unprincipled behaviour with the opposition to Incorporating Union displayed in 1705 and 1706 outside Parliament in petitions from many burghs and shires. Even Unionist writers often accepted that the bulk of the common people were opposed to the treaty: Clerk of Penicuik wrote later that 'the articles were confirmed in the Parliament of Scotland contrary to the inclinations of at least three-fourths of the Kingdom'.[18]

It appears to be implicit in Ferguson's view of events that since Scots outside Parliament were consistently opposed to Union when they had the chance to assess its merits through the pamphlet debate (which was, of course, not confined to discussing the economic merits or demerits of the case), and since leading politicians within Parliament were so vacillating and unscrupulous in their actions, then the likeliest explanation of the vote in Parliament in favour of Incorporating Union is that these were secured by political jobbery, since jobbery appears to have been the only important factor operative within Parliament and not operative outside it.

It may be, however, that the weight and depth of popular objection to Incorporating Union is commonly overestimated. There were no petitions in favour of it, but (whatever the cause) it is always easier to raise a petition of protest than one of approval, and three-quarters of the burghs and two-thirds of the shires did not in fact trouble to protest at all. There was no insurrection in 1707; a Jacobite conspiracy in 1708 relying on the unpopularity of Union was an utter flop; the rising of 1715 was little more. Even the mobs in Glasgow and Edinburgh (whose superficial excitement may have given Clerk an exaggerated view of popular opposition) never made serious trouble for the government before the Malt Tax Riots and the Porteous Riots twenty or thirty years later. Most Scots outside Parliament were apparently apathetic rather than actively hostile to what was going on within.

There are other questions that need to be raised in considering whether the Union is totally explicable as a political job. Firstly, why, if Parliament was so corruptible after the middle of 1705, had it shown itself to be hitherto the most independent-minded Parliament that had met in Scotland for generations ? Political management had been used before. Scottish politicians, especially the nobles, must have been aware from the start of the advantages that would accrue to themselves by toadying, and of the dangerous unpopularity they courted by thrusting the Act of Security, salted with obnoxious clauses, and the Act anent Peace and War upon the Queen. Yet neither Queensberry in 1703 nor Tweeddale in 1704 nor even Argyll for much of 1705 had been able to make the majority toe the line: as late as 28 June 1705 Parliament was refusing, in Ferguson's words, with 'studied nonchalance' to consider the Queen's recommendations. Is it fully plausible that the opposition lost this integrity, bloody-mindedness and nonchalance merely because the political managers became a little more skilled or tried a little harder?

Secondly, the terms that Scotland eventually secured in the Union settlement do not really suggest that the English ministers felt they had the Scottish politicians in their pockets. The treaty embodied genuine attempts to placate a wide spectrum of Scottish public opinion and would surely not have needed to take this form if the pressures of public opinion could have been avoided by astute use of corruption in Parliament alone. The independence of the Presbyterian Church of Scotland, for instance, was carefully secured by the Act of 12 November 1706. This was a real concession by England, where many were fearful of doing anything that might weaken their own established Church or encourage Dissent; it was necessary because without such an Act the Kirk's spokesmen in the pulpit and in Parliament alike would even then have refused to go into Incorporating Union, and by common consent this would have brought negotiation to a stop. The livelihood of the Scottish lawyers, perhaps the richest and most significant group in the middle class, was also preserved by those clauses in the Act of Union that guaranteed the preservation of Scots law, though this was to England an administrative inconvenience and a potential cause of future friction. In a somewhat similar way clauses in the Act of Union preserved the trading rights of the Royal Burghs, and of individuals who already possessed private rights conferring immunity from customs, excise or the regulation of trade. This reassured many who might otherwise have crept into the last ditch to oppose an infringement of their economic privileges.

Finally, the draft Act of Union itself was altered in a number of significant economic details by the Parliament of Scotland as it went through the treaty article by article in November and December 1706. All the changes were accepted in England. This would surely not have taken place if the voting had been a mere charade undertaken by a corrupted Parliament with only a passive interest in the proceedings. The same comment could be made about Defoe's pro-Union propaganda campaign: it would have been unnecessary if everything could

have been quietly arranged by political manipulation and bribery in
Parliament House.

The opinion of the present writer is that, invaluable as Dr Ferguson's
work has been in elucidating the political background to Union, the
description of the Act of Union as a 'political job' is not a helpful one, in
so far as it obscures the complexity of the making of the treaty, and
appears to imply that corruption was the main factor involved. Very
many pieces made up the jigsaw between 1704 and 1707. One was
England's determination not to have Federal Union at any price. A
second was the prospect of bloody internecine war between Jacobites
and Presbyterians in the event of a disputed succession. Scotland's
military weakness was also part of the pattern. Then there was the
demonstration of Scotland's commercial weakness, especially in 1704,
and lastly the unexpected willingness of the English to concede substantial points that made the final treaty less than completely incorporating. All these factors conjoined to make the attitude that the
Scottish Parliament had struck in the less explicit circumstances of
1703 more and more difficult to hold. At the same moment another
piece of jigsaw was provided when the Crown stepped up the scale
and determination of political management. In other words, just at the
time that there became an increasing number of pressing and honest
reasons for a man to have second thoughts about his previous attitude,
the government came forward with a tempting selection of dishonest
ones. It is hard to say that any one of the pieces of this jigsaw was
absolutely indispensable. Perhaps corruption was one essential piece:
perhaps, without corruption, Union could only have come about if
there had been bloodshed. It is, however, rather difficult to imagine that
it would not have come about at all, in or shortly after the year 1707.
The international position of Scotland in the early eighteenth century
was too isolated, her internal weaknesses and divisions were too acute
and wide-ranging, and the determination of England to protect herself
from these weaknesses by absorbing her neighbour was too strong, to
offer much rational hope north of the Border that Scotland's cherished
independence could be long preserved.

The immediate problem, however, of why men voted as they did in
the Scottish Parliament between November 1706 and January 1707 is
impossible of more detailed objective solution. Lockhart of Carnwath,
the Jacobite, watched them vote away national independence and concluded they did it all for gold and office. Clerk of Penicuik, who was a
Queensberry man, wrote later that

all the friends of the Union were so much persuaded in their consciences that they were acting for the interest of their country that they thought it as cowardly and unlawful for them to desert the measures they had engaged in as for men of virtue and honour to desert the lawful defence of their habitations when attacked by their enemies.[19]

Any rewards that he got from the government he would presumably have regarded as the just recognition of his public spirit in carrying out an unpopular but patriotic duty. What criteria can the historian conceivably use to establish whether Lockhart's or Clerk's view of events was the more correct?

To claim, therefore, that the Act of Union was approved by the Scottish members either as an act of disinterested statesmanship or as the greatest political job of the eighteenth century seems to the present writer to place upon the evidence an interpretation that it is logically unable to bear, and one which reflects, not historical fact, but the historian's own unverifiable view of what human motives are most likely to count in such a situation. The only tenable historical position, however untidy and disagreeable it may appear, is that in the last resort we cannot judge so fine a matter. You can describe how you take a horse to the water; but you cannot describe what goes on in his head while he is drinking.

BIBLIOGRAPHICAL NOTE

The best introduction to the problem of how and why the Act of Union was passed is probably to read James Mackinnon, *The Union of England and Scotland* (1896), and to follow it immediately by G. S. Pryde, *The Treaty of Union of Scotland and England 1707* (1950), and W. Ferguson, 'The Making of the Treaty of Union of 1707', in *SHR* xliii (1964). Mackinnon's narrative is still the best, most accurate and most readable of the general histories: if it is not to hand, W. L. Mathieson, *Scotland and the Union* (Glasgow, 1905), or P. Hume Brown, *The Legislative Union of England and Scotland* (Oxford, 1914), may suffice. Pryde was perhaps the last of the great Whig historians: his work may be compared with that of his noted English contemporary G. M. Trevelyan, whose *Ramillies and the Union with Scotland* (1932) is, to a degree, distorted by uncritical admiration of the Act of Union. Ferguson is a scholar of the post-Namier generation, and lives in a time when it is widely recognised that clay is a common constituent of political feet, and when the Act of Union itself is no longer admired unquestioningly.

W. C. Mackenzie, *Andrew Fletcher of Saltoun* (Edinburgh, 1935), is a partisan, but still useful, biography of the greatest of the Scottish statesmen. T. C. Smout,

Scottish Trade on the Eve of Union 1660–1707 (Edinburgh and London, 1963), and the same author's 'The Anglo-Scottish Union of 1707: 1 The Economic Background', in *EcHR* xvi (1964), are the most recent contributions to the study of the economic situation. See also A. M. Carstairs, 'Some Economic Aspects of the Union of the Parliaments', in *Scot. J. Pol. Econ.* ii (1955).

Those who want to follow contemporary sources will find the Act of Union itself printed in Pryde. For a quick selection of other material, try Baillie's correspondence (see n 12 below) and Clerk's 'Observations' (see n 7 below), along with George Lockhart, *Memoirs Concerning the Affairs of Scotland* (London, 1714), and Daniel Defoe, *History of the Union Between England and Scotland* (London, 1786). The student will certainly be better off formulating his judgements with their help than by relying upon the effusions of some popular modern historians for whom polemics and history have become richly and sadly confused.

NOTES

1. S. G. E. Lythe, 'The Union of Crowns in 1603 and the Debate on Economic Integration', in *Scot. J. Pol. Econ.* v (1958), 219–28.

2. P. J. Pinckney, 'The Scottish representation in the Cromwellian parliament of 1656', in *SHR* xlvi (1967).

3. P. W. J. Riley, 'The Scottish Parliament of 1703', in *SHR* xlvii (1968), stresses that the breakdown of the agreements between the Cavalier (Jacobite) faction and the Court party, as well as disagreements between subgroups of the Court party, had led to a political position of unusual fluidity in the Scottish Parliament of 1703. He argues that the 'anti-English' tenor of the Act of Security (as finally passed) and of the Act anent Peace and War was due to an attempt by Queensberry's party enemies to embarrass the administration, rather than to nationalist feeling.

4. Quoted in G. S. Pryde, *The Treaty of Union of Scotland and England, 1707* (1950), p. 19.

5. H. R. Trevor-Roper, *Religion, Reformation and Social Change* (1967), p. 461.

6. *Register of the Privy Council of Scotland*, 3rd ser., vii, 653; Sir George Mackenzie, *Memorials of the Affairs of Scotland* (Edinburgh, 1821), pp. 137–41.

7. 'Sir John Clerk's Observations on the present circumstances of Scotland, 1730', in *Miscellany of the Scottish History Society*, x (1965), 192. The official record merely states the decision was 'carried in the affirmative': see *Proceedings of the Estates in Scotland 1689–90* (Scottish Hist. Soc. 1954), i, 50.

8. Scottish RO, Misc. papers 260/1: Fletcher to Russell, 8 Jan 1689.

9. This clause was deleted from the statute as it appears in the *Acts of the Parliaments of Scotland* because the Queen would not sign the Act with it in.

10. Quoted by W. C. Mackenzie, *Andrew Fletcher of Saltoun* (Edinburgh, 1935), p. 167.

11. See J. Mackinnon, *The Union of England and Scotland* (1896), p. 186; Pryde, op. cit. p. 16.

12. *Correspondence of George Baillie of Jerviswood 1702–1708* (Bannatyne Club: 1842), p. 28.

13. J[ohn] S[preul], *An Accompt Current betwixt Scotland and England* (Edinburgh, 1705).

14. [Anon.], *Essay upon Industry and Trade* (Edinburgh, 1706), p. 21.

15. *Jerviswood Corr.*, p. 138.

16. Pryde, op. cit. pp. 27, 34.

17. W. Ferguson, 'The Making of the Treaty of Union of 1707', in *SHR* xliii (1964). This quotation from p. 110.

18. 'Clerk's Observations', p. 192.

19. Ibid. p. 193.

9. The Road to Peace 1710–13

A. D. MacLACHLAN

THE Tory peace-making which culminated in the Treaty of Utrecht has been given a bad press. The elder Pitt set the tone by speaking of it as the most shameful chapter in English diplomacy; and most nineteenth-century historians, anxious to repudiate such a doubtful pedigree for their Empire, have written of it as an outrage and a betrayal. Continental historians, too, have treated the negotiations either as an illustration of Albion's perfidiousness, or, in the case of chauvinistic admirers of the *roi soleil*, as a rare English incursion into the French preserve of diplomatic *realpolitik*.

Part of the objection, one suspects, is to the unheroic qualities inherent in most political arrangements. After the epic of the Grand Alliance there is something sordid about the horse-market of Utrecht. Part derives from a failure of historical imagination. The domestic history of Queen Anne's reign, under the influence of Namier, has shed its moralistic carapace, and can look the Augustan politician in the face; the diplomatic history – if it is written at all – still retains its learned innocence. Most of all, perhaps, it arises from a refusal to recognise the 'high policy' of Utrecht, with all its bewildering gyrations and almost comic *volte-faces*, as but part of the internal history of Anne's last ministry.

This essay deliberately eschews the censorial role, and attempts instead to explain through what one protagonist called 'a chain of causes' why the Tory ministers came to make peace between 1710 and 1713, why their policies were seemingly so inconsistent, and why they appeared to deceive and betray their allies. It endeavours also, by reassessing the contribution of individuals, and particularly of Robert Harley and Henry St John, to the final settlement, and above all by relating British diplomacy in these years to its domestic context, to supply the answer to Peterborough's famous quip: that the Peace of Utrecht was like 'the Peace of God, beyond human understanding'.

Between June and September 1710 Queen Anne replaced her Whig government by a ministry that was predominantly Tory. 'The great motive of all these changes', in the opinion of Jonathan Swift, 'was the absolute necessity of peace'.[1] Like many other sympathisers, he assumed that the new ministers would sooner or later initiate talks with the enemy. In the same vein, though from a very different angle, the discarded war leaders maintained that their opponents intended to reverse the foreign policy pursued with such persistence since 1703, of forcing Louis XIV's grandson off the Spanish throne and squeezing France 'until the pips squeaked'. And in a matter of months the Tory ministers did exactly as everyone predicted: by January 1711 they were fully engaged in clandestine discussions with the French; before the following December they had agreed on two sets of peace 'preliminaries', one for public consumption, the other private; and in 1713 they brought to a conclusion years of tortuous negotiation in the articles signed at Utrecht.

This later conduct of the Queen's three leading ministers, Harley, St John and Shrewsbury, has enabled most historians to accept contemporary prognostication without demur, and to dismiss protestations to the contrary as a front to deceive the allies 'until such time as they had accomplished the infamous deed they had decided upon, a secret and separate peace with France'.[2] But their intentions on coming to power demand more than squeals of outraged morality, if we are to understand the seemingly shady and devious route along which they were to lead the government and country: not least because much of the evidence on which traditional reactions are based – the shibboleths of opposition, polemical apologias or the ministers' actual deeds in office – is questionable.

The connexion between intention and action is, to say the least, unproven, especially in an age when 'policy' was so inexplicit, and with politicians as opportunistic as Harley, who never seemed to tire of telling admirers that 'policy' was not 'as is commonly supposed, the forming of schemes with remote views, but the making use of such incidents as happen'.[3] Moreover, defences of policy either made before a hostile tribunal as in the case of Harley,[4] or at the bar of history some thirty years after the event as with St John, are necessarily *ex parte* statements designed to justify, to iron out inconsistency and to invest the shifts of government with logic and reason.

Certainly, on the evidence of their statements during the years of opposition before 1710, it was legitimate to assume that they intended a radical revision of wartime policies. Although the Whig leaders spoke of the war against France in predominantly moralistic terms, and theoretically presupposed a national unanimity in 'the struggle against slavery', they were uneasily aware that the ideology they invoked had little meaning, and that the nation was no longer unreservedly on the side of the angels. For fifteen years, indeed, the debate on foreign affairs had been at the heart of party politics. During the 1690s many Tories had gradually assumed a position at variance with William III's principles of European interdependence and collective security; and they had made little effort to preserve consensus since the renewal of hostilities against Louis XIV in 1702.

Their objection to the strategy of the war, to the preference given to campaigns in Flanders over maritime, colonial or 'combined' operations,[5] was one expression of their dissent. More primitive and far more pervasive was their xenophobia. As in the 1690s, 'it needed no more than two or three campaigns to convince most Tory members that . . . the Dutch and Imperialists were prepared to suck England dry to defend their own territories while shamelessly defaulting on their treaty obligations'.[6] The Austrians were 'happy to have all Europe in arms to fight their cause' and to squander English money and English troops on their 'miserable Lord Mayor of Barcelona',[7] while Dutch evasion of trade embargoes infuriated the hard-pressed trader or over-taxed gentleman, and went a long way to corroborate St John's in-accurate but emotionally gratifying verdict: 'our trade sinks . . . and will in time be lost, while the commerce of Holland extends itself and flourishes to a great degree'.[8] Still worse, while English ministers extracted higher taxes and troop reinforcements, their Dutch and Austrian allies seemed unable or unwilling to fulfil their agreed quotas of troops and ships or even to allow 'a finishing stroke' in Flanders. The suspicions that they were being 'bubbled' by the allies, and particularly by Dutch republicans, justified long-standing prejudice against continentals. 'If you would discover a concealed Tory', recommended Shaftesbury's grandson, 'speak but of the Dutch and you will find him out by his passionate railing.'[9]

As members of the wartime administration from 1704 to 1708, Harley and St John had indicated little sympathy for squirearchal preconceptions. Their exclusion from office in 1708, however, and the growing identification of the ministry with uninhibited Whiggery was bound to drive them with more or less reluctance into the arms of the Tories. And since religious policy could provide no common ground between the two sides, the confused criticism of military strategy and carping disparagement of the allies, so popular in the country houses, inevitably formed the basis of their alliance.

Such a programme was *ipso facto* negative and indirect. 'The major business of eighteenth century governments was administration, the conduct of foreign affairs, and the methods and incidents of taxation.'[10] Significant civil legislation was rare. For an opposition this meant that there was seldom the opportunity to frame alternative policy; it could only hope, under cover of Country professions, to obstruct or dislocate the normal functioning of the executive by capitalising on its every misfortune and unpopular act. Hence the outcry over spiralling taxation, the 'butchering' of conscription bills, and the motions condemning the conduct of the war in Spain (1708); hence, above all, the criticism of bloody victories like Tournai and Malplaquet (1709), and the underlining of failure to make peace.

As early as 1707, before the Junto flooded into the ministry, Harley had become genuinely critical of the failure to make peace: 'England finds itself so oppressed by the war that a good peace would be readily embraced', he noted in a Cabinet memorandum. Though he conceded that the government should 'press as far as is reasonable to hinder the dismemberment of the Spanish monarchy', he was probably already out of sympathy with the rigid official policy of 'no peace without Spain'.[11] It was at least arguable that the strategy of the allies had got seriously out of hand. Godolphin admitted as much.[12] In the euphoric aftermath of the battle of Ramillies in 1706 anything had seemed possible: victory in Flanders had been won, the reconquest of Spain appeared certain, rebellion inside France itself was thought probable. But the blighting of optimistic plans in 1707 – fiasco in Brittany, failure at Toulon, stalemate in Flanders, and above all the 'foul miscarriage' at Almanza – produced a reaction against the war and against the assumption of international responsibilities proportionate to earlier incautious expectations. St John and Harley wished the English troops out of Spain, 'where mortality was great'; and in Flanders, they thought, 'we might war to eternity and never come to anything decisive'.[13] More than most, perhaps, they grasped the grotesque paradox of a war that could not be won because it was already won.

They were convinced that the war was no longer being fought for allied security, but for special advantages: territorial gains and trading privileges for the Austrians and Dutch, above all political domination for the English Whigs. As they and their followers saw it, 'the party that is founded on war and a senseless jargon of France, Jesuits and an invisible army of 100,000 pilgrims mounted upon elephants, have not yet acquired power enough to support themselves in that most difficult and slippery state of peace'.[14] Continued war, on the other hand, with all the attendant opportunities of financial manipulation and malversation, had created a new form of wealth out of 'the pillage of the land' and was warping the balance of political and economic power to the Whigs' advantage.[15] For behind the Junto stood crowds of bankers and stockjobbers 'who increase their wealth and secure their power by continuing a wasting war', and 'prostitute the Queen's credit for their cheats and illegal games'.[16]

As long as the war went well and food was cheap, resentment was limited to 'poor and dispirited landed men' – Blenheim was 'a pleasing spectacle to the generality, being more for their four shillings in the pound than ever they saw' – but Blenheim and Ramillies 'were not annual plants', and every barren campaign reaped the ministry bitter hostility from all sections of the rural population.[17] The terrible winter of 1708 brought acute suffering to the poor: 'though the condition of France by evident tokens appears to be miserable', noted St John the next summer, '... our own state is not much better than our enemy's; ... an unseasonable harvest would reduce our people to the same misery we triumph over'.[18] Even as he wrote, the rain-soaked harvest was being pronounced a dead loss. More alarming to the authorities than rural discontent, however, was the growing hatred of the army and the press-gang: desertion and mutiny at home and abroad became a serious problem for the first time.[19] Such signs were not lost on Harley and St John.

But more important than public opinion for a politician of the Court was the Queen's opinion. Harley and his supporters could not be voted back into power; they could only be taken back by their sovereign. Anne longed to be rid of her ministers, but she lacked the courage to do the task herself. So she had to be persuaded that action was essential to her well-being, that 'a sovereign would be in a worse position than his subjects ... if he could not deliver himself from a servant [Marlborough] ... grown dangerous by his excessive power or intolerable by his restless ambition'.[20] Anne also longed for peace; Harley was later to speak of 'her sex and Christian horror of bloodshed'.[21] But she had to be convinced of the weight of opposition against the Whiggish war – hence the demonstrations in Parliament and the propaganda from the country. These were only preconditions of the main task – a push at Court. At the head of the Tory 'gentlemen' Harley thought of himself as 'a captain of bandits'; 'those that herd[ed] with [him]' were, he said, 'naturally selfish, peevish, narrow-spirited, ill-natured, conceited of themselves, envious of any ability in others',[22] driftwood for opposition, not timber for ministerial benches. And if he was clear that they must form the backing of any new government, he was equally determined that they should not provide the leadership or monopolise the policy-making posts. To rescue the Queen from bondage he had to demonstrate that the Junto were not indispensable; to build a workable administration he had to perpetuate the traditions of 'management' moulded by Godolphin. Both demanded that he should win over the great middlemen of politics, most of them, like Shrewsbury, Whiggish in their inclinations.

These, then, were the disparate elements which underlay Harley's 'peace offensive' and qualified the 'palace revolution' of 1710: the structure of politics which forced the malcontent into faction, the economic hardship of the war and the consequent disenchantment of the 'Country', the bewildered paranoia of the gentry, the militant xenophobia of High Tory allies, and the customary tactics of court intrigue. We normally assume that words spoken in opposition bear a closer resemblance to belief and intention than those uttered in office; with an instinctive manager like Harley, and an opposition whose character was largely determined by extrinsic pressures, this is untenable. Harley's aim may well have been different, for 'to reach a northward station, a pilot may have to steer a westward course'.[23] But politics rarely allows such a divorce between means and ends: and the Whig tactics of 1710 – notably during the Sacheverell affair – determined that Harley should be accepted at Court not simply on the gentle current of royal favour, but on a national tide of High Church Toryism, and that the allies of opposition should become partners in office. The dissolution of Parliament exaggerated the situation yet further. Instead of providing the basis for a moderate Court administration supported, but not controlled, by the predominant party, the electoral landslide of 1710, coupled with the refusal of moderates such as Somerset, Cowper and Boyle to co-operate, threatened to produce a situation in which the pilots had to take their orders from the Tory party zealots below decks.[24] And the latter, only too aware of the possibility of officer defection as soon as they reached port, demanded a policy which at least approximated to their opposition professions.

Even if such an immediate policy of peace and disengagement might be theoretically attractive to the new leaders – and the domestic implications made it extremely questionable – it was impracticable in the circumstances of August 1710. The changes of the summer produced a crisis of confidence within the Alliance and a crisis of credit at home. Whatever Harley and Shrewsbury might say, it was futile to pretend that the fall of the Whigs and coming to power of factious critics of the allies was a conventional Court reshuffle. There was no doubt of the anxiety and suspicion in Vienna and The Hague caused by the latest turn in the bewildering national pastime of party politics. Anglo-Austrian understanding was at best a fragile affair, while the more substantial common purpose of the Maritime Powers now focused on the special relationship of the Dutch war leaders and the English Whigs. The frenzied Dutch efforts to save Godolphin, coupled with their known proclivity for private talks with the enemy, gave substance to reiterated warnings that the allies would rush to make what terms they could rather than wait to have them dictated by a revisionist British Parliament. Even more immediately dangerous was the threatened collapse of credit. It was hardly surprising that the Directors of the Bank of England should regard with apprehension the installation of men who had repeatedly proclaimed their hostility to sinister monetary influence. They understandably believed that a Tory ministry was bound to seek peace; and they knew that 'an insecure peace' would not only set a term to their own profits, but would enable France to recover the lucrative Spanish trade and so become formidable again. Moreover, English credit was essentially an international concern; without foreign investment, and especially Dutch investment, the over-extended war economy would have soon run down. Coming on top of the extraordinary financial strains of the past two years, the ministerial revolution was thought to endanger the whole structure of government credit. Thus, with good Whigs now threatening 'not to lend a farthing of their money'[25] and Dutch investors falling over each other to cut their English losses, the crisis of credit at home and of confidence within the alliance became one and the same.

In these circumstances it would have been suicidal to advertise radical intentions. Rather, the government had to prove its respectability, had to reassure its creditors and allies that the new ministry 'would vie with the old . . . who should go on with the most heartiness to carry on the public good and apply the public's money to most advantage',[26] and had to lay once and for all the Whig canards of its pacifism and xenophobia. However much some of the Tory publicists might relish it, Harley and Shrewsbury were alarmed at the repercussions of their palace *coup*; and they took quite seriously the warnings of Dutch desertion and City *débâcle*. To some extent, no doubt, the situation would right itself: the Dutch need for co-operation would quickly get the better of affection for departed Whig friends, while the choice between breaking Britain and backing Harley was scarcely a real one to any but the most irresponsible and partisan financiers. But for long-term security, something had to be done to attract creditors who welcomed the opportunity to take government finance out of the hands of the Whiggish bankers, but who were no more likely to be impressed by a programme of peace and homespun economy for the gentry. Similarly the Dutch had to be convinced that the new Parliament would be as able and willing as its predecessor both to support credit and to sustain the war.

But of course such tactics had little appeal to the traditional rulers of the countryside who flooded into the Commons in October 1710. To satisfy them, without endangering the stability of government, and to placate the full range of their supporters from backwoods squires to City businessmen, the ministers had to frame a 'double policy' which had something for everyone and which left maximum room for opportunism and for manœuvre. 'The most popular thing to England', Harley noted in his 'Plan of Administration', 'is to press all the allies to keep exactly to what they have agreed to do in their treaties; . . . the pressing roundly their exact perform[ance] is the likeliest way to obtain peace.'[27] Moderates, many of whom shared the criticism of allied lassitude and agreed 'that they should enlarge their charge',[28] would support a policy which seemed to promise a more energetic and thoughtful pursuit of the war, in the belief it would soon force the French to their knees; while extremists would applaud the chauvinistic self-righteousness of 'pressing roundly' in the hope that non-compliance would enable them to desert the allies. The Speech from the Throne at the opening of the new Parliament was equally bifarious: the Queen was 'sensibly touched' by 'the sufferings of this long and expensive war', and resolved to bring it to a 'safe, honourable and speedy conclusion', but she also spoke of 'carrying it on with the utmost vigour'. 'Double policy' was further complicated by the traditional Tory insistence on the superior claims of the Spanish over the Flemish theatre and by the euphoria stimulated by Stanhope's summer victories there. But when defeat at Brihuega put an end to these hopes the policy of 'pressing roundly' proved every bit as suitable for ill fortune as for good. The Austrian request for further aid was icily refused with the reminder of 'how little proportion is kept . . . by the allies', and when the Spanish ituation was debated in the Lords in January 1711 the government's onslaught on the strategy which had produced Almanza and Brihuega captured the combined votes of those who criticised the Whigs for insufficient attention to the peninsular war with those who wanted to get out of Spain altogether; it was variously interpreted as presaging a renewed onslaught against Louis in Flanders to force the evacuation of his grandson, and the acceptance of the Bourbon *fait accompli* in Madrid.[29]

Both interpretations were, in a sense, correct. If the war was to be won, it could only be won in Flanders, and war in Flanders meant re-employing the duke of Marlborough. If few of the ministers shared his conviction that the route to Madrid lay through Picardy, or believed that the Spanish knot could be untied save by partition, they saw the Flanders campaign of 1711 as the means of ensuring a reasonable base for negotiations and of further mollifying the Dutch. More than any other member of the Cabinet, Harley realised that the Dutch alliance was, and must remain, the essential prop of English foreign policy. The kernel of his conception of the European situation was an instinctive, somewhat old-fashioned Protestantism. He had never blamed the Dutch for the intransigence of the English Whigs, or shared St John's plausible fallacies about the dangers of Dutch trade or the formidable nature of the Dutch Barrier; indeed, he recognised the true nature of the alliance, that 'no one in Holland . . . has authority enough or reputation and resolution enough to give the rule',[30] and that their leaders would, within reason, follow 'cock boat behind the English battleship'. Moreover, with a myopic disregard of trading rivalry in Spanish America, he firmly believed that each country could benefit from peace negotiations without damage to the other. In his conversations with William van Huls, the Dutch confidential agent sent over on request in December 1710, he attempted to realise 'the special relationship' between them.

To begin with, van Huls was treated to a further distortion of the ministerial revolution, which was now construed as 'an absolute necessity for the maintenance of the Grand Alliance . . . a particular instance of the workings of Providence' for which the Dutch 'had good reason to thank God'.[31] Pious deceit apart, three features distinguished the talks. One may call the first 'the parallel convention', that is, the simultaneous discussion of two subjects having little bearing on one another, but enabling the participants to simulate or convince themselves of a large measure of agreement. By a similar method Harley was able to present the Dutch with both sides of ministerial policy, without committing himself to either. Thus, if he should be accused of bad faith, he could effectively claim that 'nothing was done but was privately transmitted to Holland', yet at the same time he could present any information with such a degree of mystification that he was unlikely to be tied down by Dutch conditions. The bewildered van Huls was told of the latest preparations for war and the possibility of negotiations, of the reappointment of Marlborough and of the Duke's probable supersession in the event of talks with the French, of the recovery of government credit and of the debilitating shortages which could force England out of the war. Finally, in a series of conversations early in March, Harley played his third card. The Barrier Treaty, he told van Huls, would be used by Tory zealots to envenom Anglo-Dutch relations: its commercial clauses were notoriously unpopular, and it was regarded as an impediment to peace negotiations.[32]

Meanwhile the first approaches to France were made by the earl of Jersey in his secret talks with François Gaultier, beginning in July 1710. Although he betrayed a grasp of international relations and an insight into ministerial purpose far beyond his own rather modest diplomatic talents, Jersey was given an extraordinarily free hand; hints were dropped now and then, occasionally he was given a resumé of Cabinet policy, but he did not speak to a brief. It was, in fact, typical of the inherent irresponsibility of the ministry's 'double policy' that peace negotiations should be entrusted to an unemployed Jacobite nobleman, highly critical of Court 'trimming'. Unlike Harley, Jersey recognised that a coherent campaign for peace must involve a readiness to abandon allied claims. Convinced that 'no peace without Spain' could only help the Whigs, he was only too happy to barter first Castile and then the whole Peninsula for appropriate advantages in the Indies. But these, it was clear, could be obtained only through sleight-of-hand against the Dutch. The Queen, Gaultier was told, would inform her neighbours 'that she was exhausted . . . and that she would do her utmost to obtain a speedy and honourable peace'; if they still wanted to continue the war, then she would require them to contribute full quotas.[33] And this was something the Dutch could not – or, in Tory eyes, would not – do.

Until the New Year of 1711 the Jersey talks were probably regarded as an insurance policy, to be taken out only when other measures failed. Neither Harley nor Shrewsbury wished to identify himself with perhaps treasonable negotiations; hence the inconspicuous Jersey was allowed to dangle baits which they dared not handle. After defeat in Spain had made them serious business, and cautious horse-trading replaced magnanimous peace-offerings, they were still intended to balance other plans, not to efface them.

Contacts with the French were kept private and tentative. Only a small knot of ministers – Dartmouth, Shrewsbury, Rochester and Harley – were in the know. Quite deliberately, St John was excluded from their hole-and-corner discussions. During the Election he had made himself the spokesman of anti-Dutch sentiment. Since then he had cajoled unenthusiastic colleagues with the claims of that High Tory perennial, an expedition to Canada; and he had courted 'Country' approval in the Commons with his strictures on the conduct of the allies. An admirable vehicle of 'pressing roundly', he could be a disaster to negotiations which required careful management of the allies. His clarity of thought and pungency of expression, above all his ruthless subordination of confederate to national objectives, could only lead to head-on collisions. In his able hands the negotiations were likely to be dovetailed into an energetic public attack on the Dutch or on the Austrians, which could break up the confederacy and lead to a competing downward spiral of separate offers to the enemy. To Harley and to Shrewsbury it was vital that public anger against the allies and ministerial co-operation with them should remain, as it were, on different levels. Tory xenophobia should be bottled up as much as possible, to be released only when the pressure became dangerous or allied obstinacy too glaring. Privacy was essential if the illusion of allied unanimity was to be maintained, ambiguity, if there was to be a vigorous Flanders offensive or an attack on the Spanish Empire, and stealth if the ministry was to retain the support of those as yet unwilling to renounce the objectives of the Grand Alliance. The negotiations, in fact, bore the imprint of Harley's personality – his obstinate love of secrecy, his dislike of being pinned down, and his unrivalled capacity for procrastination.

Even when St John pushed his way into the negotiations in April 1711, the confidential approach continued to play a disproportionately large role. The traditional picture of Henry St John as the new arbiter of Europe, battling with de Torcy, fighting for the ministry at the conference table, accords ill with the repeated comments of foreign ministers on his subordination.[34] It was Harley who listed English demands in June 1711 and who maintained executive control over preliminary peace talks with the French agent, Mesnager, two months later; throughout the negotiations he received copies of St John's letters to de Torcy, and conducted a private correspondence himself on points of crucial significance; and it was Harley, not St John, who handled the endless tête-à-têtes with van Huls, with Gaultier, or, further afield, with del Borgo, Maffei, Hohendorff, Eugene and Steingens, the allied and French agents who shuttled across the Channel during the Utrecht Congress. His preference for the vagaries of talk rather than the explicitness of letter-writing, his prevarication and obscurity of expression, not least his attempts when impeached in 1715 to foist the responsibility on to his erstwhile rival, coupled with St John's ostentatious use of what he knew both during the peace conferences and later in his literary remains, has led to a wild exaggeration of the Secretary's initiative and a distortion of the whole nature of the negotiations.

The intrusion of St John, however, if it never obliterated diplomacy 'by fits and starts, by little tools and indirect ways',[35] did open up the gap between Jersey's 'high road' to peace and Harley's low, and spotlight the essential incoherence of government policy: as to whether the ministers intended to negotiate a secret peace at the expense of the allies, to settle English advantages prior to the holding of a general congress, or merely to state terms and explore the ground while the other allies worked out their collective demands. If less willing than Jersey to barter away allied claims for separate peace, St John recognised that special terms could be obtained only at others' expense. While Harley vaguely hoped for English 'securities' without affront to the Dutch or without too much modification of confederate demands, St John accepted friction as inevitable, even desirable, and was ready to deride notions of 'no peace without Spain' or of a Dutch Barrier enmeshing all Flanders as 'romantic schemes which private interest formed and which sanguine temper . . . made [men] capable of embracing'. Harley entrusted van Huls in April 1711 with what he mendaciously called 'the first offers' of the enemy and spoke of Dutch participation in further peace talks;[36] St John demanded English control over the negotiations, and looked on 'treating in common' only as a means of ensuring that the allies did not 'try underhand' for special benefits, as England was doing.

Harley had won the support of the City only with disavowals of irresponsible pacifism, and latterly with promises of gain in South America. In a sense his famous South Sea scheme of May 1711[37] was a bait to the Tory 'monied men', the Janssens and the Shepheards; the fabled wealth of Spanish America was to provide the basis for a financial system that would stimulate the commercial enterprise of the nation and reward those who were ready to back the government against the giants of the Bank of England or the East India Company; and in the summer of 1711, at least, it appeared to attract some of the biggest names in the financial world – Dutchmen as well as English. Moreover, it was a further monument to Harley's 'double policy', for its expected benefits could be secured either by negotiation or force. To St John, however, 'the prospects of opening a new trade with the Spaniards and of attacking their colonies at the same time' were somewhat 'repugnant one to the other'; and in truth, the promised trading advantages to be obtained through negotiations with the French could only be made attractive so long as they were not to be shared with rapacious Dutch neighbours.[38]

Harley, of course, wanted to have his cake and eat it, to secure national benefits and keep up the appearance of collective bargaining. In this spirit he conducted his talks with Mesnager in August 1711. St John, on the other hand, spoke of English advantages as 'the sole subject of Monsieur Mesnager's visit'; allied interests should be left for the general Congress. His combination of avowed present selfishness and suggested future neutrality seemed to moderates like Shrewsbury, to 'leave her friends to shift for themselves at a general treaty in which her partiality might be liable to suspicion since she had beforehand stipulated for herself'; it even jarred rather badly with Harley's more ephemeral promises to the Dutch.[39]

St John disapproved of the carefully contrived releases and disingenuous promises eked out to Heinsius and van Huls. He preferred shock tactics – silence followed by a *fait accompli* delivered to The Hague by the hectoring ambassador, Lord Strafford. No doubt Harley's friendship with Holland was combined with the subordination of Dutch to English interests, particularly where his precious South Sea Company was concerned; no doubt, also, his efforts to win over the Dutch with offensive and defensive alliances were also endeavours to manipulate them. But his obsession with keeping up appearances, even if based on shrewd calculation as to how much English iniquity Anglophile Dutch statesmen would tolerate, made St John's struggle for extensive advantages much more difficult, and their publication for the benefit of patriotic Tories impossible. After all the South Sea euphoria, and the inspired leaks of the commercial banquet about to be spread before English merchants, the public articles signed by Mesnager in September 1711 could only appear as a bad joke. At the same time, acknowledgement of the secret concessions for England would turn the suspicion of the allies to rage, and resurrect the union of opposition Whigs and allied leaders which had imperilled the ministry the year before. Harley's solution of the dilemma was characteristic. He continued the charade of concealment long after the possibility of deception had evaporated, he performed prodigies of dissimulation to convince the Dutch that nothing had been arranged to England's advantage, and he repeatedly urged moderate opinion in England and abroad, and even the duke of Marlborough, to recognise the desirability of peace.[40]

To Jonathan Swift the whole point of the change of administration was the protection of Church and Queen and 'the absolute necessity of peace'. He lectured Harley and St John over and again on party unity, assuming, like many others, that the differences between them were personal and that they supported the same policy. He failed to realise the extent to which Harley was a Whig *manqué* and never understood the seriousness of his 'balancing projects'. But the crucial question of domestic politics in 1711 was whether the marriage of convenience between the ministers and country Tories, formed in the years of opposition, was at all desirable now that these ministers were expected to initiate and implement responsible policies. 'The ministry is upon a very narrow bottom', wrote Swift, 'and stands like an isthmus between the Whigs on the one side and violent Tories . . . We must have peace, let it be a bad one or a good one. . . .'[41] Peace, and especially a bad one, could be achieved only with the support of the Tories and at the cost of cross-party combinations. Peace, in other words, was likely to help St John in his struggle with Harley. During the Mesnager talks, the Secretary of State had refused point-blank to sit in Cabinet with the Whig courtier – now opposition fifth columnist – duke of Somerset; he had, said Swift, 'declared open war', ostensibly against undefeated Whiggery, but in reality against the Treasurer's obnoxious trimming at home and abroad.

The negotiations were St John's obvious weapon and, although he might never realise it, Swift acted as his godsent spokesman. His pamphlet *The Conduct of the Allies* (November 1711) transformed stale protests about Dutch inadequacies and sporadic snipings at Marlborough into a massive indictment of the war. But the inspiration was St John's: the violent assault on the Dutch – and Swift wrote with real hatred – was but the outcome of the Secretary's intention to make them 'swallow' the peace 'with a pox', and the destruction of 'King Marlborough', the result of his determination to rid the ministry of the one man who could frustrate his policies. These polemics may have taken their cue from Harley's presumed policies, but they went far beyond any pressure or persuasion he may have wished to put on Heinsius and Buys, and they contradicted his attempts to retain moderate support. Far from Swift's being the tool of the chief minister, the chief minister was forced to trim his sails to the hurricane produced by Swift's – and St John's – propaganda. One can see this clearly during the famous 'no peace without Spain' crisis of December 1711, when the opposition of the House of Lords threatened the government's peace programme. Swift, like St John, was convinced that Harley had been negligent and feared that the Queen might be false. He hammered away at the Dutch, lampooned and reviled Tory renegades and Whig courtiers – none of which can have delighted Harley – and when eventually Harley gave proof that 'the great work of peace' would 'go on', rejoiced to Stella that the Treasurer was 'awaked at last'.[42]

What the December crisis also showed was that the type of peace – with or without Spain, with or without the allies – would determine the character of the ministry. Rather than face a recoil into Whiggery and war, Harley acquiesced in much of St John's Tory programme. But throughout the Utrecht Congress, from January 1712 until April 1713, he continued to fight for the illusion of collective negotiations. He repeatedly disavowed the Jacobite overtones of Tory peace policy, and he insisted that the union of the French and Spanish crowns must not merely be prevented, but must be seen to be prevented. For many months he kept up the polite fiction that Spain was to fall to the Austrian candidate; and when the rash of fatalities in the French royal family made effective provision against union essential, in April 1712, he produced his 'masterstroke' – the transfer of Spain and the Indies to the duke of Savoy.

By such means, he hoped, the most telling objections to the peace would be removed and Whig irreconcilables be 'dished'. South Sea merchants, who had seen the lucrative Spanish trade slipping from their grasp, could now envisage the New World opened up to English shipping as never before. And Tories frightened off by government policy in December would be attracted back to a once more 'broad-bottomed' ministry. Even after his hypothetical European arrangements, notably the Savoy scheme, proved illusory, he held out on final settlement with Spain. Above all he refrained from publicly attacking the Dutch in the manner of St John.[43] Of course he often played Walrus to St John's Carpenter, meekly bemoaning to van Huls the Dutch morsels which St John was wolfing down in the Commons. And on occasions, notably after the Armistice of June 1712, he was prepared to join in the task of intimidation – though his methods were less direct than St John's. But he always offered to take the Dutch 'by the hand', and in one particular, the inclusion of Tournai in the Barrier, forced both the French and his colleagues to recognise their claims. In October 1712, and again in March 1713, he insisted on 'tarrying for the allies' and rejecting St John's demands for a separate peace, at the risk of splitting the Cabinet and disillusioning impatient Tories.[44]

Thus, it was an ostensible triumph for Harley's methods, when in April 1713 the Queen was able to assure Parliament that peace was general: the Dutch had signed minutes before the deadline, and Austrian consent could not be long delayed. He was able to eschew perilous reliance on Jacobite votes, and to enjoy the support of moderates at least momentarily impressed by the illusion of Anglo-Dutch co-operation and the weighty assurances of a Protestant succession.

The relative stability and continuity of sophisticated foreign policy has predisposed historians to look for the same qualities in the early eighteenth century. In fact, nothing could be more misleading than to suppose that each power attempted to implement consciously coherent programmes, or even that foreign affairs possessed a separate identity or a continuity of personnel sufficient to insulate it from the revolutions of domestic politics.

'The changing hands in England', said Walpole in 1710, 'always ends in the changing of measures',[45] and the circumstances in which Harley and St John achieved office made probable their search for peace. Convinced of Junto acquiescence in a war designed to perpetuate Whig political influence, carried into power on a wave of xenophobic Tory sentiment, they inevitably became victims of their myth and tools of their less responsible supporters.

St John was prepared to accept the logic of their position and to execute the shibboleths of refractory opposition. Friction between allies is usually a feature of the aftermath of great wars: by 1710, dissension and suspicion with the Alliance was disguised only by the common purpose of Marlborough, Heinsius and Eugene. It was easy to argue that if England did not underbid her allies, one of them was sure to defraud England and to maintain that the problem was no longer whether peace should be made and on what terms, but which power should have the making of it. The temptation to cast himself as the spokesman of the prevailing discontent, to dress up Country grumbles in elegant prose philippics, and to steal a march on the allies was irresistible to the gifted but unreflecting Secretary of State. His readiness, first to accuse and then to abandon the allies, was occasioned far more by the realisation that Tory gentlemen were eager to support such a policy, and that he was likely to benefit from it, than by any of the statesmanlike *aperçus* he later revealed to an admiring posterity.

Harley's reaction was more complex. He, too, saw the need for peace, and wanted one that would be 'solidly advantageous' for England. Yet he hoped to achieve it without cutting loose from the Alliance or losing contact with moderate Whig opinion. As one allied leader wrote of him: 'his whole object is to work up policy on two sides, so that he can choose the one which will involve him in least reproach from the nation, and to so contrive matters that he can always throw the blame on someone else'.[46] To an infinitely greater degree than has been assumed, he controlled the negotiations, even if he preferred his importance to be ostensibly eclipsed by St John's brilliant iconoclasm. And he succeeded in salvaging the Alliance against considerable odds. But his insistence on commercial advantages in the Spanish Empire – a sop to the City, but a constant impediment to Anglo-Dutch understanding – and his devious methods – so suited to the muddy waters of court intrigue, but ill-adapted to European power politics – made the illusion of collective bargaining frighteningly thin and the pretence of moderate leadership a farrago of parliamentary fact. Harley's tortuous mind and confused objectives made the Treaty of Utrecht a classic illustration of the expression 'perfidious Albion': not because he intended perfidy, but because his opportunism, his hypocrisy and his pragmatism seemed to be that to more exacting mentalities.

BIBLIOGRAPHICAL NOTE

G. M. Trevelyan, *England under Queen Anne*, iii (1934), and W. S. Churchill, *Marlborough, His Life and Times*, iv (1938), offer adequate narrative accounts of the Tory peace-making. Neither, however, attempts to analyse the basis of government policy; both are marred by ahistorical moralising. M. Foot, *The Pen and the Sword* (1957), gives a dramatic and in many ways convincing account of the struggle for peace in 1711. His reading is somewhat invalidated, however, by its uncritical reliance on Swift. D. Coombs, *The Conduct of the Dutch* (The Hague, 1958), gives the best account of Anglo-Dutch relations, but this too is distorted by inadequate use of English and Dutch diplomatic archives. I. A. Montgomery, *The Dutch Barrier, 1709–1719* (1930), shows a far less secure grasp of British politics than the preceding volume in the same book by R. Geikie. G. Holmes, *British Politics in the Age of Anne* (1967), gives the best brief account of Tory animosity to the war, while O. Klopp, *Der Fall des Hauses Stuart, 1660–1714* (Vienna, 1875–88), xii–xiv, despite obvious bias, is valuable for its grasp of diplomatic sources.

Of contemporary material, Bolingbroke's *Correspondence*, ed. G. Parke (1798), is much the most arresting, but should be read with an eye to Harley's contribution in HMC *Portland MSS*, iv, v. Serious study of the subject must, however, involve hours of archival burrowings – in a manner that would have pleased Harley's heart – into the great Portland Loan (Loan 29) at the British Museum and into the Heinsius Archives in The Hague.

I hope to develop many of the arguments outlined in this essay in my forthcoming study, *The Great Peace, 1710–1713*.

NOTES

1. *The Correspondence of Jonathan Swift*, ed. H. Williams (1963), i, 174: to Archbishop King, 9 Sept 1710.

2. N. Henderson, *Prince Eugene of Savoy* (1964), p. 181. The comment is fairly representative.

3. Swift to King, 12 July 1711, in *Corr.*, i, 238.

4. In 1715 he and his associates were impeached for their part in framing the Utrecht Settlement.

5. See pp. 20–2 above.

6. G. Holmes, *British Politics in the Age of Anne* (1967), p. 68.

7. BM Loan 29/151/12: Peterborough to Harley, 18 July 1706; Add. MS 40776, fo. 11: Shrewsbury to Vernon, 28 Oct 1706; Bodl. MS Eng. Misc. e.180, fo. 85.

8. *Letters and Correspondence of . . . Viscount Bolingbroke*, ed. G. Parke (1798), i, 17: to John Drummond, 28 Nov 1710.

9. PRO 30/24/22/2: Shaftesbury to van Twedde, 17 Jan 1706.

10. J. H. Plumb, *Sir Robert Walpole*, i (1956), 250.

11. BM Loan 29/9/37: Cabinet minutes, 22, 25 Sept 1707.

12. See p. 22 above.

13. BM Loan 29/6/1, 29/1/2; cf. HMC *Bath MSS*, i, 194.

14. HMC *Portland MSS*, iv, 516: Thomas to Robert Harley, 30 Dec 1708.

15. See pp. 135–7 above.

16. BM Loan 29/10/20: Harley to Queen Anne (draft), summer 1710; ibid./171/3: Harley to Dr Stratford, 6 Nov 1709.

17. HMC *Portland MSS*, iv, 110; Anon. *Life of Shrewsbury* (1717), p. 25.

18. Bodl. MS Eng. Misc. e.180, fo. 7: to Lord Orrery, 1 Sept 1709.

19. Plumb, op. cit. pp. 157–9; Marlborough to Godolphin, *c.* 1710, printed in G. M. Trevelyan, *England under Queen Anne*, iii (1934), 44–5.

20. BM Loan 29/10/20.

21. Ibid. 6/3.

22. Ibid. 7/1: Harley to a friend, *c.* 1701.

23. St John's description of Harley's aims to Sir William Trumbull, 1710: Berks RO. Trumbull Add. MS 133.

24. See HMC *Portland MSS*, ii, 221: Halifax to Newcastle, 26 Sept 1710.

25. Blenheim MSS E10: duchess of Marlborough to Queen Anne (draft), Dec 1710.

26. [Defoe], *Review*, Oct 1710.

27. 'Mr Harley's Plan of Administration', in *Hardwicke State Papers*, ii, 486.

28. Cowper's attitude quoted by Holmes, op. cit. p. 469 n 61.

29. SP 94/78: 'reply to Count Gallas' memorial', 10 Feb 1711; Dartmouth MSS: Cabinet minutes, 10 Feb.

30. HMC *Portland MSS* iv, 624: to Drummond, 10 Nov 1710.

31. Rijksarchief, The Hague, Heinsius MSS 1609: van Huls to Heinsius, 16 Jan 1711 (ciphered).

32. Ibid. 1609; Buys MSS, vol. ii (Harley to Buys). See also BM Loan 29/38/1: Harley's letters to Albemarle.

33. Archives Etrangères, Paris: Angleterre, 235, fo. 184; ibid. 232, folios 59–61: Gaultier to de Torcy, 17, 20 Feb 1711.

34. See ibid. 232, fo. 130; 233, folios 87–90: Gaultier to de Torcy, 15 May 1711, Torcy's memorandum, 21 July; Mellarede, 'Relatione sulle corte d'Inghilterra, 17 Jan 1713', in *Miscellanea di Storia Italia*, xxiv (Turin, 1885).

35. Bolingbroke, *Letter to Sir William Windham* (1753).

36. SP 44/213: St John to Governor Hunter, 6 Feb 1711; BM Loan 29/10/18: Harley to van Huls (draft); Heinsius MSS 2251: to same, 26 April, 3 May.

37. See p. 142 above.

38. BM Loan 29/288: St John, memorandum, *c.* June 1711.

39. *Bolingbroke Corr.* i, 335–7: Shrewsbury to St John, 27 Aug.

40. Heinsius MSS 1649: Harley to van Huls, 14 Sept; Blenheim MSS B2–7: to Marlborough, Aug–Oct 1711. For Harley's contacts with moderate Whigs see HMC *Portland MSS* v, 108, 115–16, 118, 120, 125.

41. *Journal to Stella*, 4 March.

42. For a corrective to the use of Swift's *Journal* as a reliable 'source' for government policies see I. Ehrenpreis, *The Personality of Jonathan Swift* (1958), pp. 61–75.

43. BM Loan 29/45H, 'Project for a general peace'; Heinsius MSS 1708: van Huls to Heinsius, 9 Jan, 12, 16 Feb 1712.

44. Ibid.: van Huls to Heinsius, 26 July, 2, 6, 12, 23 Aug; BM Loan 29/10/14: Harley, draft, *c.* Oct 1712; Bodl. MS Rawlinson A286: Harley to Bishop Robinson, 30 Sept.

45. Quoted in Holmes, op. cit. p. 112.

46. Haus-Hof-und Staatsarchiv, Vienna, Grosse Korrespondenz. 71: Wratislaw to Sinzendorf, 16 Aug 1712.

10. Harley, St John and the Death of the Tory Party

GEOFFREY HOLMES

In September 1714, a month after the death of the Queen whom he had served for four years as Secretary of State, the fallen Lord Bolingbroke mourned the passing of a political era: 'the grief of my soul is this, I see plainly that the Tory party is gone'. Gloomily he foresaw a future in which tens of thousands of his countrymen would continue to profess themselves Tories, but would no longer be credible competitors for power in the new Britain of George I.[1] Behind this lamentation lies one of the strangest riddles in British political history. Why did a party which commanded a natural majority of the political nation, which had enjoyed since 1710 a position of unprecedented strength in the House of Commons, and whose members had engrossed by 1714 almost every important civil office in the kingdom, thereupon disappear from the political map, as a potent force, for three-quarters of a century?

This is the problem on which this essay will focus. A possible solution, and one with much substance in it, is that the two most able Tory politicians of the day, Bolingbroke himself (the former Henry St John) and Robert Harley, earl of Oxford, engaged in a mutually destructive quarrel which divided the party, paralysed its leadership and delivered it into the hands of its enemies. A number of myths have grown up around this great political duel which can too easily befog the political scene of Anne's later years; and these we must try to dispel. But further questions will still require to be answered. Why, for instance, were there no other helmsmen ready and able to take the wheel when the captain and the first mate were swept from the bridge in that fateful summer of 1714? Is it feasible to explain the party's astonishing collapse solely in terms of leadership? Was it not the whole body, and not just the head, of Toryism that was mortally afflicted at the time of Anne's death? And, finally, can the assumption that underlies these questions – that the Tory party was indeed doomed in August 1714 – be itself sustained in the teeth of evidence which scholars have recently marshalled against it?[2]

I

To assess the contribution of Harley and St John to the Tory *débâcle* involves some understanding of the origins of their struggle, of the main stages in its development, and above all of its underlying causes. But the first necessity is to look back before the quarrel itself to the famous political friendship which preceded it. It is only when the nature of that close but strange relationship is understood that the reasons for its breakdown and for the bitter antagonism this engendered can be appreciated.

In the first place it was never an equal relationship. Harley was by fifteen years the senior, with over a decade more of parliamentary experience behind him. In the period of their closest association, during the first half of Queen Anne's reign, St John was merely the most talented member of a political group which looked to Robert Harley (Speaker in three successive Parliaments from 1701 to 1705 and Secretary of State from 1704 to 1708) for leadership and patronage. 'Robin' was the 'Master'; Harry the 'faithful' pupil. Later, when Harley formed a new administration in 1710 and St John received his first taste of Cabinet office, the latter's position remained – whether he liked it or not – that of a subordinate. Their Tory friends recognised this by the nicknames they gave the two men then, 'the colonel' and 'the captain' respectively. It is often imagined that right from the start the Queen's last ministry suffered from divided command – that it was 'the ministry of Harley and St John';[3] but this was not the case. The administration of 1710–14 was already half-way through its life when a noted confidant of its leading members wrote: 'the court is so luckily constituted at present, that every man thinks the chief trust cannot be anywhere else so well placed; neither do I know above one man that would take it, and it is a great deal too early for him to have such thoughts'.[4]

Apart from being an unequal relationship, Harley's friendship with St John had also represented, to an extraordinary degree, the attraction of opposites. Indeed, perhaps the oddest feature of their story is not that later in Anne's reign their paths so sharply diverged, but that they should ever have come together in the first place. They might never have done so but for the factious obstructionism and religious fanaticism shown by the champions of traditional High Toryism in the first two years of Anne's reign, which all but forced a disillusioned young St John into the welcoming arms of the Speaker, then casting around for Tories of every shape and size to rally them to the support of the Godolphin administration. But although their political alliance was accompanied by warm comradeship, there was never an integration of like minds and outlooks, let alone a harmony of temperaments. St John was by nature frank, impulsive, volatile; Harley secretive, oblique and phlegmatic. Their political talents were sharply contrasted, with St John the more brilliant debater and more indefatigable administrator and Harley the subtler negotiator and more skilful parliamentary manager. Their concepts of public life and its obligations were likewise very different. Harley was not only personally incorruptible, but meticulous in his attitude to public money; whereas St John, as he showed over the Quebec contracts (1711) and the commercial negotiations with Spain (1713–14), believed that nests were meant to be feathered.

Still more remarkably at variance were their basic political attitudes. To Harley the existence of party, as it had evolved by the end of King William's reign – with the deepest division that of Whig against Tory rather than of Country against Court – was a necessary evil. That is why a political spoils-system, in which party allegiance was the sole governing factor, was always unacceptable to him, particularly when it threatened the professional fields of administration. Although, in reaction against the Junto, he had severed nearly all his former Whig connexions by 1702, he consistently resisted the efforts of his friends to press him into a wholehearted commitment to Toryism, and more especially to foist on him after 1707 the mantle of party leader. Sharing as he did most of the opinions of a 'moderate Tory', such detachment became increasingly difficult to sustain as the head of a largely Tory administration between 1710 and 1714. Yet, however others saw him, he always conceived of himself as the Queen's 'manager', carrying on her business in the Sunderland–Marlborough–Godolphin tradition. St John, on the other hand, wore the habit of 'moderation' like a hair shirt. By nature and inclination he was deeply partisan, an extremist who showed his true colours in his fledgling years as an M.P. when he was a sponsor of the first two Occasional Conformity bills. His championship of right-wing policies and of unqualified single-party government later in Anne's reign was no more than a reversion to type.

The origins of the conflict between Harley and St John have long been a subject of speculation and confusion. The truth is, there was no sudden break, but rather a progressive deterioration of relations over more than six years: first a period of friction rather than direct conflict; then a period when conflict still remained to some extent below the surface, a source of embarrassment to Harley rather than a serious threat; and lastly a period when it was open and avowed, a real menace to Harley's supremacy and a dangerous source of weakness to the Tory party. The key dates emerge as 1708, 1711 and 1713.

In all three phases there were common denominators. There was disagreement over the extent to which Harley was committed, both by past promises and present professions, to the cause of Toryism. The element of personal animus was also constant throughout, limited to St John alone in the first phase, but becoming mutual in the last two. But the conventional view that theirs was essentially a clash of temperament and personality, underlain more by motives of jealousy and ambition than by a fundamental collision of principles[5] is wholly at odds with the evidence. In each phase there were major issues in dispute, and the way these issues were resolved or left unresolved was to prove of critical importance to the Tories. In the first period the argument was mainly over tactics – an argument over how the reign of Godolphin and the Whigs could best be terminated and their recovery prevented. But subsequently matters of policy and ideology became paramount, above all the issue of peace in the second period and the issue of the succession in the third.

The idea that Henry St John remained a loyal Harleyite for at least a decade must also be discounted. In fact, firm links were not forged until his third winter in the House of Commons (1703–4) and within five years these links had begun to show the first signs of stress. They were still apparently indissoluble in February 1708, when the young Secretary-at-War generously followed Harley out of office after the failure of his chief's first bid to overthrow Godolphin. Had Harley's February *coup* succeeded it was generally believed that St John would have replaced Lord Sunderland as Secretary of State for the South. This is a fact worth bearing in mind when considering St John's reaction to Harley's next attempt at a ministerial revolution, in 1710. The turning-point in their special relationship, however, had already come long before then. We can trace it back as far as the General Election of May 1708, an event which thus assumes an ominous significance for the future of the Tory cause. At this Election St John lost his seat at Wootton Bassett. All efforts to accommodate him elsewhere failed, and he was left with a strong grudge against his fellow Tories for not exerting themselves more strongly on his behalf. Some of this resentment rubbed off on Harley, although both he and his lieutenants seem to have done all they reasonably could do to assist 'the Thracian' in his plight.[6]

The next two years of enforced political inactivity, much of them passed on his country estate in Berkshire, changed the course of Henry St John's life. For one thing, they gave him prolonged insight, at first hand, into the grievances of the ordinary Tory gentleman, the private 'country esquire'. Between 1708 and 1710 the exile of Bucklebury found himself increasingly in sympathy with the attitudes of such men: with their war weariness; with their opposition to costly land operations in the Low Countries; above all with their hatred of Whiggery in all its manifestations, especially the Whiggery of the 'war profiteers' in the City. The other effect of St John's exclusion from the House of Commons was that for almost eighteen months down to the spring of 1710 it cut him off from the political mainstream, and to some extent from the Harleyite main body. While he was exhorting the 'Master' by letter to put himself 'at the head of the gentlemen of England', Harley himself was carefully preparing the ground for his second attempt to undermine the Godolphin ministry; and the agents of destruction which he planned to use (the Queen, the royal favourite Abigail Masham, and a group of discontented Whigs, the most notable of whom was the duke of Shrewsbury) were very different from the methods being advocated by his disciple. Together with the imperative need for secrecy in the work, they precluded close co-operation with St John in this vital phase.

The strain caused by these tactical disagreements was suddenly increased in March 1710, when St John discovered to his astonishment how Harley and Shrewsbury were planning to dispose of the spoils once the Godolphin ministry was overthrown, and realised that he himself had no place in their shadow Cabinet. As in 1708, Sunderland was earmarked as one of the first victims of the plot. But now there was no mention of St John among the bevy of candidates whose names were canvassed for the secretaryship before the choice fell in June on the uncontroversial Lord Dartmouth. Not until September, when Harley finally gave up his efforts to persuade an old comrade-in-arms of the 1690s, Henry Boyle, to stay on as the other Secretary of State, was the way opened for St John's promotion.[7] How can one account for this obvious reluctance to give him Cabinet office? One factor undoubtedly was the attitude of the Queen, who at this time disapproved of his political principles as well as of his unsavoury private life and his freethinking.[8] But it seems equally apparent that Harley himself, aware of St John's drift to extremism in the past two years, foresaw that it would be increasingly difficult in future to curb the younger man's natural bent. Both he and Shrewsbury realised the need for moderate policies at home while the new ministry was carrying out its first major task – that of putting peace negotiations on a firm footing, while fighting one more vigorous campaign abroad. They may even have feared that the negotiations themselves might be jeopardised with so positive a personality as St John in an office which gave him a large measure of control over the country's foreign relations.

It would have been asking too much of St John not to resent the obvious intention to exclude him from high office. His acknowledged gifts, and his self-sacrifice in 1708, entitled him to anticipate a more alluring prospect from the ministerial revolution of 1710 than an invitation to return to his old job at the War Office. His eventual appointment as Secretary of State for the North on 20 September was not in itself enough to remove the scars left by the events of the previous few months; and it should not be overlooked that two of the basic factors which were to sustain and embitter the quarrel which developed between Harley and St John in the years from 1711 to 1714, a personal grudge and a sharp divergence of political attitudes, were both present from the very start of the new ministry's life.

Friction, then, had been present since 1708. But the first real breach, disturbing to Harley's equanimity and to some extent disruptive of party unity, did not occur until 1711. It was in the spring of that year, while Harley still lay on his sick-bed following an attempt on his life by a French adventurer, that St John, jealous perhaps of the wave of sympathy for the victim, foolishly tried to detract from his colleague's near-martyrdom by claiming that Guiscard's knife had been intended for him. To Harley's anxious relatives such reckless and blatant seeking after the limelight was hard to forget and forgive; and we know that the invalid himself was deeply offended. But for him St John's indiscretion was adding insult to injury, for twice already the prime minister had been given good grounds for regretting his reluctant decision to admit his old friend into the Cabinet. Trouble had erupted in the Cabinet itself as early as January 1711, when St John, powerfully swayed by traditional Tory arguments in favour of a maritime strategy, first brought forward his proposal for an expedition to capture Quebec. Anxious not to subject the government's precarious financial position to unnecessary strain, and suspicious perhaps that the Secretary's motives were not entirely disinterested, Harley had cold-shouldered the scheme; but he had been unable to prevent the Cabinet finally approving it in the early days of his illness. Meanwhile, however, he had acquired a new and much stronger grievance against his ambitious colleague.

Early in February the House of Commons had witnessed the first concerted effort against the ministry by a formidable pressure-group of Tory backbenchers, the October Club; and Harley had good cause to suspect that St John was in some measure privy to its secrets and even involved behind the scenes in its activities.

It was common knowledge that 'the captain' sympathised with both the main aims of the Octobrists: the punishment of every Whig against whom a charge of financial malpractice in office could feasibly be brought and a total purge of that party's adherents, as he himself later put it, from all 'the employments of the kingdom, down to the meanest'.[9] It can scarcely be a coincidence that the Club's opening salvoes, including an unmistakable threat to hold up the voting of supply, were fired on 5 February 1711; and that over three years later Harley recalled to the Queen's memory, with unerring precision, that it was at 'the beginning of February 1710 [1711], there began to be a separation in the House of Commons, and Mr Secretary St Johns began listing a party, and set up for governing the House'.[10] How long St John continued to play so dangerously with fire in this way we cannot be certain. He was sobered to some extent in late February or early March by the remonstrances of a group of fellow ministers dining at his house; but during Harley's two-months' absence from the Commons after the Guiscard incident, the Secretary was seemingly tempted to at least one more major indiscretion. The humiliating fiasco over the leather duty at the end of March, when the government was defeated on a vital revenue measure by the votes of the Octobrists, and was able to recover only by the discreditable expedient of proposing the same tax the following day, disguised under a new name, was largely St John's fault. And the contemporary evidence to support a charge of connivance as well as negligence certainly cannot be lightly discounted.[11]

If by his extraordinary tactics between January and March 1711 St John had hoped to discredit Harley's administration, force his resignation and then step into his shoes, he must have been bitterly disappointed by the outcome. When Harley returned to active politics at the end of April, after his convalescence, his own star was much higher than it had been two months earlier and his ministry more firmly established, while the Secretary's stock had plummeted. In the late spring of 1711, in fact, St John's dismissal from office was confidently forecast. By great good fortune he survived. He did so mainly because Harley could at this time afford to be generous to his would-be rival. His own primacy was now unquestioned, and was soon to be confirmed when a grateful Queen made him earl of Oxford and Lord High Treasurer. Also, St John's acute mental grasp and formidable capacity for work could not lightly be dispensed with after 2 May 1711, when Lord Rochester's sudden and unexpected death deprived the government of its most experienced member; and this only a few days after the Cabinet, St John included, had been admitted to the secret that peace negotiations with France were afoot. But it is the fact of St John's survival rather than the reasons for it which is important. For this was the first of two crucial occasions during the life of Anne's last ministry when Harley allowed his erring and dangerous colleague to escape the penalty of his political sins and recover all the ground that he had lost. The second, as we shall shortly see, occurred in the autumn of 1713. Each episode appears in retrospect to have been a nail driven inexorably into the coffin of the Tory party.

The latter occasion took place shortly after the Harley–St John struggle had entered its third and most serious phase. For most of the preceding two and a half years, since April 1711, the dominant theme in the two men's relations with each other had been the making of peace. Over the same period, likewise, the government's peace policy had become the governing factor in setting the Tory party as a whole on a perilous and injurious course: 'the very work which ought to have been the basis of our strength', as the 'man of mercury' himself came to acknowledge,[12] 'was in part demolished before our eyes, and we were stoned with the ruins of it'. How St John was for long kept in ignorance of the 'Jersey stage' of the negotiations in 1710–11; how Oxford tenaciously preserved his own diplomatic control from April 1711 until the consummation in April 1713; and how St John constantly chafed and fretted at his inability to put his own stamp indelibly on the proceedings – this we learnt in the previous essay. But there are three aspects of the Tory peace-making which, because of their bearing on our own problem, merit special emphasis.

The first is that for Oxford important principles were at stake in the foreign as well as the domestic policies of his administration. From the first his Cabinet had been generally agreed on the need for peace, as well as on the fact that British interests had been sacrificed by the Whigs to those of the allies. Yet over the timing of negotiations, the methods by which peace should be sought, and the objectives it should secure, there were important ministerial differences, above all between the first minister and the Secretary for the North; and these reflected still wider differences within the Tory party at large.[13] Harley did not

exclude St John from the 'Jersey stage' because, as is sometimes maintained, he was jealous of the younger man's talents. He excluded him
primarily because he wanted the broad principles of agreement to have
been reached between Britain and France, and accepted by the allies,
before St John's own views – his unashamed anti-Europeanism, his
almost pathological hatred of the Dutch, and his consequent indifference
to the protection of most allied interests – had had the chance to obtrude
themselves. The attempt did not succeed; but the subsequent history
of the negotiations, once St John was involved in them, proved that it
was well justified.

The second point to be stressed about the personal conflict over the
peace, seen in the context of ultimate Tory disaster, is that on the one
occasion in these two years when St John broke free from Oxford's
stranglehold, during his brief mission to France in August 1712, he
committed indiscretions even more shattering than his parliamentary
frolics of 1711 and certainly more damaging in their effects. This was a
mission from which he himself expected much, as a means of breaking
down remaining obstacles to peace, but from which Oxford expected
little or nothing. The Treasurer sanctioned it only in the hope that it
would help to salve St John's wounded pride, after the Queen had con-
ferred the viscountcy of Bolingbroke on him instead of the earldom
he had expected; and he made certain that his colleague's commission
would be narrowly circumscribed. But even Oxford could hardly have
foreseen that Bolingbroke would exceed his instructions quite so
extravagantly or perpetrate the crowning solecism of allowing himself to
be seen in public with the Pretender. The result was a stormy Cabinet
meeting on 28 September 1712, at which the Treasurer succeeded in
getting Bolingbroke's actions and immediate objectives repudiated,
but at the same time discovered to his chagrin that the Secretary was
now able to command more support from other leading ministers, and
even – on some points – from the Queen, than he had imagined possible.
The importance of this Cabinet as a stage in the breakdown of ministerial
cohesion should not be overlooked.

At the same time it must be seen in perspective. For although the
ministry's peace policy added a fresh source of friction to those already
present in the relations between Oxford and St John, it was also the
main factor in postponing for so long a complete and final rupture.
Cabinet disputes over the peace there certainly were. But the overriding necessity of completing the great work to which all its members
were committed led them, on each occasion, to stifle resentments and

patch up differences which in other circumstances would have led to resignations or dismissals. Very significantly it was only after the final treaties with France had been signed in April 1713, and very soon afterwards at that, that Oxford noted the formation of the first genuine 'confederation' or 'combination' against him.[14]

This confederacy was born out of the troubles of the session of April–July 1713 (the last session of the old Parliament). Both inside and outside the ministry there were prominent Tories who by 1713 had lost faith in Oxford's leadership, or believed that now peace had come at last he had outlived his usefulness to the party. At their head, needless to say, was Bolingbroke. He and his closest allies, Lord Chancellor Harcourt and Francis Atterbury, the new bishop of Rochester, unjustly laid the onus of all the government's parliamentary difficulties – over the malt tax, the Union with Scotland and above all the commerce treaty with France – on the Lord Treasurer's shoulders, and protested that nothing positive had been done to advance the interest of the Tory party or the Anglican Church. By the end of the session, though still far from certain of the Queen's good will,[15] Bolingbroke had come to the conclusion that now was the time to make his bid for glory. 'If your brother will not set himself at the head of the Church party', he informed Edward Harley, 'somebody must'.[16]

Thus the Oxford–Bolingbroke conflict became for the first time a direct struggle for power. It was fought out in the corridors of Kensington and Whitehall during the last week in July and the first week in August, and it ended in rout for Oxford's opponents. They were forced to submit not just to his continued premiership, but to a remodelling of ministerial offices which directly curtailed their own departmental authority and placed 'Treasurer's men' at almost every strategic point available. When Oxford journeyed into Cambridgeshire at the end of August to preside over his son's marriage to Lady Harriet Holles, one of the most coveted matrimonial prizes in England, it seemed that he was setting the seal of social triumph on a great political achievement.

No-one, least of all Oxford himself, could have expected the tide of fortune at this juncture to turn so quickly against him. It did so for three reasons. The first was four weeks' almost continuous absence from Windsor by the Treasurer, which gave Bolingbroke an unexpected opportunity to rally his broken forces and to win over the influential favourite, Lady Masham. The second was Oxford's request in mid-September for the dukedom of Newcastle for his son, Edward, which caused the first real breach in the unique relationship which Oxford had enjoyed with Queen Anne since 1706. The third was Masham's betrayal of this request to Bolingbroke, who did not scruple to propagate the slander that Oxford was prepared to sacrifice all other interests, public and party, to those of his family advancement. The truth is that Oxford had been forced into this unhappy predicament mainly by the vindictiveness and self-consequence of Lady Harriet's mother.

More serious, however, than these immediate causes was the prolonged bout of apathy, verging on despair, which assailed the Treasurer from late September until well into December. This was the product partly of the damage inflicted on his relationship with the Queen (the extent of which was magnified greatly by his own paranoia), partly to a great personal tragedy he suffered in November – just when he was beginning to haul himself out of the trough – with the death of his favourite daughter. For the Tory party this phase of the Oxford–Bolingbroke struggle was to prove perhaps the most important of all. For although by December 1713 Bolingbroke had almost succeeded in convincing the Queen that his *policies* were the right ones for the government to pursue, he had still to convince her that they were best entrusted to his own hands. Anne could as yet see no obvious alternative to Oxford without turning again to the Whigs. One can only conclude that had the prime minister looked to his defences late in 1713, instead of giving way to defeatism, he would very probably have regained fairly quickly much of the ground he had lost in September; and in that case it is more than possible that he would still have been firmly in the saddle when Anne died the following August (the fact that he clung on to an infinitely weaker position till almost the end of July surely justifies this assumption). The Tory party would then not have had to face the most critical year of its existence in 1714 with a ministry which had no authoritative leadership, no clear objectives, and indeed no sense of direction.

It is this final phase of the battle for command over the Tory ministry, from January to August 1714, which has attracted most attention; and partly for this reason, partly because there is less that is new to be said about it, we may be excused for devoting the minimum of space to it here. The lack of direction in the government was nowhere more obvious, and nowhere more fatal, than in its succession policy. By the terms of the Act of Settlement of 1701, the second in line to the throne if Anne died without direct heirs was the Elector George Lewis of Hanover. Only his aged mother, the Princess Sophia,[17] stood between him and the legal Protestant succession. Ever since the winter of 1711–12 this fact had confronted the Oxford ministry with a most uncomfortable dilemma. For the Elector was a convinced supporter of the claims of the Habsburg Charles VI to the throne of Spain; he was also a soldier with a warm admiration for the duke of Marlborough. The news, that winter, of Britain's determination to abandon Spain to the Bourbons, followed by the dismissal of Marlborough from his command, had done serious damage to good relations between the ministry and the Hanoverian court. To the Elector these steps argued a favourable disposition towards the cause of the exiled Stuarts, and few Tories doubted by December 1713 that his succession would mean for them at least a temporary loss of royal favour. Had this seemed a distant prospect it would have been less disturbing. But at Christmas the Queen fell desperately ill, so ill that for two or three days her life was in genuine danger, and from every Tory, inside and outside the government, an agonising reappraisal of the succession question was called for.

Bolingbroke's priorities from now on were: first, to try to persuade the Pretender to acknowledge a purely nominal conversion to Protestantism, and second, in case this approach failed (and it had done so comprehensively by early March), to seek to ensure that Tory command of all the institutions of Church and State, and above all of the armed forces, was so unchallengeable that whoever succeeded Anne would be forced to make his terms with the party and with its leaders. Bold as he was, even Bolingbroke was not hardy enough to stake everything on the Pretender's cause. But by assiduously cultivating the Jacobite leaders in Parliament, by holding out the prospect of a repeal of the Act of Settlement and by showing himself totally unconciliatory in his attitude to Hanover, he left few politicians or observers in any doubt where his real sympathies lay. Oxford, galvanised at last into action by the Queen's illness, was convinced in the last six months of his ministry's life of the Secretary's Jacobite inclinations. He himself had never been anything but a Hanoverian at heart. And although for a month or two at the beginning of 1714 he was put so much out of patience by Hanoverian intrigues with the Whigs that he allowed himself to be associated with the appeal to the Pretender on the religious issue, his attitude towards the succession very soon became dominated by two overriding concerns.

The first was to take advantage of what parliamentary opportunities occurred (for example, over the Whig proposal to offer a reward for the Pretender's capture in June) to demonstrate his sincerity to Hanover and to the 'Hanover wing' of the Tory party. His main concern, however, was the purely negative one of clinging on to office as long as possible,

in the conviction that this was the best service he could render the
Hanoverian cause. Only twice did he veer from this course: for a few
days in March, when, under renewed attack from Bolingbroke and his
followers, he seriously contemplated throwing in his hand; and in the
last fortnight in June and the first week of July, when he saw his last
chance of destroying Bolingbroke by a vigorous counter-attack over
the conduct of the Spanish commerce negotiations. But in the main his
aim was to act, as one scholar has strikingly put it, as the 'drag anchor'
on Bolingbroke's ambitions.[18] So well did he succeed in the end in
fulfilling this self-appointed role – staving off the inevitable for four
months at least after he had totally lost the Queen's confidence, and
after his defeat had been widely predicted, and leaving his rival a mere
four days' grace before Anne's death overwhelmed him – that he is
entitled to no small share of the credit for frustrating the Pretender's
hopes. Unfortunately for the Tories, of course, the very success of this
long-drawn-out delaying action, accompanied as it was by open warfare
both in Cabinet and Parliament between Oxford and Bolingbroke
factions, further increased the possibility that the party itself would not
long survive the fall of the Lord Treasurer on 27 July 1714. Though
heavily outnumbered in the House of Commons, the Whigs had
achieved complete unity and cohesion in 1714 over the succession
question; and from the morning of 30 July, when Queen Anne, brought
by the distress and anxiety of the past few months to the end of her tiny
stock of physical resources, fell into the coma that was to mark the
start of her last illness, 'Mercurialis', the victor of the moment, saw all
the hopes and schemes of the past twelve months rendered irrelevant.
The initiative was wrested from his hands, first by the Privy Council,[19]
and secondly, after the Queen's death, by the Council of Regency for
which the Whigs had made such careful provision in the Act of 1706.
Once George Lewis had been peacefully proclaimed King at St James's
Palace gate, and it became apparent that the Jacobites were not prepared
for any swift countermove, the remorseless logic of party conflict and of
two and a half years of bad relations between the Oxford ministry and
Hanover could only mean the end of Tory government, at least in the
immediate future.

II

But did it also mean, or need it have meant, the end of the Tory party?
Certain it is that there were major obstacles in the way of the party's

revival and recovery. And none was more formidable than the poverty of its leadership.

The essence of the Tories' plight in 1714 was not that they were entirely lacking in young men with the potential of leadership: men such as Sir William Windham, the Chancellor of the Exchequer, who in the 1720s and 1730s was to become an able enough spokesman of those Tory backbenchers by then reconciled to the Hanoverian dynasty. But what the Tories needed in the aftermath of Queen Anne's death was assets that were more solid and more immediately realisable; and the sorry truth was that there was no-one who could *at once* (and this was the key point) fill the vacuum left by the fall of Oxford in July 1714 and of Bolingbroke in August. The Whigs were utterly determined to hound both these men out of public life at the earliest opportunity, using the recent peace negotiations as their excuse. In any case Oxford's constitution had already been badly undermined by illness and bouts of heavy drinking, and two years in the Tower awaiting trial from 1715 to 1717 completed the ruin of his health. As for Bolingbroke, he was still young and, for all his dissolute life, immensely vigorous (it is sometimes forgotten that he lived until 1753). But even if he had not sealed his own political fate by fleeing to France in anticipation of arrest in 1715, he would still have been out of the reckoning for several years.

The absence of any outstanding personality capable of rallying the demoralised forces of Toryism after August 1714 and, equally important, of holding them together in face of the fresh shocks they suffered over the next two years, can partly be explained on natural grounds. The most important seam of Tory leadership since 1688 – that old generation of High Church Tories whose primacy had been established by the political battles of the 1670s – had been virtually worked out. Sir Edward Seymour had died in 1708, the earl of Rochester in 1711, and the duke of Leeds (the former Danby) in 1712. The only prominent survivor of this vintage, Lord Nottingham, might have given the lead the party so desperately needed in the early months of George I's reign but for one crippling disqualification. In November 1711, prompted in part by pique, in part by principle, he had renounced his support for the Oxford ministry, made a pact with his old adversaries the Whigs, and gone into permanent opposition. Many Tories never forgave him; and even those strong pro-Hanoverians who co-operated with him in Parliament in 1714 were disillusioned when he agreed to accept a Cabinet office along with the Whigs in George I's first ministry.

Of the younger generation only three men, apart from Bolingbroke had established any real claim before 1714 to inherit the mantle of Nottingham, Rochester and Seymour. These were Sir Thomas Hanmer, one of the wealthiest commoners in England and Speaker at the time of the Queen's death; the earl of Anglesey, who had been Vice-Treasurer of Ireland under Lord Oxford; and the Northern Secretary of State from 1713 to 1714, William Bromley of Baginton. The first two had emerged since the summer of 1713 as the undisputed leaders of the Hanoverian Tories. But as fomenters of open rebellion against the ministry they had made themselves highly controversial figures, and in some Tory quarters unacceptable. Moreover Hanmer, despite a good intellect and an impressive oratorical style, remained a backbencher at heart, far more at home as a critic than as a pillar of government. The man incomparably best fitted to lead the Tory party through the wilderness in 1714 was Bromley. He had a quarter of a century of parliamentary experience behind him. Ever regarded as a staunch Churchman, he nonetheless had friends and admirers in every section of the party. In the previous four years he had filled the Speaker's Chair as well as the Secretaryship with credit. Though far more a party man than Harley, he had backed the Treasurer against the wilder excesses of Bolingbroke from 1711 almost to the end, but had refused to join in intrigues with the Whigs. Hanover believed him loyal, and he was offered a Household appointment by George I soon after his accession. Yet, with all these advantages, Bromley incomprehensibly missed the opportunity which awaited him in 1714. He continued to sit in the House of Commons until his death in 1732, but the last eighteen years were a slow downward drift into relative obscurity. Even in the Parliament of 1715–22 he became of less account on the attenuated benches of the Tory opposition than lesser figures like Windham, Shippen and Hynde Cotton. It may have been a failure of character, of ambition, or simply of faith. Whatever it was, it cost the Tory party dear; it could be argued that it cost it its best, if not its only, chance of surviving the disaster of 1714 and competing again for power.

The problem of leadership was not, of course, a new one for the Tories. It was all too familiar. The party hierarchy had never approached the cohesion which the Whigs derived from the dominance first of Shaftesbury and later of the Junto. Neither could it consistently secure united action from the lower ranks. The Country Tory backbencher and the backwoods Tory peer earned a just reputation both in William's reign and in Anne's for their independence of mind and for being unamenable to discipline. Not surprisingly, the capacity of the parliamentary Tories for fragmentation in certain circumstances was remarkable; and it was never more in evidence than in the session of 1714. The contrast with the Whigs was extraordinary. Both in 1702, when William III died, and in 1710, when the Godolphin ministry fell, the Whigs faced great difficulties and possible disintegration. That they lived to fight another day was due in no small measure on each occasion to the command which the five lords of the Junto could exercise over the party in times of adversity. In 1715–16, when three of these lords died and a fourth retired from active political life, the Whigs had a new generation of leaders ready to assume control: a generation represented by Walpole, Townshend and Stanhope and, of the younger vintage, by Pulteney and Carteret.

At the same time too much emphasis can be placed on these essentially personal factors. The Whigs survived the shocks of 1702 and 1710 not only because of talented and coherent leadership but also because in both crises the rank and file of the party were, and remained, united on essentials. Those who would maintain that the Tory party was a doomed party from the moment Queen Anne died must rest their case, at least in part, on the demonstrable lack of any comparable unity in its ranks, at least since the summer of 1713.

For a party which traditionally stood for 'Church and Crown', the Glorious Revolution, involving as it did a spectacular disavowal of the High Anglican political creed, had necessarily been a damaging experience. Yet it was one from which, to most appearances, the Tories had recovered with startling rapidity. Their great strength in the constituencies, the early favour shown them by King William,[20] and the fact that their ideological base, though undermined in 1688, had by no means been destroyed, had all played their part in this recovery. A comparison between their situation and fortunes in 1688–9 and in 1714–15 is both valid and instructive. On each occasion Tories were faced with the same basic choice – Church versus King (though in the latter case it was not the King in possession but the titular James III, 'the Gentleman over the Water', whose right was in question). On each occasion the vast majority came in the end to the same decision: they chose to reject the Stuart king in order to preserve the Anglican Church. Having made that decision once at the expense of their traditional belief in hereditary right, and what is more confirmed it thirteen years later by accepting the parliamentary exclusion of the legitimate Stuart line, the choice should logically have been much easier to make on the next occasion. In fact it proved far more difficult, and was delayed so long that the Tories were overtaken by events and, in marked contrast with 1688-9, lost control of them.

What was at the root of this dilemma? Lack of firm leadership, though of the greatest importance as we have seen, cannot have been the whole answer. Nor had the Tories experienced any diminution of their Anglican zeal in the past quarter of a century. And yet the Pretender's refusal to compromise on the religious issue in March 1714, so far from resolving their paralysis of will, only served to intensify it. Without doubt, their consciences were still sorely troubled about the Revolution and about the Act of Settlement of 1701 that had been its logical sequel. The old creed may have been denied in 1688-9; it may have seemed for some years thereafter to lose much of its relevance; but it had not been forgotten. When, for the first time since the Revolution, an oath abjuring allegiance to the Pretender was imposed on all officials and members of Parliament in 1702, it took Lord Nottingham (stout Anglican though he was, and later a doughty fighter for the Protestant succession) three months to change his first opinion, that 'the safest side *in conscience* is to refuse it'.[21] The refusal of the 'Church party' four years later to support the practical measures proposed in the Regency bill, to ensure the peaceful establishment of a Protestant successor when Queen Anne died, was another straw in the wind; and during the impeachment and trial in 1710 of Dr Henry Sacheverell for preaching a violently anti-Revolution sermon in St Paul's Cathedral, the arguments voiced by Tory after Tory proved beyond doubt that the principle of hereditary right still commanded wide support, and that even the notion of passive obedience was far from being extinct.

Such is the ideological background against which we must view the Tories' reaction to the growing breach between the Oxford ministry and the Elector of Hanover after the winter of 1711-12. Despite this estrangement, the Protestant succession still claimed its quota of genuine supporters inside the party. A handful of committed pro-Hanoverians nailed their colours to the mast as early as December 1711; more followed suit in 1712 and 1713; and by 16 April 1714 almost a quarter of the 340 Tories packed into the Commons' chamber in St Stephen's Chapel (more than had ever attended since the Revolution) were prepared to vote against the government motion that the succession was in no danger. More significant, however, was the attitude of the remainder, who either frankly repudiated or simply shirked an open commitment to Hanover. At least half the party was still torn in the spring of 1714 between the legal and religious arguments in favour of Hanover and the emotional and ideological factors, not to mention considerations of party interest, which pulled them in the opposite direction.

How this great mass of 'floaters' would have reacted in the 1714 session, had Bolingbroke been in a position to introduce – as the Jacobite members begged him to – a bill to repeal the Act of Settlement, we can only speculate. The stirring demonstration of Tory support for Edward Harley, after his unequivocal speech on 24 June in favour of a reward of £100,000 for the Pretender's capture, suggests that since April more waverers had moved towards Hanover than away from it.[22] What really mattered, however, as far as the party's future was concerned, was that so many of its adherents sat irresolutely on the fence for so long that neither Bolingbroke's hand nor Oxford's could be sufficiently strengthened by parliamentary backing to put an early end to the disastrous war of attrition at Court, a war in which there could only be one eventual victor – the Whigs.

Since the succession paralysis of 1714 was, in a sense, a delayed result of the violent shock which the Tory creed had suffered in 1688–9, it could be maintained that the party died 'from natural causes'. But taking a wider range of evidence into account, the coroner-historian would be more justified in deciding that it took its own life. It cannot be too strongly emphasised that except on the succession the Tories were not a fatally divided party in 1714. On religious policy, though some were prepared to go further than others to attack the toleration, there were no fundamental disagreements among Tory laymen, while the return of a Whig administration from August 1714 onwards lent renewed force to the old rallying cry of 'the Church in danger'. On social policy, there was still widespread acceptance of the need to shore up the landed interest against its supposed rivals in the City and in the professions, although with the end of the war the conflict of interests[23] inevitably lost something of its edge, and it would lose more as the years went by. Had Bolingbroke had his way and negotiated a new alliance with France and Spain, a serious split might conceivably have developed over foreign policy, but most Tories would have agreed in 1714 on the need for a large measure of disengagement from Europe. The death of Anne and the subsequent loss of the power it had enjoyed for the past four years did not overnight destroy the whole *raison d'être* of the 'Church party'. It still had something to live and fight for; and no less because for the great majority of Tories the succession problem virtually solved itself with the peaceful proclamation of George I. And yet, after August 1714, as for months before it, the party behaved as though the death-wish had taken possession of its spirit. Firm but judicious measures might still have resuscitated an ailing patient. Instead almost everything that was done served to hasten the end.

It is true that the final decline after August 1714 was at least partly attributable to the destructive power of the Whigs. The resignation of Shrewsbury, Oxford's successor as Lord Treasurer, within a few months of his appointment meant that for the first time since 1694 there was no 'manager' at the helm to restrain the vindictiveness of a triumphant set of party leaders or control the vast patronage of the Crown. For this reason the loss of power which the Tories suffered between August and December, first at the centre, then in the localities, was more than just a swing of the party pendulum, like those which had gone against the Whigs in 1702 and more recently in 1710. No party since the Revolution had been so dangerously exposed to the fury of its opponents as was the Tory party by the end of 1714. But at the same time no party could have done more to increase its own vulnerability. The most extra-ordinary feature of British politics in the two years following Anne's death was the well-nigh incredible folly of the Tories in squandering their last reserves of strength. By spurning the limited yet important favours which George I was prepared to bestow on them,[24] by bungling their election campaign in the winter of 1714–15 and so failing to capit-alise on a natural majority in the constituencies,[25] by withholding their support but not their sympathy from the rebels of the '15, they virtually offered themselves up as a sacrifice to their enemies.

The 1715 Election, on which the party had pinned its hopes, was not in itself a holocaust. With over 200 seats in the new House of Commons the Tories were better placed, numerically, than their opponents had been after the previous contest in 1713. But whereas the Whigs in 1713 still had their leaders, their discipline and their faith to hold them together, the Tories by 1715 lacked all three. They were also too dis-credited both at Court and in the country, especially after the disastrous decision of Bolingbroke to bolt to France in March 1715 and enlist in the Pretender's service, to escape the stigma of Jacobitism and treason when the '15 Rebellion broke out in Scotland later in the year. Even though few English Tories actively supported it, the rebellion gave the Whig ministers a perfect excuse by 1716 to carry through a purge of office-holders 'down to the meanest', such as Bolingbroke had dreamed of in 1710 but had never been strong enough to accomplish. It also enabled them to pass the Septennial Act, which on the grounds of public safety extended the maximum life of the existing Parliament from three years to seven. It was thus made impossible for the Tories to profit, with the strength remaining to them in the constituencies, from the great Whig schism of 1717 or from the South Sea Bubble scandals of 1720. From these final blows in 1716 there could be for the old Tory party no hope of recovery.

To sum up. The first Tory party did not die in 1714 but in 1716; nor even then did it die a natural death. The inquest of history, while conceding that the party's constitution had been weakened by the shocks of 1688–9 and 1701, must look elsewhere than the Revolution and the Act of Settlement for the real agents of destruction. It must find that the party was gravely wounded between 1711 and 1714 by the two men best able, in their very different ways, to give it a new lease of life; but must add the *caveat* that the protracted duel in which these injuries were inflicted was, in part at least, the reflection of broader differences of opinion among Tories at large, over basic questions of home and foreign policy. It must accept the evidence that in the months of crisis at the beginning of George I's reign the party was recklessly neglected or abused by its own physicians, and reach the verdict that at the last, despairing of the future and implacably harried by its foes, it committed suicide.

BIBLIOGRAPHICAL NOTE

No adequate full-length biography of Harley has yet been written, though several short studies are currently in preparation.[26] Recent studies of St John – e.g. S. W. Jackman, *Man of Mercury* (1965) – are of little political value, but the shrewd and vivid character judgements in H. T. Dickinson's 'Henry St John: a Reappraisal of the Young Bolingbroke', in *JBS* vii (May 1968), do something to fill the void. Making due allowance for personal bias, the contemporary apologias of the two protagonists offer the closest insight into their conflict from August 1710 onward. St John's is in *A Letter to Sir William Windham* (1717/ 1753); Oxford's in 'A Brief Account of Public Affairs . . . to . . . 8th of June 1714', printed in *Parl. Hist.* vi (1810), app. iv. For a rather different view of 'Bolingbroke's share in the Jacobite Intrigue of 1710–14' from that taken by the present writer, see H. N. Fieldhouse's article in *EHR* lii (1937).

On the Tory party in general, Sir K. Feiling, *History of the Tory Party 1640–1714* (Oxford, 1924), remains indispensable. The fullest account of its complex and fissile structure in Anne's reign is in G. Holmes, *British Politics in the Age of Anne* (1967), ch. 8. W. Michael, *England under George I: The Beginnings of the Hanoverian Dynasty* (English transl. 1936) contains the most detailed narrative of politics in the closing months of Anne's reign and the first two years of her successor's; while J. H. Plumb, *The Growth of Political Stability in England* (1967), provides a highly stimulating assessment, and A. S. Foord, *His Majesty's Opposition 1714–1830* (Oxford, 1964), a useful brief account, of the Tory dilemma of 1714–16.

NOTES

1. James Macpherson, *Original Papers containing the Secret History of Great Britain* (1775), ii, 631: to Bishop Atterbury [1 or 2 Sept].

2. e.g. J. H. Plumb, *The Growth of Political Stability in England 1675–1725* (1967), pp. 159–60; *The Divided Society*, ed. G. Holmes and W. A. Speck (1967), pp. 1–2, 33–7. For the traditional view see K. Feiling, *History of the Tory Party* (1924), p. 479.

3. This legend owes its popularity to that most widely read survey of the seventeenth century, G. M. Trevelyan's *England under the Stuarts*. See Pelican ed. (1960), pp. 484–5.

4. *The Works of Jonathan Swift*, ed. T. Roscoe (1888), ii, 483: Swift to Archbishop King, 30 Sept 1712.

5. See, for example, M. Ashley, *England in the Seventeenth Century* (1952), pp. 246–8; G. N. Clark, *The Later Stuarts*, 2nd ed. (Oxford, 1955), pp. 239, 245–6.

6. Levens MSS: St John to James Grahme, 18 July 1708; see also G. Holmes, *British Politics in the Age of Anne* (1967), pp. 319, 506 n 123.

7. HMC *Portland MSS* ii, 218.

8. Herts RO Panshanger MSS: Hamilton's diary, 21 Sept 1710, 14 Dec 1711.

9. Bolingbroke, *A Letter to Sir William Windham* (1753), pp. 21–2.

10. BM Loan 29/204: paper dated 6 June 1714.

11. See, for example, Arthur Onslow's note to Burnet, *A History of my own Time* (1833), vi, 31; Edward Harley's 'Memoirs of the Harley Family', in HMC *Portland MSS* v, 655.

12. *Letter to Windham*, p. 50; 'man of mercury' was yet another of St John's nicknames.

13. See Holmes, *British Politics*, pp. 78–80.

14. 'Set on foot against the next Parliament'. BM Loan 29/204: paper dated 15 June 1714; cf. HMC *Portland MSS* v, 466.

15. *The Lockhart Papers*, ed. A. Aufrere (1817), i, 412–13.

16. HMC *Portland MSS* v, 660.

17. Sophia died in May 1714.

18. B. W. Hill, 'The Career of Robert Harley, earl of Oxford, from 1702 to 1714' (Cambridge Ph.D. thesis, 1961), fo. 332.

19. See *The Divided Society*, ed. Holmes and Speck, pp. 176–7.

20. See pp. 120–5, 160–1 above.

21. Lloyd-Baker MSS, box 4, bundle Q55: Nottingham to Archbishop Sharp, 10 Jan 1702. My italics.

22. Staatsarchiv Hannover, CBA 24 England, 113a, folios 298–9: Kreienberg's report, 25 June; Add. MS 22201, fo. 101: [Boyer] to Stafford, 25 June.

23. See pp. 135–54 above.

24. Add. MS 47027, pp. 342–8. Of particular importance was the rejection by Bromley, Hanmer and the latter's friend and ally Ralph Freeman of the King's invitations to join the Nottinghamites in the ministry (Oct 1714). Unlike Nottingham, these three leaders had no past sins to purge, and their acceptance would have ensured, as nothing else could, that the Tories did not fight the General Election of 1715 as a truculent opposition faction.

25. A spectacular example of their indiscreet electoral propaganda was Francis Atterbury's 'English Advice to the Freeholders of England' (1714). See *Somers Tracts* (1815), xiii.

26. Elizabeth Hamilton, *The Backstairs Dragon: A Life of Robert Harley, Earl of Oxford* (1969), was published after this Bibliographical Note was written.

NOTES ON CONTRIBUTORS

G. V. BENNETT, Fellow, Chaplain and Tutor in Modern History, New College, Oxford; formerly Lecturer in History, King's College, London (1954–9); graduate of Cambridge; ordained in 1956 and is an Honorary Canon of Chichester; author of *White Kennett, Bishop of Peterborough* (1957) and editor of *Essays in Modern English Church History in Memory of Norman Sykes* (1966); is soon to publish a new life of Francis Atterbury.

JENNIFER CARTER, Lecturer in History, University of Aberdeen; formerly Lecturer at Makerere College, East Africa; graduate of London; author of a doctoral thesis, 'The Administrative Work of the English Privy Council, 1679–1714' (London, 1958) and of an article on the Cabinet in the reign of William III.

E. L. ELLIS, Lecturer in History, University College of Wales, Aberystwyth; formerly Tutor at Ruskin College, Oxford (1949–62); graduate of Aberystwyth; author of a doctoral thesis on 'The Whig Junto' (Oxford, 1962), now being prepared for publication, and of a forthcoming centenary history of the University College of Wales.

G. C. GIBBS, Lecturer in History, Birkbeck College, London; graduate of Liverpool; author of articles and essays on British foreign policy in the early Hanoverian period; at present engaged on a study of European sources for parliamentary history in the reign of George I and on an introduction and a new index to Luttrell's *Brief Historical Relation of State Affairs*.

GEOFFREY HOLMES, *see cover*, Reader in History, University of Lancaster; graduate of Oxford; author of *British Politics in the Age of Anne* (1967) and co-editor (with W. A. Speck) of *The Divided Society* (1967).

HENRY HORWITZ, Associate Professor of History, University of Iowa; graduate of Haverford College; author of *Revolution Politicks: The Career of Daniel Finch, Second Earl of Nottingham 1647–1730* (1968) and of articles on seventeenth-century ecclesiastical and political history. Currently working on a study of Parliament under William III.

ANGUS McINNES, Lecturer in History, University of Keele; graduate of Aberystwyth; author of articles, and of a recently completed book, on Robert Harley; now working on the history of Shrewsbury between 1500 and 1800.

A. D. MACLACHLAN, Senior Lecturer in History, University of Sydney; graduate of Cambridge; author of a doctoral thesis on the negotiation of the Utrecht settlement (Cambridge, 1964), and is at present preparing for publication his book, *The Great Peace*.

T. C. SMOUT, Reader in Economic History, University of Edinburgh; graduate of Cambridge; author of *Scottish Trade on the Eve of the Union 1660–1707* (1963) and of *A History of the Scottish People 1560–1830* (to be published 1969).

W. A. SPECK, Lecturer in History, University of Newcastle upon Tyne; formerly Tutor at Exeter University (1962–3); graduate of Oxford; co-editor of *The Divided Society* (1967); author of *Swift* (1969) and of a forthcoming book, *Tory and Whig: The Struggle in the Constituencies 1701–1715*.

Index

Judiciary, 43, 46, 93, 156
Junto, Whig, 18, 46, 101, 102, 105,
  108–10 *passim*, 122, 123, 125–9,
  130, 165–6, 168, 172, 200–2, 212,
  218, 230–1

Kentish Petition, 54, 72, 130
Kenyon, Professor J. P., 112, 133
King, Gregory, 2–3, 4–5, 10, 23,
  34 n 2, 86

La Hogue, battle of (1692), 124
Lancashire, 3, 81–2
Land: social and political importance
  of, 6, 106, 136–7, 146; fiscal
  importance of, 23–4, 140–1, 201;
  ownership of, 32, 138, 147; price
  of, 139–40, 147
Land Bank, 83, 136
Land Tax, *see* Taxation
'Landed interest', 135, 147–50, 233
Law and legal system, of England,
  12, 42, 43, 54–5, 83–4, 93. *See
  also* Judiciary
Liberty, personal, 54–5, 81
Liverpool, 3, 30
Local government, 9, 53–4
Locke, John, 84, 86, 88, 89, 93, 117
London, 3, 4, 25, 30, 53, 85, 90–1,
  139, 144–5, 167, 170, 172; 'the
  City', *see* 'Monied interest'
Lords, House of, 17, 40, 41, 45, 104–
  6 *passim*, 161, 171, 173–4, 186,
  189, 204–5, 211
Lords Justices, 51
Louis XIV, King of France, 2, 21,
  41, 59–65 *passim*, 68, 70–1, 74, 75,
  82, 130, 197, 198

Macaulay, T. B. (Lord), 14, 132
Malplaquet, battle of (1709), 150,
  200
Managers, political, 50, 125–6, 131,
  202, 218
Marlborough, duke of, 20, 21, 22,
  50, 130, 137, 167, 201, 205, 210,
  212, 218, 227
Mary II, Queen of England, 40–1,
  42, 50–1, 108, 118, 120, 121, 125,
  131, 133 n 4, 159–60
Masham, Abigail, Lady, 220, 225–6

Merchant marine, English, *see* Ship-
  ping
Mesnager, Nicolas, 207, 209, 210
Methuen Treaties (1703), 65
Monarchy, character and theories of,
  39–42 *passim*, 47, 55, 89, 132, 155–
  6, 160, 169–70, 231
'Monied interest', 5–6, 13, 83, 135–
  7, 142, 144–5, 147–51, 201, 203–4,
  208–9, 220, 233
Montague, Charles, 82, 123, 125,
  126
Morgan, Professor W. T., 96, 97
Musgrave, Sir Christopher, 109, 110

Namier, Sir Lewis, 14, 96–7, 98,
  101, 111, 194, 197
Navigation Acts (1651, 1660), 27, 28,
  29, 178, 180
Navy, Royal, 19, 21, 29, 52, 124,
  126
Nef, Professor J. U., 27–8
Netherlands, Spanish, 64, 71, 124,
  199, 200, 205, 208, 220
Newcastle, John, duke of, 139, 140;
  heiress of, 225–6
Newcomen, Thomas, 32
Newton, Sir Isaac, 10, 90, 92
Nonconformists, Protestant, *see* Dis-
  senters
Nonjurors, 159–60, 161, 169, 173
Norwich, 3
Nottingham, Daniel, earl of, 64, 101,
  102, 121, 122–5 *passim*, 146, 149,
  158, 160–2, 167–8, 172, 229–30,
  232, 237 n 24

Oaths: Coronation Oath, 40–1;
  Oath of Allegiance, 41, 160, 161–
  2; Abjuration Oath, 41, 110, 232
Occasional Conformity, 167, 172;
  bills against, 49, 168, 172, 218
October Club, 222
Offices, government (and office-
  holders), 5, 10–11, 41, 97, 98–9,
  105–7, 126, 135, 144–5, 216, 234–5
Oxford, earl of, *see* Harley

Parliament, of England and Great
  Britain, 11, 13, 15, 16, 39, 40–50